Praise for
# FROM HERE TO THERE:
## THE STAUGHTON LYND READER

"Staughton Lynd's work is essential reading for anyone dedicated to implementing social justice. The essays collected in this book provide unique wisdom and insights into U.S. history and possibilities for change, summed up in two tenets: Leading from below and solidarity."
—Roxanne Dunbar-Ortiz, author of *Red Dirt* and *Outlaw Woman*

"This remarkable collection demonstrates the compassion and intelligence of one of America's greatest public intellectuals. To his explorations of everything from Freedom Schools to the Battle of Seattle, Staughton Lynd brings lyricism, rigour, a historian's eye for irony, and an unshakable commitment to social transformation. At this moment of economic crisis, when the air is filled with ideas of 'hope' and 'change,' Lynd guides us to understanding what, very concretely, those words might mean and how we might get there. These essays are as vital and relevant now as the day they were written, and a source of inspiration for activists young and old."
—Raj Patel, author of *The Value of Nothing* and *Stuffed and Starved*

"I met Staughton and Alice Lynd nearly fifty years ago during an exuberant time. As a young man, I was greatly impressed by their combining of serious academic work with Quaker morality and willingness to throw themselves into a social movement. It has been many years since that time, but Staughton's reflective and restless life has never ceased in its exploring. This book is his great gift to the next generation."
—Tom Hayden

"*From Here to There: The Staughton Lynd Reader* is a veritable treasure chest of Lynd's unparalleled brilliance and respect for rank-and-file movements. If you're interested in broad social change and meaningful democracy, you simply must read Staughton Lynd."
—Daniel Gross, IWW Starbucks organizer, co-author of *Labor Law for the Rank and Filer*

"Staughton Lynd's life of non-violent accompaniment with workers and the poor has been marked by a prodigious literary output. While immersed in the world and its struggles, he, with the steady involvement of his wife and partner Alice in their extensive joint work, has consistently recorded, studied, and written about social change from the viewpoint of workers and the poor. History, analysis, and the faithful transcription of the voices of struggle that emerged out of the 1960s and '70s civil rights and antiwar campaigns, out of the resistance to the mill and factory shutdowns in the north in the 1980s and '90s, give flesh and blood to the dry bones of theory. No one has better balanced an understanding of traditional Marxist and anarchist revolutionary theory with American traditions of democratic rights and individual liberty."

—Charles McCollester, former chief shop steward at Union Switch & Signal, author of *The Point of Pittsburgh*

# FROM HERE TO THERE

*The*
*STAUGHTON LYND*
*Reader*

# FROM HERE TO THERE

*The*
*STAUGHTON LYND*
*Reader*

*edited by* **Andrej Grubacic**

PM Press 2010

*From Here to There: The Staughton Lynd Reader*

ISBN: 978-1-60486-215-7
Library of Congress Control Number: 2009912422

Copyright © 2010 Staughton Lynd
This edition copyright © 2010 PM Press
All Rights Reserved

PM Press
PO Box 23912
Oakland, CA 94623
www.pmpress.org

Cover Design by John Yates/Stealworks.com
Layout by Josh MacPhee/Justseeds.org

Printed in the USA on recycled paper.

# CONTENTS

To begin with, apologies to sisters in the movement that until about 1970 I used masculine pronouns—"he," "his"—to refer to all human beings. I find that Eleanor Roosevelt defended this practice when helping to draft the Universal Declaration of Human Rights after World War II. More remarkably, Barbara Deming, a colleague on the editorial board of *Liberation* magazine and, in my opinion, the most perceptive commentator on nonviolence that our movement produced, did the same in the Sixties. No matter. It was wrong. I apologize.

About half of the essays in this volume are talks that never appeared in print. With one exception (a chapter in a book), the remainder appeared in periodicals that may be difficult to access and in some cases no longer exist.

For better or worse I have had fundamentally the same outlook on things since I turned twenty-one in 1950. (That was also the year I met my wife, Alice. See our joint autobiography, *Stepping Stones*, published by Lexington Books in 2009.) That is, I have advocated nonviolence during years when it was the radical thing to do to call policemen "pigs"; I have celebrated the decentralization of decision-making, also known as "participatory democracy," whether in a movement, a trade union, or a nation; and I have insisted that, whatever you believe, you must act on it: put your body where your mouth is, as we used to say.

This last article of faith—do it now—becomes more challenging to practice as I approach and pass eighty. I hope I have avoided telling other persons to do things that I am no longer able to undertake.

For readers who may have encountered one or more of these essays before, I need to explain the following: As I have thought about a matter and gradually clarified my ideas, I have built an argument from one talk or essay to the next. Inevitably, the result is repetition. In a first presentation I would highlight hypothesis A, and then repeat it in my next presentation while adding two new theses, B and C. In offering successive presentations in this *Reader* I have sometimes eliminated the repetition of an argument in a second or third elaboration of a theme.

Occasionally I have made slight corrections in a text that may have come into being fifty years ago. I have also sometimes added an explanation in brackets to clarify a word or phrase that would have been obvious to an audience at that time, but may no longer be self-explanatory.

Finally, I should like to acknowledge that like our previous joint venture, *Wobblies and Zapatistas*, this book is in significant part the product of Andrej Grubacic as well as of myself. It was his idea that there should be a "Reader" made up of unpublished talks and articles in obscure journals. And his Introduction, beside being extremely generous, paid me the compliment of focusing on ideas rather than personal characteristics.

That's about it. Have fun.

# INTRODUCTION:
## LIBERTARIAN SOCIALISM FOR THE TWENTY-FIRST CENTURY
### ANDREJ GRUBACIC

In November 2008, French academic Max Gallo argued that the great revolutionary parenthesis is closed for good. No more "magnificent barefoot men marching on a dazzled world" whom Victor Hugo had once admired. Any revolutionary transformation, Gallo said, inevitably means an eruption of violence. Because our societies are extremely fragile, the major responsibility of intellectuals and other public figures is to protect those fragile societies from such an eruption.

Gallo is hardly alone in putting forth this view, either historically or within the current moment of discussion and debate. Indeed, his cautionary plea was quickly echoed by another man of letters, and another notable French leftist, historian François Furet. Furet warned that any attempt at radical transformation was either totalitarian or terrorist, or both, and that the very idea of another society has become almost completely inconceivable. His conclusion was that we are, in a certain sense, condemned to live in the world in which we live.

And then, only one month later, in December, there was the Greek rebellion. The Greek miracle. Not a simple riot, most certainly not a "credit crunch rebellion," but a rebellion of dignity and a radical statement of *presence*: of real, prefigurative, transformative and resisting alternatives. Rebellion that was about affirming the preciousness of life.

I am writing this Introduction on the anniversary of the murder of Alexis Grigoropoulos, the act that put the fire to the powder keg of the Greek December. While writing, I am reminded of words from Staughton Lynd in a personal communication written to me during those days:

> At the same time, just as we honor the gifts of the Zapatistas, we should ceaselessly and forever honor the unnamed, unknown men, women and children who lay down their lives for their comrades and for a better world. There sticks in my mind the story of a Salvadoran campesino. When the death squad arrived at his home, he asked if he might put on his favorite

soccer ("football") shoes before he was shot. The path to a new
world cannot be and will not be short. Any one of us can walk
it only part of the way. As we do so we should hold hands, and
keep facing forward.

But how do we walk? How do we begin walking?

The aim of this Introduction is to suggest the relevance of
Staughton Lynd's life and ideas for a new generation of radicals. The
reader will undoubtedly notice that it has been written in a somewhat
unconventional tone. My intention is to describe the process that led
myself, an anarchist revolutionary from the Balkans, to discover, and
eventually embrace, many of the ideas espoused by an American historian, Quaker, lawyer and pacifist, influenced by Marxism. This task is
not made any easier by the fact that Staughton, through the years of our
friendship, has become a beloved mentor and co-conspirator. Staughton
Lynd, for many good reasons that you are about to discover in reading
this collection, has earned a legendary status among people familiar with
his work and struggles.

It is impossible even to begin to conceive of writing a history
of modern day American radicalism without mentioning the name of
Staughton Lynd. He lived and taught in intentional communities, the
Macedonia Cooperative Community and the Society of Brothers, or
Bruderhof. He helped to edit the journal *Liberation* with Paul Goodman
and David Dellinger. Together with Howard Zinn he taught American
history at Spelman College in Atlanta. He served as director of SNCC-
organized Freedom Schools of Mississippi in 1964. In April 1965, he
chaired the first march against the Vietnam War in Washington, D.C.
In August 1965, he was arrested together with Bob Moses and David
Dellinger at the Assembly of Unrepresented People in Washington, D.C.,
where demonstrators sought to declare peace with the people of Vietnam
on the steps of the Capitol. In December 1965, Staughton—along with
Tom Hayden and Herbert Aptheker—made a trip to Hanoi, in hope of
clarifying the peace terms of the North Vietnamese government and the
National Liberation Front of South Vietnam. He was one of the four
original teachers at Saul Alinsky's Industrial Areas Foundation Training
Institute founded in 1968-1969. He stands as one of the original protagonists of the New Left assertion of "history from the bottom up," which
is today so celebrated and widely appreciated. He fought as a lawyer for
the rank-and-file workers of Youngstown, and for prisoners at the supermaximum security prison in Youngstown who know him as "Scrapper."
Staughton has been and remains a guru of solidarity unionism as practiced by the Industrial Workers of the World.[1]

This list could very easily go on. But I do not set out here to write a history of Staughton's life. There are other books and articles that have done that.[2] Rather, I would like to describe how my own politics have changed in the course of my intellectual engagement and friendship with Staughton Lynd, and why I today believe in, and continually profess the need for, a specific fusion of anarchism and Marxism, a political statement that I refused for much of my life as a militant, self-described, and unrepentant anarchist. The aim of this short Introduction is to explain why I believe that the ideas of Staughton Lynd are crucially important for the revolutionaries of my generation, and to offer some suggestions for a possible new revolutionary orientation, inspired by his ideas.

I was born to a family of revolutionaries. I come from Yugoslavia, or what is left of Yugoslavia. It is called something else now. Although I moved to the United States in 2005, I was already a foreigner well before that moment. I became a foreigner as early as the beginning of the 1990s, when the political ideas of inter-ethnic cooperation and mutual aid as we had known them in Yugoslavia were destroyed—disappeared in the combined madness of ethno-nationalist hysteria and humanitarian imperialism. Yugoslavia, for me, and for people like me, was never just a country: it was an idea. Like the Balkans itself, it was a project of inter-ethnic co-existence, a trans-ethnic and pluricultural space of many diverse worlds.

The Balkans I know is the Balkans *from below*. A space of bogumils—those medieval heretics who fought against Crusades and churches—and a place of anti-Ottoman resistance, a home to hajduks and klefti, pirates and rebels, a refuge of feminists and socialists, of anti-fascists and partisans, a place of dreamers of all sorts struggling both against provincial "peninsularity" as well as against occupations, foreign interventions and that process which is now, in a strange inversion of history, often described with that fashionable phrase, "balkanization."

My family was a microcosm of *this* Balkan reality. My grandparents were socialists and Titoists, partisans and anti-fascists, dreamers who believed in self-management and the Yugoslav "path to socialism."[3] This idea—and especially the Yugoslav and Balkan dream of an inter-ethnic, pluricultural space—was dramatically dismantled in the 1990s, when I found myself living in a country that was no longer my own. It was ruled by people I could not relate to, local tyrants that we used to call "aparatciki," bureaucrats of ideas and spirit. That was the beginning of my struggle to understand my own identity and the problem of Yugoslav socialism. I went on to look for another path to what my grandparents understood as communism. It seemed to me that the Marxist-Leninist way of getting "from here to there," the project of seizing the power of the

state, and functioning through a "democratically" centralized party organization, had produced *not* a free association of free human beings but a
bureaucratized expression of what was still called by the official ideology
of a socialist state, "Marxism." Yugoslav self-management was, like so
many other failures in our revolutionary history, a magnificent failure, a
glimmer, not unlike those other ones that Staughton Lynd and I discuss
in our book, *Wobblies and Zapatistas*.

Being thus so understandably distrustful of Marxism, I became,
very early on, an anarchist. Anarchism, to my mind, means taking democracy seriously and organizing prefiguratively, that is, in a way that
anticipates the society we are about to create. Instead of taking the power
of the state, anarchism is concerned with "socializing" power—with creating new political and social structures not after the revolution, but in
the immediate present, in the shell of the existing order. With the arrival
of the Zapatistas in 1994, I dedicated all of my political energy to the
emerging movement that many of us experienced as a shock of hope,
and what journalists would later come to describe as a potent symbol of a
new "anti-globalization movement." This journey took me from villages
of Chiapas and social centers in Italy, to such networks and forums as
Peoples Global Action, the World Social Forum, as well as to many other
revolutionary projects, local and global, of this new generation of anabaptists trying to turn the globalized world upside down.[4] I survived the
violence of the Yugoslav wars and NATO interventions but, in the end, it
was my political work in Belgrade , in the country that I still refuse to call
by any other name than Yugoslavia, that made it difficult for me to stay
there. With the kind help of many generous friends, I found a refuge in
the United States, as well as an opportunity to finish my graduate studies
at SUNY Binghamton and its Fernand Braudel Center. It is here in the
libraries of Binghamton State University, in fact, where the story of my
friendship with Staughton Lynd should properly begin.

One day, as I was working in the university library—and quite by
accident, or with the help of what Arthur Koestler calls library angels—
my eyes were drawn to a shelf in front of me and a book with a somewhat tacky cover.[5] There was an American eagle, an image I did not
particularly like, and a title that I was similarly not immediately fond
of: *Intellectual Origins of American Radicalism*. This was not my cup of
tea. I wanted to write about "coloniality," post-structuralism, and other
exotic things that academics seem to find interesting. As I started reading it, however, I simply could not make myself put it down. What I had
in my hands was the best kind of a history-from-below: a breathtaking
reconstruction of American radicalism, a moving story of anabaptists
and abolitionists, of communal experiments and direct democracy, of the

"ordinarily inarticulate," a tradition of "my country is the world." It spoke of "bicameralism from below," a vision that is "not simply a utopian vision but a means of struggle toward that vision." At the heart of this vision is revolution understood as a process that

> begins when, by demonstrations or strikes or electoral victories in the context of supplementary direct action, the way a society makes its decisions is forced to change. That is something very real even when the beginnings are small. It means, not just that a given decision is different in substance, but that the process of decision-making becomes more responsive to the ordinarily inarticulate. New faces appear in the group that makes the decision, alternatives are publicly discussed in advance, more bodies have to be consulted. As the revolutionary situation deepens, the broadening of the decision-making process becomes institutionalized. Alongside the customary structure of authority, parallel bodies—organs of "dual power," as Trotsky called them—arise. . . . [A] new structure of representation develops out of direct democracy and controlled by it. Suddenly, in whole parts of the country and in entire areas of daily life, it becomes apparent that people are obeying the new organs of authority rather than the old ones. . . . The task becomes building into the new society something of that sense of shared purpose and tangibly shaping a common destiny which characterized the revolution at its most intense.[6]

These institutional improvisations are made easier if there are pre-existing organizations of the poor, institutions of their own making, such as the "clubs, the unorthodox congregations, the fledgling trade unions" that are "the tangible means, in theological language the 'works,' by which revolutionaries kept alive their faith that men could live together in a radically different way. In times of crisis resistance turned into revolution, the underground congregation burst forth as a model for the Kingdom of God on earth, and an organ of secular 'dual power.'"[7]

I remember reading, again and again, the last passage of the book. "The revolutionary tradition is more than words and more than isolated acts. Men create, maintain, and rediscover a tradition of struggle by the crystallization of ideas and actions into organizations which they make for themselves. Parallel to Leviathan, the Kingdom is dreamed, discussed, in minuscule form established. Within the womb of the old society—it is Marx's metaphor—the new society is born."[8]

I don't think I had ever before encountered a more lucid and beautiful description of a revolutionary process. Years later, I find myself going back to these words often. And it was this magnificent little book that ultimately made me decide to change the subject of my thesis and to write about experiences of inter-racial and inter-ethnic mutual aid in American history instead. Quite an ambitious project for a young historian from Yugoslavia to take up, and thus a further testament to the level of inspiration I drew from this book.

At its very roots, Staughton's approach resonated with my perspective as an anarchist and how I understood anarchism. And very interestingly enough for me, this was what was drawn from the work of an explicitly self-identifying *Marxist* historian! But could there be a better way of writing history from the perspective of an *anarchist* historian? Is there a more apt way of being an anarchist historian than practicing what Staughton Lynd calls "guerrilla history" as it is described in "Guerrilla History in Gary" and "A Vision of History" (Essays 14 and 15)? And could there be a more urgent topic for someone from Yugoslavia, someone struggling to understand the intertwined legacy of inter-ethnic conflict and inter-ethnic solidarity? Soon after I put *Intellectual Origins* back on the shelf, I went to look for Staughton Lynd. I found him in Youngstown, Ohio.

I remember vividly our first meeting. We met in New York, a few hours before he gave the talk at the War Resisters League included in this *Reader* under the title, "Someday They'll Have a War and Nobody Will Come" (Essay 24). I will never forget Staughton's question to me: "How can I join your movement?" After a long conversation I made him the promise that I would help him to do that, but also that I would join his. Two years later, after meeting a group of young activists in Portland who were reading with excitement our *Wobblies and Zapatistas*, I felt I had made good on my promise.

Staughton still likes to ask me why it is that I went to see *him*. Why didn't I look for some famous Italian or French radical theorist? I suspect that he knows the reason well, but I indulge him nonetheless, by answering that we all make mistakes. Still, the question deserves a longer response. After all, I was one of the activists and writers who advocated a "new anarchism": a movement free of the burden of the traditional political practice, but rather emerging out of the organic practice of contemporary, global and networked struggles. I penned article after article criticizing the "weight of the old."

However, the truth is that I moved to the United States, to use an expression that Staughton likes, as a broken-hearted lover. Networks and connections that were built during the cycle of the 1990s were still in place, but 9/11 in the United States, and Genoa in Europe, as well as some profound mistakes made by the movement, brought us to a situation where there was not a coherent response to imperial globality and neo-liberal violence. The World Social Forum was in a serious crisis, and Peoples Global Action had more or less disappeared from the revolutionary horizon. Groups with which I used to work, like Direct Action Network in New York, were nowhere to be found, and the global movement was in a process of a search for a new orientation. Networks were becoming notworks. It became clear to me that, at least in the long term, we should not anchor our efforts in the hope for encounters and summits. The lifestyle of activists who "summit hop" from one brief-lived action to the next is, in the long run, unsustainable. There was a need for a new emancipatory program. It was my feeling that in running away from traditional models of organizing we ended up running too far, and far too quickly.

The whole context that David Graeber and I optimistically described as a coalescing "new anarchism" was in a state of evident confusion.[9] Even today, in times that are perceived by most as a serious crisis of the capitalist system, the movement in the United States is still far from having achieved any strategic clarity. The Left is without the movement. Or the movement is without the Left. Wobblies and Socialists are not organizing "encampments" in rural Oklahoma, as they used to do before the inter-racial Green Corn Rebellion of 1917. Times are as serious as they were then, if not more so, but somehow there are no "penny auctions" this time around. Meanwhile, intellectuals are writing serious political essays that no one who hasn't spent years in graduate school can hope to understand. Ivy league professors are telling us that to hope and work for an inter-racial movement is a waste of time. White workers are irrevocably generalized as racists, class is "multitude," and we are all part of the post-alpha generation suffering from the pathologies of "semiocapitalism."

On the other side of the world, news from Yugoslavia, or whatever other name local elites and foreign embassies now use to describe it, was and remains equally disconcerting. The new, former state-socialist republics were neo-liberalized, privatized or colonized, caught in an uneasy tension between sclero-nationalism and neo-liberalism. A foreigner with papers to prove it, I remain an outsider trying to make sense, from the outside, of what has happened to my movement and to the country from which I came. I felt and feel that we need a revolutionary synthesis of a new kind. And at the same time, I found and find myself as a Yugoslav to be a man without a country; but also, as an anarchist, a man without a state. That is why I went to find Staughton Lynd. I went to Youngstown to listen, to try to understand what went wrong, and I found myself in a conversation.

In the forthcoming years of our friendship and intellectual partnership, we came up with a suggestion for a new revolutionary orientation that would be premised on a fusion, or synthesis, of what we recognized as indispensable qualities of both anarchism and Marxism. It would perhaps be accurate to say that, in the process, I became a bit of a Marxist and Staughton a bit of an anarchist. In *Wobblies and Zapatistas*, we offered the following approach:

> What is Marxism? It is an effort to understand the structure of the society in which we live so as to make informed predictions and to act with greater effect. What is anarchism? It is the attempt to imagine a better society and insofar as possible to "prefigure," anticipate that society by beginning to live it out, on the ground, here and now.
>
> Isn't it perfectly obvious that these two orientations are both needed, that they are like having two hands to accomplish the needed task of transformation?[10]

These two viewpoints had been made to seem to be mutually exclusive alternatives. They are not. They are Hegelian moments that need to be synthesized.

We argued that in North America there is a tradition we termed the Haymarket synthesis, a tradition of the so-called "Chicago school" of anarchism, represented by Albert Parsons, August Spies, and the other Haymarket martyrs, all of whom described themselves as anarchists, socialists, and Marxists. This tradition was kept alive by the magnificent band of rebels known as the Wobblies, and today by rebels in Chiapas, the Zapatistas. Our responsibility today, in the United States, is to revive the Haymarket synthesis, to infuse it with new energy, new passion and new insights. To discover *libertarian socialism for the twenty-first century*. To rekindle dreams of a "socialist commonwealth," and to bring socialism, that "forbidden word," into a new and contemporary meaning. It is my belief that the ideas collected in the *Reader* before you present an important step in this direction. They suggest a vision of a libertarian socialism for the twenty-first century organized around the idea and practice of *solidarity*.

The essays in this collection do not tell us about one and only one way of getting "from here to there." As Staughton writes in "Toward Another World" (Essay 25), "I am glad that there does not exist a map, a formula or equation within which we must act to get from Here to There. It's more fun this way, to move forward experimentally, sometimes to stumble but at other times to glimpse things genuinely new, always to be open to the unexpected and the unimagined and the not-yet-fully-in-being."

In this spirit, without offering or imposing blueprints, I would like to suggest that libertarian socialism for the twenty-first century, a contemporary reworking of the Haymarket synthesis, could be organized around three important themes:

1. *Self-activity.* In creating a libertarian socialism for the twenty-first century we should rely not on a fantasy that salvation will come from above, but on our own self-activity expressed through organizations at the base that we ourselves create and control.

2. *Local institutions or "warrens."* Crucially important for a new revolutionary orientation is what Edward Thompson called a warren, that is, a local institution in which people conduct their own affairs.

3. *Solidarity.* We need to build more than a movement, we need to build a community of struggle.

### 1. SELF-ACTIVITY

We can understand self-activity in two ways. One is through what the Industrial Workers of the World call "solidarity unionism." In different parts of this *Reader*, Staughton describes solidarity unionism as a horizontal expression of workers' self-activity. In "Toward Another World" (Essay 25), he explains:

> An easy way to remember the basic idea of solidarity unionism is to think: Horizontal not vertical. Mainstream trade unionism beyond the arena of the local union is relentlessly vertical. Too often, rank-and-file candidates for local union office imagine that the obvious next step for them is to seek higher office, as international union staff man, regional director, even international union president. The Left, for the past seventy-five years, has lent itself to the fantasy that salvation will come from above by the election of a John L. Lewis, Philip Murray, Walter Reuther, Arnold Miller, Ed Sadlowski, Ron Carey, John Sweeney, Andrew Stern, or Richard Trumka.
>
> Instead we should encourage successful rank-and-file candidates for local union office to look horizontally to their counterparts in other local unions in the same industry or community. This was labor's formula for success during its most creative and successful years in memory, the early 1930s. During those years there were successful local general strikes in Minneapolis, Toledo, San Francisco, and other, smaller industrial towns. During those years local labor parties sprang up like mushrooms across the United States. Today some organizers in the IWW, for example in Starbucks stores in New York City, once again espouse solidarity unionism.

Instead of following the top-down, bureaucratic traditions of the founding fathers of the labor movement, and their fascination with national unionism, we should follow another path, the one that, as Staughton points out in "From Globalization to Resistance" (Essay 19), "takes its inspiration from the astonishing recreation from below throughout the past century of ad hoc central labor bodies: the local workers' councils known as 'soviets' in Russia in 1905 and 1917; the Italian factory committees of the early 1920s; solidarity unions in Toledo, Minneapolis, San Francisco, and elsewhere in the United States in the early 1930s; and similar formations in Hungary in 1956, Poland in 1980-1981, and France in 1968 and 1995." What is important, he explains, is that these "were all *horizontal* gatherings of all kinds of workers in a given *locality*, who then form regional and national networks with counterpart bodies elsewhere."

A second form of self-activity, closely related to the practice of solidarity unionism, is the Mayan idea of *"mandar obediciendo"* that informs the contemporary practice of the Zapatistas. This vision of a government "from below" that "leads by obeying" calls for separate emphasis, as Lynd says in his concluding essay, "because of the preoccupation of socialists for the past century and a half with 'taking state power.'" As I read the communiques from the Lacondón jungle, he writes, "I realized that at least from a time shortly after their initial public appearance, the Zapatistas were saying: We don't want to take state power. If we can create a space that will help others to make the national government more democratic, well and good. But our task, as we see it, is to bring into being self-governing local entities linked together horizontally so as to present whoever occupies the seats of government in Mexico City with a force so powerful that it becomes necessary to govern in obedience to what Subcomandante Marcos calls 'the below.'"

What the Zapatistas mean by this is an intention, an active effort to create and maintain a horizontal network of self-governing communities. This is what a new kind of libertarian socialism would look like. As Staughton writes on the last page of *Wobblies and Zapatistas*: "imagining a transition that will not culminate in a single apocalyptic moment but rather express itself in unending creation of self-acting entities that are horizontally linked is a source of quiet joy."[11]


## 2. *LOCAL INSTITUTIONS OR "WARRENS"*

As for warrens, in "Edward Thompson's Warrens" (Essay 21)—one of the most important pieces in this collection—we learn about a metaphor that is central to Thompson's understanding of a revolutionary process: a rabbit warren, that is, a long-lasting local institution. I remember once reading somewhere about a Spanish revolutionary and singer who said that we lost all the battles, but we had the best songs. I never liked this attitude, as noble and poetic as it might be. Any new revolutionary perspective ought to go beyond this. For much of my life as a revolutionary I have been haunted by what I call "Michelet's problem." Michelet was a famous French historian, who wrote the following words about the French revolution: "that day everything was possible, the future was the present and time but a glimmer of eternity." But, as Cornelius Castoriades used to say, if all that we create is just a glimmer of hope, the bureaucrats will inevitably show up and turn off the light.[12] The history of revolutions is, on the one hand, a history of tension between brief moments of revolutionary creativity and the making of long-lasting institutions. On the other hand, the history of revolutions often reads like a history of *revolutionary alienation*, when the revolutionary was, more than anything else, ultimately and almost inevitably alienated from his or her own creations. Michelet's problem is about resolving this tension between brief epiphanies of revolutionary hope and the hope for long-term institutionalization of revolutionary change.

The crucial question then is how to create such lasting institutions, or better yet, an ongoing culture of *constructive* struggle. In *Wobblies and Zapatistas*, Staughton asserts that "every single one of the ventures or experiments in government from below that we have been discussing existed for only a few months or years. In many societies they were drowned in blood. In most cases underlying economic institutions, that provided the matrix within which all political arrangements functioned, did not change. The leases on Hudson Valley manors after the Revolution did not differ dramatically from such leases before the Revolution."[13] So what is missing? How can we try to approach the answer to what I have called Michelet's problem?

In the contemporary anarchist movement, if we can speak of one, there is a lot of talk about "the insurrection" and considerable fascination with "the event."[14] The French accent and sophisticated jargon are perhaps new and in fashion, but these are not new topics. They appear to crop up, with disturbing regularity, with every new generation of revolutionaries. The old refrain that organizing is another word for going slow is being rediscovered by some of the new radicals. This is the topic of "The New Radicals and Participatory Democracy" and, especially, "Weatherman" (Essays 6 and 8).

I think we can say that there are, risking some oversimplification, two ways of thinking about revolution. In his essay on Thompson's warrens, Staughton says that "Thompson implicitly asks us to choose between two views of the transition from capitalism to socialism." One is expressed in the song "Solidarity Forever" when the song affirms, "We can bring to birth a new world from the ashes of the old." In this perspective, "the new world will arise, phoenix-like, after a great catastrophe or conflagration. The emergence of feudalism from pockets of local self-help after the collapse of the Roman Empire is presumably the exemplar of that kind of transition." This is the negative idea of revolution, very much present in contemporary movement literature.[15]

A second view of the revolution is positive, comparing it to the transition from feudalism to capitalism.

> The preamble to the IWW Constitution gives us a mantra for this perspective, declaring that "we are forming the structure of the new society within the shell of the old."
>
> Thompson opted for the second paradigm. . . . For a society to be criss-crossed by underground dens and passageways created by an oppositional class is, in Thompson's 1960s vocabulary, to be "warrened." British society, he wrote, is "warrened with democratic processes—committees, voluntary organizations, councils, electoral procedures." Because of the existence of such counter-institutions, in Thompson's view a transition to socialism could develop from what was already in being, and from below. "Socialism, even at the point of revolutionary transition—perhaps at this point most of all—must grow from existing strengths. No one . . . can impose a socialist humanity from above."

We have here an image of a constructive, not apocalyptic, revolution: built on the positives of a socialist commonwealth emerging from existing creations improvised from below. In Thompson's words:

> [S]uch a revolution demands the maximum enlargement of *positive* demands, the deployment of constructive skills within a conscious revolutionary strategy—or, in William Morris' words, the "making of Socialists." . . . Alongside the industrial workers, we should see the teachers who want better schools, scientists who wish to advance research, welfare workers who want hospitals, actors who want a National Theatre, technicians impatient to improve industrial organization. Such people do not want these things only and always, any more than all industrial workers are always "class conscious" and loyal to their great community values. But these affirmatives exist, fitfully and incompletely, with the ethos of the Opportunity State. It is the business of socialists to draw the line, not between a staunch

but diminishing minority and an unredeemable majority, but between the monopolists and the people—to foster the "societal instincts" and inhibit the acquisitive. Upon these positives, and not upon the debris of a smashed society, the socialist community must be built.

We should always cherish these beautiful words. But what is Thompson's warren? And why do I insist that it represents a formula for success? It is, first and foremost, a local institution in which people conduct their own affairs—an immigrant center or local union, for example—that expands in time of crisis to take on new powers and responsibilities, and then, after the revolutionary tide ebbs, continues to represent, in institutionalized form, an expanded version of what existed to begin with.

It would be impossible to understand the Russian revolution—the long Russian revolution (from 1890 to 1920)—without looking at the middle-class convocations, the student demonstrations, the workers' petitions: all forms of direct action, within the context of pre-existing and new "warrens," such as local unions, universities, and soviets. After the failure of the December 1905 uprising in Moscow and Petrograd, soviets lived on in popular memory until they were re-created by workers in 1917. In American labor history the most important meetings and organizations, including the ones that led to formation of the CIO in the 1930s, took place in pre-existing local institutions, such as fraternal societies, credit unions, burial associations, singing clubs, churches and newspapers.

In "Remembering SNCC" (Essay 4), an essay that ought to become required reading for anyone interested in the movement of the Sixties, we discover that one cannot hope to understand what happened in the South and in the civil rights movement without understanding that student action emerged from pre-existing warrens such as African American churches and college campuses. In the last section of the *Reader*, we learn that the Zapatistas provide perhaps the clearest example of all: hundreds if not thousands of years of life in pre-existing *asambleas*, and a decade of as yet unchronicled "accompaniment" by a group of Marxists-Leninists from the universities of Mexico City.

A way of looking at what happened in all these cases is that revolutionaries can often light a spark—not a prairie fire!—but whether or not a fire will catch hold depends on the response of people in their pre-existing local unions, factory committees, benefit associations, and other local institutions. Some of the self-governing institutions will be old entities (warrens) that have taken on new powers and objectives. In Chiapas, Mayan *asambleas* play this role. In Russia, soviets were the heart of the revolution. The nature of a revolutionary process is such that the distinction between old and new local institutions becomes blurred. The role of libertarian socialists is above all to nurture the creation, the spread, and the authority of local "warrens," to defend the existence, the legitimacy, and the autonomy of such formations.

### 3. SOLIDARITY

Finally, how do we do that? How do we build communities of struggle?

If capitalism developed as a practice of the idea of contract, libertarian socialism should be developed as a practice of *solidarity*. There are several kinds of solidarity. On the one hand, we might say, solidarity can be defined as drawing the boundary of our community of struggle as widely as possible. There are many examples of solidarity thus defined. In "Henry Thoreau: The Admirable Radical" (Essay 1) and especially in "The Tragedy of American Diplomacy" (Essay 23), Staughton speaks very fondly of Thoreau, who, in his essay on civil disobedience, famously observed that the fugitive slave, and the Mexican prisoner on parole, and the Indian come to plead the wrongs of his race, should find good citizens in the only house in a slave state in which a free man can abide with honor, namely, in prison behind bars.

This is one way of understanding solidarity. Another way of understanding solidarity is by pointing out, as Staughton does in his essay "From Globalization to Resistance" (Essay 19), is that there is a problem with the concept of organizing. There are several ways to organize. One way is Leninist vanguardism: the idea that the working class, left to itself, is able to develop only trade-union consciousness. The proper revolutionary consciousness could only be brought to workers "from without." In the United States, during the 1930s and 1970s, this process was known as "colonization." Revolutionaries would go to a factory and "colonize" the workplace. It is not all that different with trade-union organizers, irrespective of how courageous or resourceful they might be: when they organize in a way that implicitly assumes an "outside," it creates a certain inequality between organizer and organized.

The anarchist response to this, in the last couple of decades, was twofold. One way was to offer a perspective of "contaminationism." As David Graeber explains, "On a more immediate level, the strategy depends on the dissemination of the model: most anarchists, for example, do not see themselves as a vanguard whose historical role is to 'organize' other communities, but rather as one community setting an example others can imitate. The approach—it's often referred to as 'contaminationism'—is premised on the assumption that the experience of freedom is infectious: that anyone who takes part in a direct action is likely to be permanently transformed by the experience, and want more."[16]

The other, loosely-defined anarchist approach was to behave like a social worker, tending the communities from the outside, not as a fellow student or a fellow worker with a particular understanding of a situation shared with others, but as an "activist" or professional in social change—a force outside of society, organizing those "inside" on their own behalf. There are many successful and admirable examples of this kind of organizing. However, the same problem of an implicit inequality still stands.

A far better alternative than these two responses, and one that I would like to advance here, is a process that Staughton calls "accompaniment." Revolutionaries should accompany workers and others in the creation and maintenance of popular self-governing institutions. In this process, we should not pretend to be something we are not. Rather, we can walk beside poor people in struggle just as we are, hopefully providing support and certain useful skills.

I experienced this vision of accompaniment while I was still living in Yugoslavia. A few of us, students from Belgrade University, recognized that the only organized resistance to the encroaching tide of privatization and neo-liberalism was coming from a group of workers in the Serbian countryside. We decided to go to northern Serbia, to a city called Zrenjanin, and approach the workers. These workers were very different from ourselves. Some of them had fought in the recent Yugoslav wars. Most of them were very conservative, patriarchal, and traditional. We went there and offered our skills. We had a few. We spoke foreign languages. We had internet access and know-how in a country where only 2 percent of the people used this service. We had connections with workers and movements outside Serbia. Some us were good writers. A few had legal expertise. These workers were grateful but understandably quite skeptical, as were we. Soon, however, something like a friendship emerged. We started working together and learning from each other. In the process of struggle against the boss, the private armies he sent to the factory, and the state authorities, we started to trust each other. We both changed—workers and students. Today, after ten years of accompaniment, the same group of students plays an important role in the Coordinating Committee for Workers Protests in Serbia, where five Strike Committees represent workers from three cities and five branches of industry.

Staughton and his wife Alice encountered the notion of accompaniment in Latin America. In "From Globalization to Resistance" (Essay 19), we find these lines:

In Latin America—for example, once again, in the work of Archbishop Romero—there is the different concept of "accompaniment." I do not organize you. I accompany you, or more precisely, we accompany each other. Implicit in this notion of "accompañando" is the assumption that neither of us has a complete map of where our path will lead. In the words of Antonio Machado: "Caminante, no hay camino. Se hace camino al andar." "Seeker, there is no road. We make the road by walking."

Accompaniment has been, in the experience of myself and my wife, a discovery and a guide to practice. Alice first formulated it as a draft counselor in the 1960s. When draft counselor meets counselee, she came to say, there are two experts in the room. One may be an expert on the law and administrative regulations. The other is an expert on what he wants to do with his life. Similarly as lawyers, in our activity with workers and prisoners, we have come to prize above all else the experience of jointly solving problems with our clients. They know the facts, the custom of the workplace or penal facility, the experience of past success and failure. We too bring something to the table. I do not wish to be indecently immodest, but I will share that I treasure beyond any honorary degree actual or imagined the nicknames that Ohio prisoners have given the two of us: "Mama Bear" and "Scrapper."

In "Toward Another World" (Essay 25), Staughton writes:

> In the annual pastoral letters that he wrote during the years before his assassination, Romero projected a course of action with two essential elements. First, be yourself. If you are a believing Christian, don't be afraid of professing it. If you are an intellectual don't pretend that you make your living by manual labor. Second, place yourself at the side of the poor and oppressed. Accompany them on their journey.
>
> . . . One last point about accompaniment is that it can only come about if you—that is, the lawyer, doctor, teacher, clergyman, or other professional person—stay in the community over a period of years. . . . I feel strongly that if more professionals on the Left would take up residence in communities other than Cambridge, New York City, and Berkeley, and stay there for a while, social change in this country might come a lot more quickly.

"The Two Yales" (Essay 12) and "Intellectuals, the University and the Movement" (Essay 13) are perhaps the most radical critique of the arrogance of campus intellectuals I ever came across. In *Wobblies and Zapatistas*, Staughton added:

> I have a hard time with theorizing that does not appear to arise from practical activity or lead to action, or indeed, that seems to discourage action and consider action useless.
>
> I don't think I am intellectually inept. Yet I confess that much of what is written about "post-Marxism," or "Fordism," or "deconstruction," or "the multitude," or "critical legal studies," or "whiteness," and that I have tried to read, seems to me, simply, both unintelligible and useless.
>
> What is the explanation for this universe of extremely abstract discourse? I yearn to ask of each such writer: What are you doing? With what ordinary people do you discuss your ideas before you publish them? What difference does it make, in the world outside your windows and away from your word processor, whether you say A or B? For whom do you consider yourself a model or exemplar? Exactly how, in light of what you have written, do you see your theoretical work leading to another world? Or would it be more accurate to suggest that the practical effect of what you write is to rationalize your comfortable position doing full-time theorizing in a college or university?[17]

In the pages of the same book Staughton offers a similarly trenchant critique of some anarchist practices:

> As a lifelong rebel against heavy-handed Marxist dogmatism I find myself defending Marx, and objecting to the so-called radicalism of one-weekend-a-year radicals who show up at a global confrontation and then talk about it for the rest of the year.
>
> These are harsh words. But I consider them deserved. Anarchists, above all others, should be faithful to the injunction that a genuine radical, a revolutionary, must indeed swim in the sea of the people, and if he or she does not do so, is properly viewed as what the Germans called a "socialist of the chair," or in English, an "armchair intellectual."
>
> It is a conspiracy of persons who make their living at academic institutions to induce others who do the same to take them seriously. I challenge it and reject it. Let them follow Marcos to the jungles of Chiapas in their own countries, and learn something new.[18]

In this project of "accompaniment," the model should be that of the Mexican intellectuals, students and professors, who went to live in the jungle, and after ten years came forth as protagonists of a revolution from below. The Zapatistas were not footloose: they went to a particular place and stayed there, in what must have been incredibly challenging and difficult circumstances, for a decade of accompaniment. The central component of accompaniment is that we should settle down in particular places so that when crises come we will already be trusted friends and members of the community.

When I argue for accompaniment in my university talks I am usually accused of proposing a practice that defers, without criticism, to whatever poor and oppressed people in struggle believe and are demanding at the moment. It is to these critiques that Staughton answers in *Wobblies and Zapatistas*:

> In his fourth and last Pastoral Letter, written less than a year before his death, Romero says that the preferential option for the poor does not mean "blind partiality in favor of the masses." Indeed:
>
> > In the name of the preferential option for the poor there can never be justified the machismo, the alcoholism, the failure in family responsibility, the exploitation of one poor person by another, the antagonism among neighbors, and the so many other sins that [are] concurrent roots of this country's crisis and violence.
>
> I submit that the foregoing is hardly a doctrine of unthinking subservience to the momentary beliefs or instructions of the poor.
>
> I challenge those who offer this critique of "accompaniment" to explain, in detail, how they go about relating to the poor and oppressed. I suspect that they do not have such relationships at all. That makes it easy to be pure: without engagement with the world, one need only endlessly reiterate one's own abstract identity.
>
> "Accompaniment" is simply the idea of walking side by side with another on a common journey. The idea is that when a university-trained person undertakes to walk beside someone rich in experience but lacking formal skills, each contributes something vital to the process. "Accompaniment" thus understood presupposes, not uncritical deference, but equality.[19]

It is interesting to note the similarity between accompaniment and another form of praxis emerging from Latin America. In some parts of the continent anarchists have developed a praxis of involvement in social movements that they call "Especifismo." The mainstay of Especifismo is the engagement called "social insertion." This means activists being focused on activity within, and helping to build, mass organizations and mass struggles, in communities and neighborhoods, in various social spheres. This does not mean people from outside intervening in struggles of working people, but is about the focus of organizing radicals within the communities of struggle. Various struggles can include strikes, rent strikes, struggles for control of the land, struggles against the police and gentrification, struggles against sexism, for the right to abortion, against bus fare increases, or any other issue that angers working people and moves them to act.[20]

But accompaniment can be taken even further, to the very issue of revolutionary agency. In "From Globalization to Resistance" (Essay 19) we encounter a hypothesis, further developed in "Students and Workers in the Transition to Socialism" (Essay 20), that

> the concept of "accompaniment," in addition to clarifying the desirable relationship of individuals in the movement for social change to one another, also has application to the desirable relationship of groups. A great deal of energy has gone into defining the proper relationship in the movement for social change of workers and students; blacks and whites; men and women; straights and gays; gringos, ladinos and *indígenas*; and no doubt, English-speakers and French-speakers. An older wave of radicalism struggled with the supposed leading role of the proletariat. More recently other kinds of division have pre-occupied us. My question is, what would it do to this discussion were we to say that we are all accompanying one another on the road to a better society?

It appears that in Hungary, as well as later in France and the United States, and before that in revolutionary Russia, students came first, and workers subsequently joined in.

> Why do students so often come first? One can speculate. To whatever extent Gramsci is right about the hegemony of bourgeois ideas, students and other intellectuals break through it: they give workers the space to think and experience for themselves. Similarly, the defiance of students may help workers to overcome whatever deference they may be feeling toward supposed social superiors.

It is of great importance to stress that solidarity must be built outside of the university library and on the basis of practice, not shared ideas. Solidarity only can be built on the basis of action that is in the common interest. In the pages of "Nonviolence and Solidarity" (Essay 17) we learn that in "the world of poor and working-class resistance . . . action often comes before talk, and may be in apparent contradiction to words that the actor has used, or even continues to use in the midst of action. The experience of struggle gives rise to new understandings that may be put into words much later or never put into words at all." In these situations, "Experience ran ahead of ideology. Actions spoke louder than organizational labels."

The most convincing example of this is the prison uprising at Lucasville, Ohio, a rebellion inside a maximum security prison which Staughton discusses in "Overcoming Racism" (Essay 18).[21]

> The single most remarkable thing about the Lucasville rebellion is that white and black prisoners formed a common front against the authorities. When the State Highway Patrol came into the occupied cell block after the surrender they found slogans written on the walls of the corridor and in the gymnasium that read: "Convict unity," "Convict race," "Blacks and whites together," "Blacks and whites, whites and blacks, unity," "Whites and blacks together," "Black and white unity."
>
> The five prisoners from the rebellion on death row—the Lucasville Five—are a microcosm of the rebellion's united front. Three are black, two are white. Two of the blacks are Sunni Muslims. Both of the whites were, at the time of the rebellion, members of the Aryan Brotherhood.

Could Lucasville's example provide us with glimpses of how to create an inter-racial movement?

> In the 1960s and early 1970s, the self-organized protest movement of blacks created a model for students, women, workers, and eventually, soldiers. In the same way, the self-organized resistance of black and white prisoners can become a model for the rest of us in overcoming racism. Life will continue to ask of working people that they find their way to solidarity. Surely, there are sufficient instances of deep attitudinal change on the part of white workers to persuade us that a multi-ethnic class consciousness is not only necessary, but also possible.

This is one of the aspects of Staughton's thought that influenced me the most. I started exploring American history and, while falling short of discovering many examples of a "usable past," I was able to discern a current of inter-racial, inter-ethnic mutual aid that we could follow from the early days on the frontier to the inter-racial unionism of the Wobblies in Pittsburgh and Philadelphia, SNCC, and Lucasville. The important thing is not to romanticize these experiences. Not to succumb to the temptation that I call "conspiracy optimism," a temptation that makes us see the Many-Headed Hydra of resistance raising her head everywhere. No. A legacy of conquest and a legacy of mutual aid co-exist in American history and American politics, just as they do in the Balkans. A new anti-capitalist inter-racial movement is possible only in the context of practical, lived solidarity, that transcends differences and overcomes. Libertarian socialism for the twenty-first century needs to be built on the understanding that the only movement worthy of that name is an inter-racial movement built on the process of accompaniment.

What about solidarity in the context of internationalism? In *Intellectual Origins* Staughton explores the tradition articulated by a series of working-class intellectuals in the United States whose credo was, "My country is the world." In one of the most beautiful passages of *Wobblies and Zapatistas*, Staughton says the following:

> Surely this is the form of internationalism we should espouse. It makes it possible for us to say, "Yes, I love my country! I love the fields of New England and Ohio, and also the mist-covered mountains and ravines of Chiapas and Nicaragua. I love the clarity of Thoreau, the compassion of Eugene Debs and the heroism of Bartolomeo Vanzetti, the paintings of Rembrandt, the music of Bach. I admire the conductors of the Underground Railroad and the self-organizing peasants and artisans in revolutionary Spain. My country is the world."

Finally, there is another kind of solidarity, one that must be nurtured not only in struggle but in our communities of struggle. This is very hard but necessary. If we can't build an organization in which human beings trust one another as brothers and sisters, why should anyone trust us to build a better society? Within the pages of *Wobblies and Zapatistas*, Staughton urges:

> We need to proceed in a way that builds community. There must be certain ground rules. We should practice direct speaking: if something bothers you about another person, go speak to him or her and do not gossip to a third person. No one should be permitted to present themselves in caucuses that

define a fixed position beforehand and are impervious to the
exchange of experiences. We must allow spontaneity and experiment without fear of humiliation and disgrace. Not only
our organizing but our conduct toward one another must be
paradigmatic in engendering a sense of truly being brothers
and sisters.

In my years as an anarchist organizer, one of the most disturbing patterns
I noticed is exactly the problem Staughton describes here: the inability to
practice comradeship to keep our networks, our social centers and affinity
groups alive. I would see one group after another destroyed by corrosive
suspicion and distrust. In order for us to be effective as revolutionaries,
our communities of struggle must become *affective communities*—places
where we practice direct dialogue and prefigurative relationships.

The new generation of revolutionaries has a huge responsibility
today, most of all in the current crisis of capitalist civilization. We need
to muster imagination and prefigurative energy to demonstrate that
radical transformation of society is indeed possible, despite the words
of those two distinguished professors mentioned at the beginning of
this Introduction. That another world is conceivable, *without* eruptions
of violence. For this we need a new kind of synthesis. Perhaps the one
that I tried to propose: a reinvented and solidarity-centered libertarian
socialist synthesis that combines direct democracy with solidarity unionism. Strategy with program, accompaniment with warrening, structural
analysis with prefigurative theory arising from practice; stubborn belief
in the possibility of overcoming racism with affective anti-sectarianism.
This proposed synthesis is, perhaps, woefully inadequate, simplistic or
naive. Even if this is so—even if this is not that map which will take us
safely from here to there—I hope that it can at least provoke and inspire
a conversation moving toward these ends and ideals.

George Lukács ends his book, *Theory of the Novel*, with the sentence, "the voyage is over, now the travel begins." This is what happens at
the moment when the revolutionary glimmer has been extinguished: the
voyage of a particular revolutionary experience may be over, but the true
travel is just starting. At this very moment, I hear that the Polytechnic
school in Athens has been occupied once again. People are in the streets.
The spirit of December, one year after the rebellion, is everywhere.

Marxist political economists say that capitalist civilization is crum-
bling. This might be so. If it is, good riddance. We should hear the voice
of Buenaventura Durruti speaking to us, across decades, that we should
not be in the least afraid of its ruins. But the path to a new world that we
carry in our hearts, a path to a free socialist community, can be built only

on existing strengths, and not "upon the debris of a smashed society." Upon the positives, with our collective prefigurative creativity, we should venture to re-make another world. It is indeed a long journey. But as Staughton Lynd never ceases to remind us—as we walk we should hold hands, and keep facing forward.

## ENDNOTES

1   Because of his advocacy and practice of civil disobedience, Staughton was unable to continue as a full-time history teacher. The history departments of five Chicago-area universities offered him positions, only to have the offers negated by the school administrations. In 1976, Staughton became a lawyer. He worked for Legal Services in Youngstown, Ohio from 1978 until his retirement at the end of 1996. He specialized in employment law, and when the steel mills in Youngstown were closed in 1977-1980 he served as lead counsel to the Ecumenical Coalition of the Mahoning Valley, which sought to reopen the mills under worker-community ownership and brought the action *Local 1330 v. U.S. Steel.* He has written, edited, or co-edited with his wife Alice Lynd more than a dozen books. The Lynds have jointly edited four books. They are *Homeland: Oral Histories of Palestine and Palestinians* (New York: Olive Branch Press, 1994); *Nonviolence in America: A Documentary History,* revised edition (Maryknoll, NY: Orbis Books, 1995, now in its sixth printing); *Rank and File: Personal Histories by Working-Class Organizers,* third edition (New York: Monthly Review Press, 1988); and, most recently, *The New Rank and File* (Ithaca: Cornell University Press, 2000), which includes oral histories of labor activists in the past quarter century. Their memoir of life together is published under the title *Stepping Stones* (Lanham, MD: Lexington Books, 2009).

2   See especially Carl Mirra, *The Admirable Radical: Staughton Lynd and Cold War Dissent, 1945-1970* (Kent, OH: Kent State University Press, 2010).

3   See my book *Don't Mourn, Balkanize* (Oakland: PM Press, 2010).

4   A very good introduction to the anti-globalization movement is News from Nowhere, *We Are Everywhere* (New York: Verso, 2004).

5   Staughton Lynd, *Intellectual Origins of American Radicalism*, new edition (Cambridge: Cambridge University Press, 2009).

6   *Intellectual Origins*, pp. 171-172.

7   *Intellectual Origins*, p. 173.

8   *Ibid.*

9   David Graeber and Andrej Grubacic, "Anarchism, or the Revolutionary Movement of the Twenty-first Century," http://www.zmag.org/znet/viewArticle/9258.

10 Staughton Lynd and Andrej Grubacic, *Wobblies & Zapatistas:*

*Conversations on Marxism, Anarchism and Radical History* (Oakland: PM Press, 2008), p. 12.

11 *Wobblies & Zapatistas*, p. 241.

12 Cornelius Castoriadis, *Political and Social Writings* (Minneapolis: University of Minnesota Press, 1993), p. 131.

13 *Wobblies & Zapatistas*, p. 81.

14 See Invisible Committee, *The Coming Insurrection* (Los Angeles: Semiotext(e), 2009).

15 See Derrick Jensen, *A Language Older than Words* (White River Junction, VT: Chelsea Green, 2004).

16 David Graeber, *Direct Action: An Ethnography* (Oakland: AK Press, 2009).

17 *Wobblies & Zapatistas*, p. 215.

18 *Wobblies & Zapatistas*, p. 23.

19 *Wobblies & Zapatistas*, p. 176.

20 See Michael Schmidt and Lucien Van Der Walt, *Black Flame: The Revolutionary Class Politics of Anarchism and Syndicalism* (Oakland: AK Press, 2009).

21 Staughton Lynd has written about the Lucasville rebellion in "Black and White and Dead All Over," *Race Traitor*, no. 8 (Winter 1998); "Lessons from Lucasville," *The Catholic Worker*, v. LXV, no. 7 (Dec. 1998); and "The Lucasville Trials," *Prison Legal News*, v. 10, no. 6 (June 1999). This work is gathered together in *Lucasville: The Untold Story of a Prison Uprising* (Philadelphia: Temple University Press, 2004). Staughton has also contributed to a play by Gary Anderson about the Lucasville events.

# THE SIXTIES

W hat caused "the Sixties"? How did the uprising of African Americans, students, and ultimately, women, soldiers in Vietnam, and prisoners, come about? Remember that the movement to be explained was international, and outside the United States—as in France in 1968—involved workers, too.

No one appears to have an adequate answer. Perhaps the explanation that came closest was Paul Goodman's in his book *Growing Up Absurd*.

And why did the organizations of the Sixties, like the Student Nonviolent Coordinating Committee (SNCC) and Students for a Democratic Society (SDS), crash and burn before the decade ended? This, too, is a mystery demanding its historian.

As we await comprehensive accounts, perhaps we can seize and hold particular patches of historical terrain.

Henry Thoreau, whom Ralph Waldo Emerson called an "admirable radical," was the patron saint of all those who resisted arbitrary authority in the Sixties. He was the man who retreated for a year to Walden Pond and who called together fellow residents of Concord, Massachusetts to hear him speak in praise of Captain John Brown. Students who sat-in at segregated lunch counters and war objectors who tried to climb aboard nuclear submarines invoked Thoreau. "Henry Thoreau: The Admirable Radical" appeared in *Liberation* magazine in February 1963.

In my first year as a graduate student in history I wrote "How the Cold War Began," a review essay that drew on several books that had been recently published. Although SNCC and SDS were repeatedly denounced as Communist, in fact, as this essay shows, we kept our distance from both sides in the Cold War. "How the Cold War Began" was published in *Commentary* in November 1960. It is reprinted with the permission of Commentary, Inc.

The Sixties are rightly remembered for particular achievements, such as winning the right to vote for African Americans in the South and helping to end the Vietnam War. However, we were always multi-issue. Indeed we knew, early on, that the many single issues we confronted were products of an economic system. Speaking to the first mass protest against the Vietnam War, in Washington, D.C. in April 1965, Paul Potter, president of SDS, said that we must "name that system." But as was generally true in the Sixties, he did not name it. I tried to fill in the blank with "Socialism, the Forbidden Word," published by *Studies on the Left* in Summer 1963.

The signature campaign of the Sixties was Mississippi Freedom Summer in 1964. I was coordinator of Freedom Schools, improvised summer high schools for African American young people. Every one seemed to take pride in the Freedom Schools and in "Every School A Freedom School" I try to say why. "Every School A Freedom School" was an address to an organization of radical teachers called the Rouge Forum in May 2009, and is reprinted with permission.

In "Remembering SNCC," I commented on the strategy underlying the summer, which was to seat delegates from the Mississippi Freedom Democratic Party (MFDP) in place of delegates from the all-white state party at the Democratic National Convention. "Remembering SNCC" was a talk to the Organization of American Historians in March 2003. It was delivered at the motel in Memphis where Dr. King was murdered, which has been made over into a museum.

The words "participatory democracy" appeared in the SDS founding manifesto, the Port Huron Statement (1962). Like the song "We Shall Overcome" the term has spread all over the world. Wherever ordinary people demand accountability from their representatives, as throughout Latin America today, they often use the polysyllabic mantra bequeathed by SDS.

SDS published "The New Radicals and Participatory Democracy" as a pamphlet, reprinted from the Summer 1965 issue of *Dissent.*

The last two pieces in this section address the question: What can we learn from the Sixties so that, if given another chance, we can do better? "The Cold War Expulsions" was an address to an extraordinary gathering of the Pennsylvania Labor History Society at the Community College of Allegheny County in September 1998. The occasion brought together Catholics who had tried to expel Communists from the new unions of the CIO and members of the United Electrical Workers (UE) who had fought the expulsions.

"Weatherman" is a somewhat expanded version of a review of Mark Rudd's book that was previously published in *The Sixties: A Journal of History, Politics and Culture*, v. 2, no. 2 (September 2009), and is used with permission.

# 1. HENRY THOREAU: THE ADMIRABLE RADICAL

Henry Thoreau has become the patron saint of new radicals and of all unadjusted Americans. The existentialist doctrine of committed action, Martin Buber's concept of "encounter," and of course Gandhi's practice of civil disobedience, were all clearly anticipated by the retiring Concord surveyor. Like the young men of Concord in the 1840s, we find it natural to ask regarding this or that question of the day, What does Henry Thoreau think? Still more is he an oracle for those who, in choosing a life-work, turn aside from some "good thing" to launch out by dead reckoning on a wild course impossible to justify to friends and relatives. And for those drawn to direct confrontation with the Slave Powers and Mexican Wars of our own times, Thoreau's spare sentences, driven like nails into the heart of the matter, are Gospel and Baedeker for these forbidding regions.

Emerson, in his essay "The Transcendentalist," called "admirable radicals" those "intelligent and religious persons [who] withdraw themselves from the common labors and competitions of the market and the caucus, and betake themselves to a certain solitary and critical way of living." Emerson described their motives with his friend Thoreau in mind: "They are striking work, and crying out for something worthy to do! [Their attitude is:] If I cannot work, at least I need not lie." The weak soul among them, Emerson continued, uses up his strength in denial: "It is well if he can keep from lying, injustice, and suicide." But the strong spirits "overpower those around them without effort. Their thought and emotion comes in like a flood, [they] lose no time, but take the right road at first."

Thoreau appeals today to those who in greater or less degree feel driven to withdraw themselves from the common labors and competition of the market and the caucus, as he did. In the retrospect of the century since his death, he seems a strong spirit who, without wasting his strength on denial, chose the right road at first. Society as he found it, with its anxious competition and soul-exhausting materialism, repelled him. Institutionalized reform, full of talk without action, repelled him no less. He said "no" to both the Establishment and its organized opponents, and found his own way through to say "yes" before his God.

## I

Yet the nature of Thoreau's dissent remains unclear. He is usually regarded as both a pacifist and an anarchist. In fact he was neither.

Thoreau is commonly considered a pacifist because Gandhi acknowledged the impact of "Civil Disobedience" on the shaping of *satyagraha*. Thoreau's actual position, however, was the one he imputed to John Brown: a resolve that "he would never have anything to do with any war, unless it were a war for liberty." In 1854, Thoreau wrote: "Show me a free state, and a court truly of justice, and I will fight for them, if need be." In 1859, he said:

> It was his [John Brown's] peculiar doctrine that a man has a perfect right to interfere by force with the slaveholder, in order to rescue the slave. I agree with him. . . . I shall not be forward to think him mistaken in his method who quickest succeeds to liberate the slave. I speak for the slave when I say, that I prefer the philanthropy of Captain Brown to that philanthropy which neither shoots me nor liberates me.

All of us, Thoreau continued, are protected by violence every day in the form of the jail, the gallows, the handcuffs and billy of the policeman. "So we defend ourselves and our hen-roosts, and maintain slavery." Why shrink from violence when for once it is employed in a righteous cause? "I do not wish to kill nor to be killed, but I can foresee circumstances in which both these things would be by me unavoidable." Nor was this attitude toward violence a late development in contradiction to an earlier Thoreau: while in all his writings the regular soldier stands for conscienceless servility, the embattled soldier at Concord Bridge always stands for manly independence. What Gandhi took from Thoreau was not pacifism (this influence came rather from Tolstoy), but the concept of civil disobedience.

Thoreau was not an anarchist, either. He wrote in "Civil Disobedience": "to speak practically and as a citizen, unlike those who call themselves no-government men, I ask, not at once no government, but *at once* a better government." "The only government that I recognize," he repeated in "A Plea For Captain John Brown," "— and it matters not how few are at the head of it, or how small its army—is that power that establishes justice in the land." True, Thoreau was not content to wait on the usual political methods of voting and petition. He felt contempt for the politician's tendency to avoid fundamental questions: "The available candidate," Thoreau observed, "is invariably the Devil." However, Thoreau's decision to sever allegiance from the United States Government sprang not from a contempt for government in general, but from the conviction that this particular government was inherently corrupt because its very constitution (Article I, Section 2 and Article 4, Section 2) sanctioned slavery. Petitioning might be well, but "the State has provided no way; its very Constitution is the evil." In an America that was a "slave-ship," in a Massachusetts that was one of the "confederated overseers," the just man had no choice but total opposition.

As Thoreau himself made clear, this was not anarchism but revolution. "All men recognize the right of revolution," he writes in "Civil Disobedience," but they say that while it was right to revolt over a tax on tea, it is wrong to revolt over slavery. "I think," rebuts Thoreau, "that it is not too soon for honest men to revolt and revolutionize."

Thoreau's position in the late 1840s and 1850s was similar to Garrison's, who publicly burned the Fugitive Slave Law and the Constitution of the United States. These were the days when Congress required every citizen of the North to assist in capturing fugitive slaves, on pain of imprisonment; when the Supreme Court (in the Dred Scott case, 1857) ruled that a Negro could not be a United States citizen; when pro-Southern Presidents openly connived in extending the area of slavery. Thoreau was only one of many who, under these circumstances, resolved to transfer allegiance from the United States Constitution to a still "higher law" of universal morality. Sumner, Seward or Wendell Phillips could have said, as Thoreau did:

> I would remind my countrymen that they are to be men first, and Americans only at a late and convenient hour. No matter how valuable law may be to protect your property, even to keep body and soul together, if it do not keep you and humanity together [then break the law].

In rejecting the government of the hour, Thoreau appealed, in the classical manner of revolutionaries, to the people at large. "When, in some obscure country town, the farmers come together to a special town-meeting, to express their opinion on some subject which is vexing the land, that, I think, is the true Congress." Of the Mexican War which occasioned "Civil Disobedience," Thoreau remarked that it was "the work of a comparatively few individuals using the standing government as their tool; for, in the outset, the people would not have consented to this measure." Just how deeply-felt was Thoreau's sense of involvement in his country is suggested by a passage from "Slavery in Massachusetts." Here the occasion was the forcible return to slavery of the fugitive Anthony Burns in 1854. "I have lived for the last month," Thoreau wrote,

> —and I think that every man in Massachusetts capable of the sentiment of patriotism must have had a similar experience— with the sense of having suffered a vast and indefinite loss. I did not know at first what ailed me. At last it occurred to me that what I had lost was a country.

"I had never respected the government near to which I lived," Thoreau continued, "but . . . I have found that hollow which even I had relied on for solid."

> I am surprised to see men going about their business as if nothing had happened. I say to myself, "Unfortunate! They have not heard the news." . . . No prudent man will build a stone house under these circumstances, or engage in any peaceful enterprise which it requires a long time to accomplish. . . . It is not an era of repose. We have used up all our inherited freedom. If we would save our lives, we must fight for them.

Five years earlier, in "Civil Disobedience," Thoreau had said: "If I devote myself to other pursuits and contemplations, I must first see, at least, that I do not pursue them sitting on another man's shoulders." Now the author of *Walden* cried out: "I walk toward one of our ponds; but what signifies the beauty of nature when men are base? . . . The remembrance of my country spoils my walk."

In short, this gentle man was ready to resort to violence rather than live with the organized violence of slavery; this patriot (like Martin Luther King today) was ready to break the law to make the law more just. Neither a pacifist nor an anarchist, then, but—what? A revolutionary? Of course, but what sort of revolutionary? Let us approach this question a little more at our leisure.

## II

Two broad approaches have dominated Thoreau criticism. One sees in Thoreau the poet-naturalist, the bridegroom of nature, the Concord recluse, the solitary whittler, the self-appointed inspector of swamps and snowstorms This view takes as its texts *Walden* and *A Week on the Concord and Merrimac Rivers*, the two books Thoreau published in his lifetime. The other approach to Thoreau views him as a social radical increasingly drawn to abandon the study of nature for the emancipation of man. This view finds its point of departure in the reform essays already copiously quoted.

It will be obvious from the foregoing that, in my opinion, Thoreau's radicalism must not be regarded as something incidental or peripheral in his life. On the other hand, those who approach Thoreau by way of his concern for nature are quite right in saying that he often regarded public affairs as an irritating diversion from his principal business. Consider how, in *Walden*, Thoreau speaks of the night he spent in jail for refusing to pay a tax to support the Mexican War. The incident had occurred while he was living at the pond. "I had gone down the woods for other purposes. But, wherever a man goes, men will pursue and paw him with their dirty institutions, and, if they can, constrain him to belong to their desperate odd-fellow society." His response is not so much resistance as indifference. Let the state come after him if it will. "It is true, I might have resisted forcibly with more or less effect, might have run 'amok' against society; but I preferred that society should run 'amok' against me, it being the desperate party." When Thoreau emerged from his night in Concord jail, he did not go to the nearest soapbox, he went huckleberry-picking.

An adequate conception of Thoreau's life and mind must do more than either the botanical or the political approaches can do. It must set the man in a framework which holds together his passion for the water-lily and his concern for the auction-block. It must leave him, as he certainly was, whole.

Thoreau's writing testifies to this wholeness. He used the same words and images to express what he wanted to say about both nature and social justice. "I went to the woods," begins the best-known paragraph he ever wrote, "because I wished to live deliberately, to front only the essential facts of life." The sin of politics, similarly, was that "those who have been bred in the school of politics fail now and always to face the facts. . . . The fact which the politician faces is merely, that there was less honor among thieves than was supposed, and not the fact that they are thieves." John Brown was great because of his courage to "stand right fronting and face to face to" the fact of slavery. He was, Thoreau thought, "true as the voice of nature is."

The power of the naked truth is a grand theme of both *Walden* and the plea for John Brown. "Be it life or death, we crave only reality. . . . Any truth is better than make-believe." With this conviction Thoreau had gone to Walden to drive life into a corner. Thus he thought John

Brown, cornered in the Harpers Ferry armory, spoke to his captors as they stood over him.

Those who think the individual action thrown away uselessly, Thoreau wrote in "Civil Disobedience," "do not know by how much truth is stronger than error." Thoreau as much as Mill or Milton believed in the winnowing of truth from error. He saw the process not as an exchange of ideas, but as a confrontation of lives. Life based on principle, wherever and however lived, was "transcendentalism." To Thoreau, John Brown was "a transcendentalist above all." When Brown and his little band acted, "the North . . . was suddenly all transcendental." For the effect of this action, as of Thoreau's sojourn at Walden, was to drive the mind from formulae to "original perceptions."

Both in his approach to nature and in his approach to slavery, Thoreau insisted that a man begin where he is. He felt no need to leave Concord, for he sensed undiscovered continents in his own soul. And when in 1854 he attended an anti-slavery meeting of the town, he was "disappointed to find that what had called my townsmen together was the destiny of Nebraska, and not of Massachusetts." "I had thought," he went on, "that the house was on fire, and not the prairie [but] it was only the disposition of some wild lands a thousand miles off, which appeared to concern them. The inhabitants of Concord are not prepared to stand by one of their own bridges, but talk only of taking up a position on the highlands beyond the Yellowstone River." In this perspective Thoreau's intense localism, like Gandhi's comparable concept of *swadeshi* (home industry), was not quite so parochial as sometimes supposed.

Thoreau's predilection for the near-at-hand made him as skeptical of the reformer who attended only to "the gross but somewhat foreign form of servitude called Negro Slavery," as he was of the botanist who imported exotic plants which could, in fact, be found on a stroll through Concord woods. Closer to home was the capitalism which laid its rails on the bodies of Irishmen, and the spirit of capitalism which led the Concord farmer to creep down the road of life, pushing before him a barn seventy-five feet by forty.

Going to the pond was an act of social rebellion. It sprang from love of nature, but also from the stubborn conviction that "trade curses everything it handles," from a refusal to join his Harvard classmates in settling for a conventional career; from an utter distaste for the "lying, flattering, voting, contracting yourself into a nutshell of civility, or dilating into an atmosphere of thin and vaporous generosity," of organization men in the economy of the day. In "Life Without Principle," Thoreau presented the frenetic antagonists of a profit-oriented society, separated from each other as they labor within arm's reach, in this memorable image:

After reading Hewitt's account of the Australian gold-diggings one evening, I had in my mind's eye, all night, the numerous valleys, with their streams, all cut up with foul pits, from ten to one hundred feet deep, and half a dozen feet across, as close as they can be dug, and partly filled with water—the locality to which men furiously rush to probe for their fortunes—uncertain where they shall break ground—not knowing but the gold is under their camp itself—sometimes digging one hundred and sixty feet before they strike the vein, or then missing it by a foot—turned into demons, and regardless of each other's rights, in their thirst for riches—whole valleys, for thirty miles, suddenly honeycombed by the pits of the miners, so that even hundreds are drowned in them—standing in water and covered with mud and clay, they work night and day, dying of exposure and disease.

Here were men more desperately circumstanced than the "silent poor" of the city slums evoked in *Walden*, for their fate was self-willed. The application of the Fugitive Slave Law to Massachusetts made Thoreau cry out, in the same year that "Life Without Principle" was delivered as a lecture, that he was living "*wholly within* hell." But clearly a man who, believing that "you must get your living by loving," saw the ordinary free society of his day as "the activity of flies about a molasses-hogshead," would not have felt transported to heaven merely by the emancipation of the slave.

Love of nature and rebellion against society were very practically blended in Thoreau because he made his living by manual labor. It was his occupation by choice, and he continued it throughout his adult life: I do not believe this can be said of any other man of letters in American history. His preference of silence to words, his insistence (which we shall come to in a moment) on action, his feeling for tangible realities—"hard bottom and rocks in place, which we can call *reality*, and say, This is, and no mistake; and then begin"—are bound up with these years of manual labor. In the *Week*, for instance, he eulogizes the farmers on the bank,

> men you never heard of before, whose names you don't know ...
> rude and sturdy, experienced and wise men, ... teaming up their
> summer's wood, or chopping alone in the woods, men fuller of
> talk and rare adventure, than a chestnut is of meat; who were not
> only in '75 and 1812, but have been out every day of their lives.
> ... Look at their fields, and imagine what they might write, if
> ever they should put pen to paper. Or what they have not writ-
> ten on the face of the earth already, clearing, and burning, and

scratching, and harrowing, and plowing, and subsoiling, in and in, and out and out, and over and over, again and again, erasing what they had already written for want of parchment.

More intimately and convincingly, Thoreau struck the same note in *Walden*, in his portraits of the Canadian woodchopper and other unlettered visitors. It sounds again in the great affirmation of "Civil Disobedience" that prison is where "the fugitive slave, and the Mexican prisoner on parole, and the Indian come to plead the wrongs of his race, should find" the man of principle. One may shrug off as romanticism this sense of abstract identity with other workingmen. It was very real to Thoreau. Writing of Carlyle, Thoreau declared: "Above and after all, the Man of the Age, come to be called workingman, it is obvious that none yet speaks to his condition, for the speaker is not yet in his condition. Like speaks to like only; labor to labor, philosophy to philosophy, criticism to criticism, poetry to poetry."

Both as naturalist and as reformer, Thoreau turned away from the ordinary life of the intellect as well as from the ordinary life of the market-place. Life in the woods was a rejection of the academic round, of scholars who "sell their birthright for a mess of learning." At or away from Walden, the doctrine of doctrine in Thoreau's cosmology was action.

## III

Action, not mere activity. Thoreau, of course, could sit for hours watching ants, or listening to the hum of a telegraph wire; he did just as little gainful labor as he could do so as to have "freedom left for my proper pursuits"; he believed that "the truly efficient laborer will not crowd his day with work, but saunter to his task, surrounded by a wide halo of ease and leisure." The inaction Thoreau abhorred was hypocrisy: the failure to act as one talked.

"There are thousands," Thoreau wrote of the Mexican War, "who are *in opinion* opposed to slavery and to the war, who yet in effect do nothing to put an end to them; who, esteeming themselves children of Washington and Franklin, sit down with their hands in their pockets, and say that they know not what to do, and do nothing; who even postpone the question of freedom to the question of free-trade, and quietly read the prices-current along with the latest advice from Mexico, after dinner, and, it may be, fall asleep over them both." They vote, but with a strip of paper not the whole of themselves. "They hesitate, and they regret, and sometimes they petition; but they do nothing in earnest and with effect." If they are Christians, so much the worse for them:

The modern Christian is a man who has consented to say all
the prayers in the liturgy, provided you will let him go straight
to bed and sleep quietly afterward. All his prayers begin with
"Now I lay me down to sleep," and he is forever looking forward to the time when he shall go to his "*long* rest."

Here again the Thoreau of *Walden* and of "John Brown" are one
man. What is *Walden* but a long plea ("perhaps more particularly addressed to poor students") that we not accept lives of quiet desperation,
that we venture out in faith as one who "advances confidently in the direction of his dreams"?

On the eve of World War II, Gandhi wrote to a friend in Europe
that if one man in Europe truly understood nonviolence he could stop
the war. This was Thoreau's faith exactly. "When one man has reduced
a fact of the imagination to be a fact of his understanding," he wrote in
*Walden*, "I foresee that all men will at length establish their lives on that
basis." One man, he wrote in "Civil Disobedience," who withdrew his
allegiance from the slave-catching state and went to prison for it, could
"be the abolition of slavery in America." Ten years later at Harpers Ferry,
Thoreau thought he had found his man; and the historian pondering
the effect of that one man in a century's retrospect can only gasp at the
accuracy of the prediction.

Thoreau valued thought only as it opened up new ways to act. The
philosopher, he argued, must "solve some of the problems of life, not only
theoretically, but practically. The success of great scholars and thinkers
is commonly a courtier-like success, not kingly, not manly. They make
shift to live merely by conformity, practically as their fathers did, and
are in no sense the progenitors of a nobler race of men." Authors should
put themselves into their books, or else put down their pens. "We do not
learn much from learned books, but from . . . frank and honest biogra-
phies." "The word which is best said came nearest to not being spoken at
all, for it is cousin to a deed which the speaker could have better done."
Seventeenth-century English literature was full of life because "the little
that is said is eked out by implication of the much that was done." Right
action for Thoreau was more than rational, it was the intuitive gesture of
the whole man.

Consistently, too, Thoreau invoked the New Testament as a gospel
of the act, not the Word. Thoreau was a foe of religious doctrines; like
Emerson, he sought to come out of church into God's universe; more
than Emerson, he celebrated his pantheism with aggressively heathen
hymns to health and a good conscience. But he gladly called Brown a
Puritan, and was in fact very much of a Puritan himself. "There is no such

thing as sliding up a hill. In morals, the only sliders are backsliders." Thus he rapped the knuckles of the Massachusetts judges who condoned the rendition of fugitive slaves. The New Testament for Thoreau was one of those facts which cleaves a man to his marrow. "There are, indeed, several things in it which no man should read aloud but once, things like 'Lay not up for yourselves treasures on earth,' and 'For what is a man profited, if he shall gain the whole world, and lose his own soul?' They never *were* read, they never *were* heard. Let but one of these sentences be rightly read from any pulpit in the land, and there would not be left one stone of that meeting-house upon another."

Each of Thoreau's reform essays is built, unobtrusively and with irony, upon one of these sentences. "Men labour under a mistake," Thoreau writes early in *Walden*. "By a seeming fate, commonly called necessity, they are employed, as it says in an old book, laying up treasures which moth and rust will corrupt and thieves break through and steal." "The question is," he says in "Slavery in Massachusetts," "not whether you or your grandfather, seventy years ago, did not enter into an agreement to serve the Devil, and that service is not accordingly now due; but whether you will not now, for once and at last, serve God . . . by obeying that eternal and only just CONSTITUTION, which He, and not any Jefferson or Adams, has written in your being." And above all, in "Civil Disobedience":

> If I have unjustly wrested a plank from a drowning man, I must restore it to him though I drown myself. This, according to Paley, would be inconvenient. But he that would save his life, in such a case, shall lose it. This people must cease to hold slaves, and to make war on Mexico, though it cost them their existence as a people.

## IV

But can the watcher by the pond, even the bell-ringer in the meetinghouse, give us more than vague and nostalgic encouragement today? One wonders how Thoreau, tough and gritty as he was, would have "fronted the fact" of the gas chamber or the mushroom cloud. Solitary men of principle seem at first glance irrelevant to the mindless bureaucracies which threaten to destroy us.

To laud Thoreau in general and for yesterday but to deny his pertinence in particular and at present is (as he said of parlor Abolitionists) to give Godspeed to the right as it goes by us. For all over the world, a new radicalism is rediscovering the spirit of Thoreau. Non-aligned individuals appear everywhere, refusing to torture Algerians, hurling bricks at Soviet tanks, clambering aboard Polaris submarines, choosing jail without bail in Mississippi. How similar are the words they use to the century-old sentences of Thoreau! Thus Schweitzer has written that example is not the main means of persuasion, it is the only means.

I recently quoted to a civil-rights leader Thoreau's statement that one wholly-committed man could abolish slavery. To our mutual astonishment, he replied that he had often said to his co-workers that one man unafraid of death could abolish racial discrimination in Mississippi. Surely such rediscovery of Thoreauvian principles by persons unaware of his writings, is strong testimony to his continued relevance.

Thoreau's writings, however, could help the new radicals to sharpen their thinking. Probably most new radicals would define their ideology so as to include the three elements of 1) direct action, 2) civil disobedience, 3) nonviolence. They tend to regard these three elements as parts of an inseparable whole. Hence, when their direct action is obviously coercive, as in the case of economic boycotts, they continue to regard it as an expression of love; or when the whole strategy of their movement rests on a Supreme Court decision, they nonetheless consider themselves the heirs of "Civil Disobedience."

We have seen that what was central for Thoreau was neither nonviolence nor civil disobedience, but direct action: the absolute demand that one practice—right now, and all alone if necessary—what one preaches. My own impression is that this imperative is also the essential quality of the new radicalism. Would it not be more truthful for the young radicals to say that they believe in nonviolence when possible, civil disobedience if necessary, but direct personal action in all cases whatsoever? That was Thoreau's view, and it enabled him to support John Brown in 1859 and Abraham Lincoln in 1861, to oppose the Mexican War but approve the Civil War, without hypocrisy or inconsistency. (In contrast, Garrison had abruptly to abandon nonviolence and Wendell Phillips to change his views of the Constitution, in order to support the Union when the war came.) No less significant than the material simplicity Thoreau espoused was his ideological simplicity. The one precept of direct action—the principle, in Paul Goodman's words, of, "If not now, when?"—was his only intellectual baggage. Thus stripped for action, he remained flexible to grow and change.

Thoreau's personal strategy was to escape from under society by simplifying his wants. But are we all to go to Walden and grow beans?

Perhaps a clue lies in the fact that what Thoreau sought at Walden was to avoid the perpetual consciousness of things and money which filled the minds of the mass of men he knew. In his view it was not so much the work men did as their anxiety about work which made them quietly desperate about their lives. Thoreau observed the housing of the poor, he protested the exploitation of the railway laborer, but his audience was principally those who had only themselves for overseer. Like Veblen, whom he resembles in so many ways, Thoreau opposed the spirit of capitalism and the psychology of materialism, more than poverty or exploitation as such. As he says in "Life Without Principle," he wanted making a living to be an unconscious function of society, like digestion in the body. He resented above all being asked to scheme and haggle and fret over matters which seemed to him inferior business for the human soul.

Seen in this way, the doctrine of *Walden* can be squared with the Industrial Revolution. It can even be squared with socialism. If Thoreau could have made his living in a public workshop as casually or matter-of-factly as he used the Concord library or the town meeting-hall, I think he would have been content. In a fugitive review of a book entitled *Paradise (to Be) Regained*, Thoreau once commented on the Fourierist schemes for potential material abundance which were popular in the 1840s. He had no objection to them; he only urged that in attending to the unused energies of machines and matter, the greater unused energy of love be not forgotten. Nor was he altogether an anti-statist in cultural matters. Several glowing pages of *Walden* are devoted to the dream of Concord village as a patron of learning and the arts.

Thoreau was a practical man who urged his readers to keep their castles-in-the-air but build foundations under them. The foundation for his dreams today might have to be different than the hut at Walden. The possibility of a socialist Thoreau is suggested by the fact that the British Labor Party in the generation of Tawney, Cole and Laski took *Walden* as its Bible, as by Gandhi's remarkable statement, a year before his death, that "truth and *ahimsa* must incarnate in socialism." My point here is not to appropriate Thoreau for a particular political philosophy, but simply to underline his continued amplitude and fecundity in a world of bureaucracies and machines. No doubt whatever institutional apparatus we suggested to the grey old rebel, he would respond that there was still more day to dawn.

At the banquet which closed the Yalta conference, Roosevelt, Churchill, and Stalin all offered toasts. When it came Churchill's turn, he

> addressed himself to the years ahead. He felt, he said, that all
> were standing on the crest of a hill with the glories of great
> future possibilities stretching before them; that in the mod-
> ern world the function of leadership was to lead the people
> out from the forests into the broad sunlit plains of peace and
> happiness. He felt that this prize was nearer their grasp than
> at any time in history, and that it would be a great tragedy if
> they, through inertia or carelessness, let it slip from their grasp.
> History would never forgive them if they did.[1]

We live today amid the ruins of that hope. Any responsible inquiry into the present controversies between the United States and the Soviet Union must find its way back, from the U-2 to Hungary and Suez, thence to Korea, Czechoslovakia, the Marshall Plan, and the Truman Doctrine, and so, finally, to that time and that failure. In those months of early 1945 which Herbert Feis, in his new book,[2] has called "between war and peace," the hard core of difference between East and West is to be found.

None of us can presume to discuss this question without anxiety or passion. One finds it peculiarly difficult to bring to bear on the problem of the cold war the intellectual discipline which, say, the Spanish-American or even the First World War can now readily call forth. The shrill and strained atmosphere, the partisan interpretations of war and quasi-war have been with us for an uninterrupted quarter of a century. We live, move, and have our intellectual being in a habitually clamorous climate of opinion.

Yet how precious would be the gift of seeing the cold war, now, with the kind of perspective which commonly comes only after the passage of much time. There are very few international crises which in the historian's retrospect altogether justify the ideology or behavior of any of the participants. We know now that the war of 1812 began days after, on the other side of the Atlantic, the English Orders in Council which occasioned it had been revoked. Today many of us would be ready to join Henry Thoreau in his Concord jail to protest the war against Mexico. Years after the Spanish-American War, experts examined the torn hull of the battleship *Maine* and concluded that the explosion had taken place not outside the boat but within. The blundering or hypocrisy or chicanery which brought on these wars seems to us today inadmissible. In short, if we could only approximate the historians' collective judgment, a generation hence, concerning the cold war, we might be helped in our understanding of the practical alternatives that are presently before us.

In search of objectivity the American student may attempt to balance the work of Westerners by consulting Soviet accounts. He will be disappointed. It is true that Soviet historians are far more familiar with English, French, and German sources than Westerners are with publications in Russian. For example, V. I. Israelyan's *Diplomatic History of the Great Patriotic War* (Moscow, 1959; in Russian) cites ten American collections of documents and over sixty memoirs and historical works in English. It is also true that the skeleton of events narrated by a work like Israelyan's is full and accurate. But time after time crucial interpretations are woodenly self-justificatory. Human blundering and groping on both sides of the Iron Curtain are underestimated. Thus Stalin's attitude toward the treatment of postwar Germany is made to seem consistent at all times; and he is said to have refused Churchill's famous proposal in October 1944 to divide Eastern Europe into British and Soviet spheres of influence because "the Soviet Union in correspondence with its policy of non-interference in the inner affairs of other nations rejected all plans for division of Eastern Europe into spheres of influence." Inversely, the Soviets tend to portray American policy as changing from white to black after the death of Roosevelt, whereas among Western scholars even those who are most sympathetic to Soviet behavior in the cold war have stressed the vacillations and ambiguities in Roosevelt's dealing with the USSR.[3]

One turns back, perforce, to Western scholarship. Here two first-class scholars have been at work: Feis, in the two books already cited, and William McNeill of the University of Chicago, in his brilliant earlier account, *America, Britain and Russia: Their Cooperation and Conflict, 1941–1946* (London, 1953). These works have a quasi-official character. Feis's books were, so he tells the reader, in part inspired by Averill Harriman, America's wartime ambassador to the Soviet Union. They draw both on unpublished papers of Harriman's and on the unpublished papers of the State Department (these have just been closed to scholars). McNeill's volume, similarly, was commissioned by the Royal Institute of International

Affairs and scrutinized before publication by "a number of individuals familiar with the events narrated." Thus the works of Feis and McNeill are something more than individual interpretations. To a degree they represent the collective memory of British and American officialdom about their wartime alliance with Soviet Russia and how it broke down.

Perhaps because of their quasi-official character the Feis and McNeill books display the same defect as their Soviet counterparts. They narrate, but they do not really interpret. They do not face squarely the childlike and penetrating question, Why did the cold war start? Some of McNeill's sharpest observations are buried in footnotes. Feis concludes *Between War and Peace* with the moving sentence: "To choose life, the great nations must one and all live and act more maturely and trustfully than they did during the months that followed the end of the war against Germany." Moving, but also banal. Feis does not go beneath the surface of events in search of the specific men and motives that obstructed the choice for life, the inarticulate major premises which led each side to a point from which further retreat seemed inadmissible.

To go beneath the surface means, as I have said, going back. The climactic events of the six months after Yalta—the defeat of Germany, the San Francisco and Potsdam conferences, the testing and use of the atom bomb, all shadowed and confused by the death of Roosevelt and the political defeat of Churchill—brought into the open the conflict in objectives between England and America and the Soviet Union. But this conflict had existed in embryo from the first tentative discussions in 1941 of postwar aims among the three military partners. While the war lasted, each side, intensely needful of the other's military aid, tended to avoid direct confrontation of the latent political tensions. Even at Teheran (1943), perhaps the high point of Big Three harmony, McNeill comments that "Allied co-operation could be and was founded upon agreement on military strategy. Agreement on post-war issues was not genuinely achieved. All important decisions were left for the future after only vague explanation of the issues involved." Victory over Germany, together with the decision of the Truman cabinet that Soviet military assistance was not essential to the defeat of Japan, lifted the lid of a Pandora's box.

The characteristic, continuing objectives of each of the three powers had in fact become quite clear within a year of the German attack on the Soviet Union. When the Red Army, to the surprise of the highest military personnel in both England and America, survived into the winter of 1941-1942, serious negotiations as to postwar goals began. Then as later Stalin underscored the fact that twice in thirty years Russia had been invaded through Poland, and insisted on a more westerly frontier (incorporation of the Baltic nations and the Curzon Line in Poland)

and a friendly postwar Polish government. Then as later Churchill, also thinking in terms of his nation's security, showed himself ready to bargain with the Soviet Union on a *quid pro quo* basis but equally ready to invoke the threat of force if negotiation seemed inadequate; it was at this time that Churchill, having just signed the Atlantic Charter with its promise of democracy for "all the men in all the lands," told Parliament that the phrase was not meant to apply to the British Empire. In December 1941, Foreign Minister Anthony Eden went to Moscow to seek an accommodation of Soviet and British diplomatic objectives.

Here American diplomacy intervened in a way which foreshadowed future Soviet-American tension. That December, and again in May 1942 when Molotov visited London and Washington, Secretary of State Hull brought strong pressure on the English government to avoid territorial commitments until a postwar peace conference. On the latter occasion, indeed, he threatened to issue a public statement dissociating the United States from any such agreement reached between Britain and the Soviet Union. The American objective, for Roosevelt and Hull as for Woodrow Wilson years before, was to prevent dictation to small nations so that they might determine their own destinies through democratic processes; and to substitute for the balance-of-power arrangements which seemed inevitable and natural to America's European partners, an international organization to keep the peace. Thus in the Second as in the First World War, American diplomacy sought nothing less than a diplomatic new deal, an altogether new start in the conduct of international relations.

Not only in objectives but in ways and means American diplomatic behavior in this first year of the war was symptomatic of much that was to follow. Avoiding hard bargaining on specific issues, America sought—in the words of a Hopkins memo—to "take the heat off" the Soviet territorial demands by pushing hard for a second front (as well as by talking of a postwar international organization in terms which were, as Feis says, "vaguely magnificent rather than sturdy"). The United States of course had other substantial reasons for desiring a second front. But Feis and McNeill make it clear that the Americans found it a "happy coincidence" that the military strategy which they favored, a direct assault on Germany through France, was at the same time the form of assistance which the Soviet Union desired above all others. The American hope, Feis writes, was that "the Soviet government was to be lured away from one boon by a choicer one, away from its absorption in frontiers by the attraction of quick military relief."

By championing the second front and postponing to a later day the inherent conflict between the American concern for worldwide democracy and the Soviet preoccupation with the security of its borders, Roosevelt established himself, by the middle of 1942, as a mediator between Churchill and Stalin. As McNeill observes in a remarkable footnote, this relationship was a personal tour de force which rested on a peculiar and indeed artificial basis of fact:

> The British public was perceptibly warmer in its feeling toward Russia than was the American public, among whom repugnance to socialism and consciousness of Russia's failure to join in the war against Japan were far greater than in Britain. On the other hand, the American Government in general assumed a more indulgent attitude toward Russia on current questions (for instance Lend-Lease), combined with a more rigid attitude on long-range issues (for instance, the question of the Baltic states) than did the British Government. The secret of this curious contradiction lay mainly in the fact that Churchill and Eden thinking largely in terms of a balance of power, wanted to bargain with Stalin, whereas Roosevelt and Hull thought in terms of abstract principles to which they hoped Stalin could, if treated indulgently enough by his wartime allies, be committed.

When in 1942 and again in 1943 Roosevelt failed to deliver on a second front, a foundation was laid for future ill will.

Viewed in this way, Roosevelt's approach to the Soviet Union appears fundamentally similar to that of Wilson and to that of Eisenhower; personalities fall away, and the thread of a shared tradition stands forth. All three Presidents attempted to eschew diplomatic settlements based on a balance of power. Like Wilson at Versailles, and indeed in conscious recoil from Wilson's entanglement in secret wartime agreements, Roosevelt and Hull during World War II sought to brush aside concrete, immediate points of difference in order to establish agreement on general principles of world organization. Feis says of Hull in 1943:

> Over each disjointed problem the interested and rival powers were poised—ready to contest, bargain and threaten. This had been the customary way in the past by which questions of frontiers, political affiliations and the like got settled. He wanted to bring it about that all such exercises in national power and diplomacy would in the future be subordinated to rules of principle.

The Americans, McNeill agrees,

> tended to think of the establishment of an international orga-
> nization as a sort of talisman which would possess a powerful
> virtue to heal disputes among the nations. Instead of regarding
> international politics as essentially and necessarily an affair of
> clashing interests and struggle for power, Americans, both of-
> ficials and the general public, tended to think that international
> politics were, or at least should be, a matter of legal right and
> wrong, and that the common interest of all men and nations
> in the maintenance of peace was so obvious and so compel-
> ling that only hardened criminals would think of transgressing
> against it.

Alike in placing too much reliance on the forms of international organization, Wilson, Roosevelt and Eisenhower also have shared a tendency to evolve simplistic solutions to the internal problems of foreign nations. For all three men the sovereign nostrum for the domestic ills of other nations has been, "When in doubt, hold a free election." Roosevelt grasped the awakening of the colonial world but conceived it one-sidedly in formal political terms; less than Wendell Willkie did he perceive the universal challenge to the big house on the hill. Land reform, for example, was as germane to the emergence of democracy in Eastern Europe as were free elections. Indeed land reform was a principal bone of contention between the Soviet-sponsored Lublin government and the Polish government-in-exile. Yet the Big Three paid it scant attention in their interminable discussion of the Polish question.

One cannot avoid the suspicion that Roosevelt's intermittent demand for freedom in Eastern Europe did not altogether escape the tragi-comic quality of Wilson's insistence that the revolutionary Huerta regime in Mexico conduct a plebiscite on its own legitimacy, or—*reductio ad absurdum*—President Eisenhower's recent proposal for a worldwide referendum on communism and democracy. In each of these incidents, the American President expressed a sincere and idealistic concern, but a concern which did not really represent a practical alternative in the given situation. McNeill points out that "neither Roosevelt nor Churchill seems frankly to have faced the fact that, in Poland at least, genuinely free democratic elections would return governments unfriendly to Russia." Therefore, he continues,

> the democratic process on which so many eulogies were ex-
> pended could not produce governments in Eastern Europe (or

in many other parts of the world) that would further the harmony of the Great Powers and prove acceptable to all of them. Men were not so uniform, so rational, nor possessed of such good will, as the democratic theory presupposed; and in talking of Eastern European governments which would be both democratic and friendly to Russia the Western Powers were in large part deluding themselves.

George Kennan has written in much the same vein of the American Open Door policy in the Far East. "Our constant return to these ideas," Kennan says, "would not serve really to prevent the conflict of interests in China from living themselves out pretty much in accordance with their own strategic, political, and economic necessities." Just so the State Department policy toward Europe during World War II, according to Feis, "tried to arrest the march of armies, the clash of civil wars, the forays of diplomacy by repeated affirmations of the view that principle should govern European postwar settlements."

This syndrome of American attitudes—a syndrome which Walter Lippman has called "Wilsonian" and E. H. Carr "Utopian," and which has been best characterized by Kennan—threw up significant obstacles to the making of a peace. To say this is not to belittle the American dream of democracy and world organization. It is not so much the American goals in World War II but the lack of realism with which they were elaborated in specific circumstances that is disturbingly prophetic of much which liberals now like to think of as uniquely Eisenhowerian. How similar to latter-day criticisms of American diplomacy's lack of "initiative" are these words of McNeill describing Roosevelt's passivity as the need for postwar decisions bore down on him:

> From early in 1942 the American Government had repeatedly proclaimed the principle that no final decision on matters of post-war frontiers or systems of government should be made until the end of the war. The theory that a political vacuum could be maintained in Europe was absurd on its face; but this principle helped to hide from American officials the daily necessity of making decisions.

American indecision in the closing years of the war diminished the chances for post-war settlements in both Poland and Germany. Long before Hungary [in 1956], United States foreign policy was encouraging hopes in Eastern Europe which it had no concrete plans to support. Thus, early in 1944 Roosevelt refused to "back in an unambiguous manner" the proposals for Poland agreed on at Teheran, instead

contenting himself with amiable sentiments about "freely negotiated" and "friendly" settlement of the Soviet-Polish dispute.
Clearly Roosevelt did not wish to grasp the nettle, hoping that
Stalin and the Poles would come to terms of their own accord.
But his attitude only confirmed the Poles in their obstinate
disregard of the realities of their situation, and allowed them to
cling to the belief that Roosevelt would come to their rescue.

"In this instance," McNeill continues, "and throughout the following year,
Roosevelt tried to avoid the responsibilities of the new American power,
and by not making himself clear to the Poles he stored up trouble for the
future." Thus in 1944, when Mikolajczyk went to Moscow to consult
with Churchill and Stalin about Poland, he was astonished to learn that
everyone but himself had thought that Roosevelt at Teheran essentially
accepted the Curzon line. At Yalta, Admiral Leahy warned Roosevelt
that the vagueness of the accord reached on reorganizing the Polish government would permit the Russians to make their own interpretation: the
President could only wearily reply, "I know, Bill, I know."

Of Germany, McNeill writes that "the American Government,
because of its internal disputes and indecision, prevented even the discussion of a common Allied policy for Germany." Alarmed by the furor
occasioned by the Morgenthau Plan, Roosevelt put a stop to all efforts to
make postwar plans for Germany from late 1944 until his death. "This
ostrich attitude towards the future," says McNeill, "prevented whatever
chance there may have been for arriving at Allied agreement upon policy
toward Germany through the European Advisory Commission or in any
other way, and left the subordinate American officials who were charged
with the task completely at sea."

In default of an American initiative, what planning for peace took
place in 1943-44 consisted chiefly of British and Soviet attempts to divide Europe between them into spheres of influence. The story of these
attempts is an important one, for it suggests that the Soviets, like the
West, felt in 1945 that past understandings between the Big Three concerning Eastern Europe were betrayed.

The pattern for postwar spheres of influence in the liberated European
countries was established in Italy, however, not in Eastern Europe, and by
England and America rather than by Russia. In theory the three military
partners were committed to joint decision-making and to democratic self-
determination within every European country, regardless of whose armies
were occupying it. But in fact, the Big Three tacitly recognized and accepted spheres of influence all over the world. In China, Feis writes, "Stalin

and Churchill seemed willing to have the American government take the lead in directing the political evolution of that country; and the American government was assuming it. Similarly, it was understood that Britain could be to the fore in dealing with Southeast Asia." And Churchill said of South America: "We follow the lead of the United States in South America as far as possible, as long as it is not a question of our beef and mutton." The habits twined about these long-standing arrangements proved too strong to be offset in meeting the challenge of liberated Europe when it first presented itself in Italy.

England took the lead. Churchill wanted to keep the monarchy in Italy, and deprecated any statement about self-determination. Russia's desire to take an active role through a tripartite military-political commission was deflected by the fact that Western commanders retained power, and when Russia established independent diplomatic relations with the Italian government, its move was strongly resented and protested by the West. The powers which Russia wanted, however, were the very ones that England and America were later to demand in Eastern Europe and which the Soviets denied, pointing persistently to Italian precedents. Some Westerners foresaw the result of the West's behavior in Italy; thus Ambassador Winant wrote in July 1943, that "when the tide turns and the Russian armies are able to advance we might well want to influence their terms of capitulation and occupancy in Allied and enemy territory." But this view did not prevail and the outcome was, in McNeill's words, that "in Italy, Russia had been effectively excluded from participation in Allied decision-making, and the Western Allies could hardly expect to be treated differently by the Russians in Rumania."

As German resistance began to crumple and the Allied armies poured into Festung Europa, the volume and pace of political decision-making in occupied territory necessarily increased. England began making independent approaches to the Soviet Union looking toward an agreement on spheres of influence which would safeguard the Mediterranean lifeline and put some limit to the Red Army's advance. "Experience," Feis comments,

> was showing how hard it was to apply the rule of common consent in each of these unstable situations. And decision would not always wait. In brief, the diplomatic methods in use began to seem defective or unsuitable—awkward for war, ineffective for peace. Hence both diplomats and soldiers began to wonder whether an arrangement which made one or the other Allies the dominant authority in each of these situations was not the sensible way to end the discussion.

Churchill, more tersely, stated that in each of the occupied countries someone had to play the hand, and with this in mind he journeyed to Moscow in October 1944 to make his division of Eastern Europe with Stalin, and thus safeguard British predominance in Greece.

As in 1941-42, so in these negotiations of 1943-44 the United States preferred to remain, in the words of the Monroe Doctrine, an "anxious and interested spectator." Harry Hopkins intervened to change the text of Roosevelt's cable to Churchill referring to the latter's Moscow trip, so that the American President, rather than empowering Churchill to speak for him, insisted on retaining "complete freedom of action." The reserved American veto imparted a provisional character to the Churchill-Stalin agreement. Thus it was that Western policy toward Eastern Europe in 1945 wavered because England and America had not reached full agreement, but the Russians, as in the similar case of the second front, interpreted the wavering as simple bad faith. Stalin protested that he had no idea whether the governments of Belgium and France, created under Western aegis, were democratic; he simply accepted them. Did not the accord of October 1944, although expressly limited to provisional arrangements until German surrender, give him by implication a similar free hand in Eastern Europe?

The first test of the new arrangement came in Greece. In his effort to make the agreement with Churchill stick, Stalin stood aside while British troops crushed Communist-led Greek guerrillas: in Churchill's words, Stalin "adhered very strictly to this understanding." At the same time—as Feis, McNeill, and Williams all agree—he attempted to curb the Communist parties in Western Europe, Yugoslavia, and China from bidding for power, lest such an attempt spark off armed conflict between the great powers. It was therefore something of an irony when the Chinese revolution seemed to the West to confirm its image of the irresistible expansionism of Russian Communism.

In the absence of firm tripartite agreements, particularly about Poland, the British government, hitherto the advocate of realistic acceptance of a Soviet sphere of influence in Eastern Europe, at war's end found itself imploring American military assistance to contain the expansion of Soviet power. The upshot was as paradoxical as it was tragic. A sequence of events familiar in Anglo-American diplomatic history then took place. As in the formulation of the Monroe Doctrine, as in the formulation of the Open Door policy, the British government suggested to America a joint declaration of policy for reasons altogether in the realm of *Realpolitik*. As in the two preceding instances, so in 1945-47 the United States government proclaimed the policy as its own and lent it the panoply of a moral crusade. Ten years later, in consequence, England was in the position of trying to restrain the partner which but yesterday it had to prod.

Looking back, it is still difficult to assign responsibility with any sureness for this critical turn of events. America, which realized the importance of creating the United Nations before the bonds of wartime partnership were relaxed, failed to see the comparable importance of more humble agreements about governments and frontiers, and this failure complicated the already inherent difficulty where two men so different in their points of view as Churchill and Stalin had to reach firm agreements. A number of prominent Americans, including Roosevelt and Hopkins, were deeply impressed by England's determination to retain its empire: this made them slow to accept Churchill's growing fear of Russian expansion, just as it blinded them to the truth that, in actual hard fact, America had always depended on the English empire to shield it from potential aggressors. Had the Soviet leaders been less suspicious and dogmatic than they were, they might well have been confused in responding to an England which did not have the strength to enforce its realism, and an America which did not seem to realize that idealism must be supported by something more than documents.

For the Soviets, such indecision on the part of the West must have encouraged the hope, championed by Trotsky after World War I, of carrying the revolution westward on the bayonets of the Red Army. Advocates of the Russian interpretation of these events have quoted the Forrestal diaries to show that military leaders in the West did not really fear Soviet attack;[4] but these quotations begin no earlier than 1946, when the readiness to mobilize military force to deter such attack had already shown itself. Feis and McNeill reiterate that we possess very little material with which to interpret Soviet intentions in the spring of 1945. But there seems no good reason to doubt that the Russians were prepared to carry their influence as far westward as they could safely go without risking the danger of war.

The inertia acquired by supposedly temporary military arrangements, their tendency then to turn into a political status quo unless deflected by new agreements for which, after Yalta, the Big Three alliance suddenly seemed no longer capable, posed for the West a genuinely "agonizing reappraisal." It seemed that to keep on a friendly footing with Russia it was necessary to betray (as it appeared to the West) the Polish people on whose behalf England had gone to war. Roosevelt and Truman were not as different in their reactions to this problem as extremists of both the right and the left would have one think: the President who sent the two most pro-Soviet men in American governmental circles (Davies and Hopkins) as his first envoys to Churchill and Stalin cannot have been, initially, bitterly anti-Soviet.

The course ultimately adopted was, of course, containment, and its error lay, surely, in making such a "posture" the *whole* of one's foreign policy. In itself, containment was simply the normal practice of diplomacy which sought to maintain a balance of power, and supported this effort with the threat of force; England has certainly never practiced anything else, and when the United States has tried to follow another course—as between 1801 and 1812 in our dealings with England and France—it has altogether failed. Containment was startling only in contrast with the Wilsonian idealism, today almost hard to remember, which preceded it.

What was novel and alarming was the exaltation of containment from one among many means to the entire substance of a policy. There was nothing in the idea of containment itself which would have precluded, for example, long-term credits for postwar reconstruction to the Soviet Union. Even if this had seemed impossible for domestic political reasons, such loans might have been offered to Eastern Europe. When in the Marshall Plan proposals the offer was finally made, the international atmosphere had become embittered, Communist parties had strengthened their hold throughout Eastern Europe, and it was too late. In a sense, Eastern Europe was the first underdeveloped area where we failed.

In its sudden, totalistic shift from a reliance on ideals alone to a reliance only on the threat of war, American policy after 1945 exhibited a characteristic tendency to go from one one-sided solution to its opposite, equally one-sided. The Darlan and Badoglio deals, the unconditional surrender formula, the dropping of the atom bomb, also suggest an extremism of expediency and violence which all too frequently was the sequel to the benevolent extremism of America's first intentions.

George Kennan has shown how this tendency of American international behavior to oscillate between extremes of idealism and violence is magnified by our habitual self-righteousness.[5] "It does look," Kennan observes,

> as though the real source of the emotional fervor which we Americans are able to put into a war lies less in any objective understanding of the wider issues involved than in a profound irritation over the fact that other people have finally provoked us to the point where we had no alternative but to take up arms. This lends to the democratic war effort a basically punitive note, rather than one of expediency.

Again Kennan says, commenting on the intrinsic connection between self-righteousness and total war:

> Whoever says there is a law must of course be indignant against the lawbreaker and feel a moral superiority to him. And when such indignation spills over into military contest, it knows no bounds short of the reduction of the lawbreaker to the point of complete submissiveness—namely, unconditional surrender. It is a curious thing, but it is true, that the legalistic approach to world affairs, rooted as it unquestionably is in a desire to do away with war and violence, makes violence more enduring, more terrible, and more destructive to political stability than did the older motives of national self-interest. A war fought in the name of high moral principle finds no early end short of total domination.

Instances of such behavior are legion. One recalls how the "peace without victory" position which Woodrow Wilson proclaimed in January 1917—which meant, if it meant anything, a negotiated peace—gave way in three short months to the complete conviction that autocratic governments could not be dealt with and must therefore be destroyed to "make the world safe for democracy." Again, McNeill has caught this quality in Roosevelt's attitude toward fascist Germany:

> The conviction that Germany should be made to suffer for the wrongs done to the world by the Nazis was in a sense the obverse of Roosevelt's belief in the goodness and rationality of mankind at large. If a nation somehow failed to exhibit goodness and rationality, thus challenging Roosevelt's general belief about human nature, it endangered its claim to belong to humanity and deserved, Roosevelt came to feel, the severest sort of punishment.

It is as if, to sum up, the failure of reality to respond to innocent intentions (a lack of forethought as to means being itself considered a kind of innocence) calls forth a thirst for vengeance; then hope may give way to fear of an opaque reality which seems suddenly out of control; and reality be made to suffer for its intransigence.

This transition was the more inevitable after 1945 because English and American policy-makers had persistently underestimated Soviet strength, and the awakening to the real nature of the postwar balance of power came as something of a traumatic shock. One reason for the slow Anglo-American response to Soviet postwar demands in 1941 had been, as Churchill and Hull candidly confess in their memoirs, the conviction that Russia would grow weaker as the war went on. The colossal Red Army rolling east and west from Soviet borders in the spring and summer of 1945 caused latent anti-Communism to come quickly to the surface of opinion and seem sensible policy.

Only then did many sincere and thoughtful persons in the West recall that Soviet ideology, pressed on to the heroic defensive as it had been since 1941, nonetheless envisioned the transformation of capitalism to socialism throughout the world. Revolution from within was the classical means towards this end; but Marx had never imagined a situation in which socialism and capitalism, represented by different groups of countries, would duel for the allegiance of the rest of the world; and it was a still more basic tenet in the Marxist tradition that means were, in any case, secondary. This underlying tension between opposing social systems facilitated the transformation of cautious cooperation into hostility at a time when public opinion still basked in the glow of victory, and even the leaders of the three victorious powers had far from lost hope in peaceful negotiation. As McNeill puts it: "Each of the Big Three wanted peace and security and recognized that only their continued cooperation could secure these goals. But what seemed an elementary precaution to safeguard the security of the Soviet Union to the one side seemed Communist duplicity and aggression to the other."

If then, we return to the question, Why did the cold war start? the most fundamental answer might be: Because for the first time the challenge of authoritarian socialism to democratic capitalism was backed by sufficient power to be an ever-present political and military threat. It is a far more complicated and potent challenge than that represented by Germany in 1914 or Japan in 1941; it is the kind of challenge associated with the break-up of empires and the transformation of whole societies rather than with the ordinary jostling of diplomatic intercourse. In this sense, those who now speak of negotiation and disarmament as simple nostrums are being superficial, and those who invoke the American way of life are more nearly correct.

Yet containment, while recognizing the seriousness of the problem, would appear to be an inadequate response. Even before the possession of atomic weapons by both sides made reliance on military reprisal archaic, containment was a one-sidedly negative policy which could lead only to slow defeat, and, by way of the frustration and fear thereby engendered, to war. It involved and still involves an identification of the United States with governments whose only qualification for our friendship is their anti-Communism, and which in every other respect go against rather than with the grain of worldwide aspiration. Only a narrow and superficial realism can look to such alliances for strength in the long run.

Is there a moral to be drawn from this alternation between the extremes of Wilsonian idealism and military "realism"? Ten years after he formulated the containment policy, George Kennan saw a moral clearly. "I should like today to raise the question," Kennan stated in 1957,

> whether the positive goals of Western policy have really receded so far from the realm of practical possibility as to be eclipsed by the military danger, whether we would not, in fact, be safer and better off today if we could put our military fixations aside and stake at least a part of our safety on the earnestness of our effort to do the constructive things, the things for which the conditions of our age cry out and for which the stage of our technological progress has fitted us.

"Surely everyone," Kennan continued,

> our adversary no less than ourselves, is tired of this blind and sterile competition in the ability to wreak indiscriminate destruction. The danger with which it confronts us is a common danger. The Russians breathe the same atmosphere as we do, they die in the same ways. . . . Their idea of peace is, of course, not the same as ours. . . . But I see no reason for believing that there are not, even in Moscow's interpretation of this ambiguous word, elements more helpful to us all than the implications of the weapons race in which we are now caught up. And I refuse to believe that there is no way in which we could combine a search for those elements with the pursuit of a reasonable degree of military security in a world where absolute security has become an outmoded and dangerous dream.[6]

### ENDNOTES

1   Herbert Feis, *Churchill, Roosevelt, Stalin: The War They Waged and the Peace They Sought* (Princeton: Princeton University Press, 1957).

2   Herbert Feis, *Between War and Peace: The Potsdam Conference* (Princeton: Princeton University Press, 1960).

3   See the final chapters of William Appleman Williams' *American-Russian Relations, 1871-1947* (New York: Rinehart & Co., 1952) and *The Tragedy of American Diplomacy* (Cleveland and New York: World Publishing Co., 1959).

4    See Carl Marzani, *We Can Be Friends: Origins of the Cold War* (New York: Topical Book Publishers, 1952) as well as the books of W. A. Williams previously cited.

5    These quotations are from *American Diplomacy, 1900-1950* (Chicago: University of Chicago Press, 1951). In his writings of that date Kennan altogether failed to apply his general critique of American foreign policy to its dealings with the Soviet Union. Whereas he could say of American conduct toward Imperial Germany in World War I that "you could have refrained from moralistic slogans, refrained from picturing your effort as a crusade, kept open your line of negotiation to the enemy, declined to break up his empire and overthrow his political system . . ." yet these were the very goals that Kennan advocated for our policy toward the USSR. Whereas in general he counseled America to "admit the validity and legitimacy of power realities and aspirations, to accept them without feeling the obligation of moral judgment, to take them as existing and inalterable human forces, neither good nor bad, and to seek their point of maximum equilibrium rather than their reform or their repression"—"reform or repression" of the Soviet system were the very goals which Kennan's influential writings of these years urged. Finally, whereas in treating America's relations with Japan before World War II Kennan noted how American policy tended to bring about "the final entrenchment of the power of the military extremists," he notably failed to see that the policy of containment he then advocated would have the identical effect on Moscow.

6    These quotations are from George Kennan, *Russia, the Atom and the West* (London: Oxford University Press, 1958).

Last spring, several thousand students who had come to the capitol to protest American resumption of nuclear testing sat on the wet grass around the Washington Monument to hear Emil Mazey, Norman Thomas and other speakers pass on the torch of radicalism from the older generation to the new. The students were somber; they had just filed silently through the Arlington Cemetery; when Thomas, the concluding speaker, came white-haired and open coated to the microphone, the students rose to their feet in spontaneous tribute. As Thomas threw gibe after gibe at the insanity of the arms race, the students roared with appreciation. Then Thomas, thinking to cap these sallies, quipped: "How can there be a Vital Center in Washington, when there is no Left?" The students were silent. They did not know what "the Left" was.

The previous summer I was part of a committee which sought to make possible travel to Cuba. The committee, like the Cuban issue itself, had drawn together persons from both the pacifist and Marxist traditions of dissent. One side of the room would query: "What about help from the F.O.R., the W.R.L., and the A.F.S.C.?" "What are they?" responded the other side. Then the latter suggested: "Shouldn't we approach the S.P. or the S.W.P.?" The pacifists in their turn asked for a translation.

Thus the New Left has not yet identified its usable past, nor found a vocabulary with which to express its inchoate impulses. Freud had a theory to explain this kind of blockage which makes the past inaccessible and the present inarticulate: he thought the inhibiting factor was the taboo on sex. I suggest that in the case of the New Left the obstacle to intellectual coherence is the taboo on socialism. Who has not sat through countless conversations wherein, about midnight, someone would blurt out: "Of course, the real answer to the problem we're discussing is socialism"? My argument is that a cultural prohibition keeps us from seeing and matter-of-factly saying that socialism is the natural inheritor of the currents of dissent which have lately accumulated in America.

What I mean by socialism is comprehensive planning, involving maximum popular participation, based on public ownership of all major industries. In a recent issue of *The New Statesman and Nation,* Arthur Schlesinger, Jr., stated that socialism thus defined is "politically irrelevant and intellectually obsolete"; and if anyone knows what is politically relevant, it is certainly Mr. Schlesinger. Meantime the funeral of ideology has been repeatedly celebrated by a variety of writers. But I believe that the idea of socialism, like Joe Hill, ain't dead.

It was interesting, for example, that the same issue of *The New Statesman* which contained Schlesinger's article on "The Administration and the Left," began with an editorial entitled, "No Substitute for Planning." As a matter of fact there is no substitute for planning. Whichever of the single issues espoused by liberals one takes hold of, a persistent effort to find a truly adequate solution will end at the threshold of comprehensive public ownership and planning. That is why the Left, forced into single issue advocacy by the witch hunt after World War II, must sooner or later resume its commitment to a program which will change the basic social structure.

Consider civil rights. There is a growing recognition in the Southern student movement that freedom which is merely legal and political freedom is inevitably token freedom. Equality requires a redistribution of wealth as well as the right to vote. As James Baldwin put it in "Letter From A Region Of My Mind": "There is simply no possibility of a real change in the Negro's situation without the most radical and far-reaching changes in the American political and social structure."

This is not to say that the right to vote is unimportant. But even to induce Negroes to take the risk of registering to vote, it is necessary to suggest how the vote can be used to solve more tangible problems. Voter registration must be accompanied by concrete local programs, presented by independent candidates, which confront the fact that the average acreage of farms owned by Negroes in Georgia is fifty-two acres, or the circumstance that in some communities of the Mississippi Delta the average annual income of Negro *families* is $1,000.

The new horizon for nonviolence in the South is the winning-over of the Southern poor white to a social and economic program benefiting poor people of all colors. But Tobacco Road will not welcome integration until it can be shown that uniting with the Negro means a bigger slice of the pie for Tobacco Road. Unless the opening of new opportunities for the Negro is accompanied by the creation of new jobs, integration will increase the fear of whites that they will lose their jobs. In the old days before we knew Marxism was wrong, such paradoxes were called contradictions of capitalism.

The most visible evidence of the need for comprehensive public ownership and planning in America is the state of our cities. Recent administrations have perverted the intention of the New Deal's public housing act, so that what began as a program for slum-clearance has become a program of slum-creation. When $200-a-month apartments are built on sites where low-income tenants used to live, the total supply of low-rent housing is diminished, and displaced site-tenants, by doubling up with dwellers in other ghettoes, hasten the blight of these other neighborhoods. Urban renewal has strengthened rather than weakened segregation in urban housing, the basis of discrimination in the North. Any rational program of housing and slum clearance must leave behind the single project perspective of the private entrepreneur and take its stand on the old and honorable proposition that land, even choice central-city land, is the gift of God to mankind as a whole. Authoritative estimates inform us that twice the sum spent annually on defense could wipe out all the slums in America. But—"this is socialism."

The over-arching inefficiency of the hard-headed pragmatism advocated by Mr. Schlesinger is that for thirty-four years its managers have produced their fluctuating modicum of prosperity only by spending on armaments. It is difficult to decide which is the more utter failure of the Kennedy administration: its inability to "get the economy moving again"; or the fact that, coming into office with brave talk of "turning the tide" of world Communism, it has spent two years mounting and dismounting offensives against seven million Cubans. Both failures follow directly from habitual reliance on the narcotic of armaments as the solution for all foreign and domestic ills. Perhaps pragmatism cannot be blamed for its inability to think strategically, a kind of thinking it eschews on principle: yet the condition of man, perpetually dangling over the nuclear precipice, calls for more than expedients. What we must recognize is that in the long run peace does not offer a solution to the former corporation lawyers who staff the United States State Department. Co-existence and disarmament are *technically* possible in a capitalist society. In *practice*, as Rostow observes, "generally men have preferred to go down in the style to which they had become accustomed rather than to change their ways of thinking and looking at the world." So long as our policy-makers insist that foreign aid must basically take the form of private investment, and that public works must be non-competitive with private profits, just so long will there be no peace this side of socialism.

As always, the paradoxes of our national life are most visible in the South. The South is characteristically and mistakenly viewed as something separate from American society and history. Thus liberal historians write of the absence of feudalism in our national experience, forgetting that some of us were slaves; and liberal reformers embark on the transformation of under developed, one-party, caste-ridden societies elsewhere on the globe, without asking themselves whether, in light of our demonstrated failure to transform such a society in our own country, we are likely to do it anyplace else. To put it bluntly, American capitalism appears unable to bring democracy to the South. It seems a good deal more likely that this American Bavaria will barbarize the rest of the nation.

And it is not only the South which needs to be democratized. Public ownership and planning is the technical side of socialism, but the deeper purpose of American socialism has always been the completion of the American Revolution. As Harvey Wheeler put it in *The Nation* a year ago, the "permanent program" of the American Left "has been to devise organizational and governmental devices to release the suppressed potentialities of the masses." American socialists, traditionally, made their distinctive contribution by insisting that the people must take into their own hands the control of industry if they hoped to retain the control of government.

Pick up any of the classics of Anglo-American radicalism in the late nineteenth century, and you will find that socialism is presented as the fulfillment of democracy. Thus G.B. Shaw wrote in his preface to the *Fabian Essays:* "The writers are all Social Democrats, with a common conviction of the necessity of vesting the organization of industry and the material of production in a State identified with the whole people by complete Democracy." In America the argument for a second American Revolution was more explicit. "The reform I have proposed," said Henry George in *Progress and Poverty*, "is but the carrying out in letter and spirit of the truth enunciated in the Declaration of Independence. They who look upon Liberty as having accomplished her mission when she has abolished hereditary privileges and given men the ballot, have not seen her real grandeur. We cannot go on prating of the inalienable rights of man and then denying the inalienable right to the bounty of the Creator." When Julian West awoke in *Looking Backward*, Doctor Leete's explanation of the new society ran in similar terms:

> In a word, the people of the United States concluded to assume the conduct of their own business, just as one hundred odd years before they had assumed the conduct of their own government. At last the obvious fact was perceived that no business is so essentially the public business as the industry and commerce on which the people's livelihood depends, and that to entrust it to private persons to be managed for private profit is a folly similar in kind, though vastly greater in magnitude, to that

of surrendering the functions of political government to kings
and nobles to be conducted for their personal glorification.

The essential charge against the capitalist was not what he did to the
workingman, but what he did to American democracy. Henry Demarest
Lloyd found a characteristically consummate way of saying this in *Wealth
Against Commonwealth*, where he wrote that Standard Oil had done everything to the Pennsylvania legislature except refine it.

Thus it was no accident that W. J. Ghent and others envisioned the
new industrial plutocracy as a new feudalism. An analogy of capitalism to
feudalism, and of the coming revolution against capitalism to the old and
glorious revolution against kings, was the archetypal metaphor of vintage
American socialism: the robbers were robber *barons*, and Veblen's leisure
class had inherited its routine of force and fraud from

the higher states of the barbarian culture; as, for instance, in
feudal Europe or feudal Japan.

This older vocabulary, in which America was seen as a house divided between economic aristocracy and an endangered political democracy had
a richness somewhat lacking in terms such as "the warfare state," "the
military industrial complex," or "Fascism."

One of the many sensibilities dulled in modern America is the
awareness of when democracy is in danger. Surely the drift of the political process has been toward a kind of government adapted to industrial
aristocracy: a government in which initiative has passed to what might
accurately be called an elected constitutional oligarchy. Democracy, as
William Appleman Williams has said, is more than the ability to say "No";
democracy at its best is (in the words of Tom Hayden of the Students for
a Democratic Society) a "participatory democracy" in which each citizen
acts "as a potential sharer in the governing of society." But what democracy has become in our society is merely a residual right of dissent to
the more outrageous policies which They propose. Sometimes, as in the
Cuban [missile] crisis, there is no time even for that. A more simple age
might have suggested that if democracy and push button warfare were
incompatible, push button warfare would have to go. To say this today is
socialism and subversion.

Any identification of socialism and democracy must confront the
massive indoctrination of the last twenty years to the effect that socialism and democracy are incompatible. If American government is tending
toward the divine right of Presidents, it will be said, the trend is justified

because of the qualitatively different horrors of the totalitarian antagonist. Norman Thomas remarks that when he began his career as a socialist propagandist, opponents never attempted to argue that capitalism was morally good: they said that socialism could not work. Nowadays, Thomas observes, capitalism is defended as the necessary basis for an ethical society. The historian C. Vann Woodward has compared the change in American attitudes toward capitalism since the 1930s to the change in Southern attitudes toward slavery between the 1820s and the 1840s. In each case, an institution once considered a deplorable necessity came with astonishing rapidity to be regarded as a positive good.

One recalls how, under the dual impact of German Fascism and Soviet purges and forced labor camps, such thinking got started. As a high-school student during World War II, I read Edmund Wilson's *To the Finland Station* and Burnham's *The Managerial Revolution* on the New York City subways. I can even remember the subway stops where enlightenment as to the meaning of each book occurred. Appropriately enough, Wilson's vision of Marxism as the humanism of the future became clear to me in the daylight north of Dykman Street, while the impact of Burnham's pessimism about centralization came home to me in the dark near the 14th Street station. For me, and I believe for many others, the years of coming to maturity after World War II involved a continuing dialogue between the hard-boiled centralizer and the sensitive anarchist, the Commissar and the Yogi, the Marxist and the pacifist, a dialogue which (at least in my own case) expressed itself in a most erratic sequence of personal actions. Books such as Silone's *Bread and Wine* which seemed to achieve some synthesis between the two viewpoints became treasured talismans. In such an atmosphere of schizophrenia on the Left, it was easier for defenders of the Establishment to come on stage as champions of freedom and the individual.

The insistence that capitalism rather than socialism offers the more hospitable environment for democracy has lately begun to lose conviction. For one thing, on Burnham's own logic it becomes increasingly obvious that institutional governments in mass societies, whatever their labels, have certain grave common problems. Democracy is a matter of more or less. The American citizen whose political participation is confined to the annual act of pulling a lever in a little curtained room, is on a different level of Inferno from the Soviet citizen; but neither one is in Paradise. In the United Auto Workers, Walter Reuther tries out proposals in his "caucus" before taking them to the convention, and by "straw vote" before formal decision: decisions are usually unanimous, but only those policies are proposed for which unanimous assent can be predicted. This is a political process not so *very* far removed from the "plebiscitary democracy" of totalitarian states (in the one direction), or from the poll-sensitive managed democracy of the Kennedy administration (in the other).

Administration intellectuals such as Rostow and Kennan often write as if American institutions were infinitely malleable. As the years go by, and the Soviet Union, haltingly and awkwardly but according to all accounts irresistibly, continues to grow more liberal and flexible, while New Frontiers on this side of the Atlantic turn out to be damp squibs, it becomes simply impossible to cling to the notion that the Soviet Union is uniquely rigid compared to the "open society" of the United States.

Not only do Soviet and American citizens face the common problem of an overgrown institutional environment, they also have a shared ideological tradition on which to draw. The Communist ideal of the withering away of the state resembles, as has often been observed, the liberal ideal of the night-watchman state. Moreover, at the turn of the century, when modern bureaucracy was making its traumatic debut, a current of concern ran throughout the Western world which involved personalities as different as Robert LaFollette and Rosa Luxemburg. The French "syndicat" and the Russian "soviet," guild socialism and political pluralism, the I.W.W. and the direct primary, were all parts of an attempt by the most varied reformers to manage the bureaucratic beast. Verbally, at least, recent Soviet statements suggest that a return is underway to the goal of direct democracy presupposed in Lenin's image of a state so simple that cooks could run it. Participatory democracy in a Communist society might emphasize administration rather than legislation. In any case, as a technology of abundance makes regions more self-sufficient and citizens more leisured and sophisticated, the objective conditions will exist for a far more decentralized decision-making process than occurs today in either the Soviet Union or the United States.

Could such a participatory democracy find new roots in our city streets, a number of ancillary problems would begin to solve themselves. We know now that prejudice can be destroyed by massive "equal status contact" between members of previously separated groups. The block meeting to shape neighborhood responses to urban renewal, the shop meeting to discuss production goals of a common plan, could continue into adult life the child's experience in an integrated school. The deeper meaning of nonviolence, I think, is closely akin to the central faith of democracy: the insistence that decisions should come about through a process of personal confrontation and encounter. Participatory democracy is therefore an ideal which catches up both the democratic mythos of the older radicalism and the Gandhian ideology of the newer.

Finally there is the matter of socialist internationalism. Like the protagonist of *Catch-22*, we have all been obliged to recognize that men of power on "our side" (whichever side we may have thought was ours) threaten us just as much as their counterparts on the other. No longer can there be a temptation to identify universal human values with the interests of any nation state. I believe the third essential ingredient of a revived American socialism—besides recognizing the housekeeping necessity of planning, besides envisioning socialism as the fulfillment of democracy—is clear and unequivocal assertion that there is an interest of humanity distinct from all national interests. We must learn again from Paine to feel that our country is mankind. We must learn from Thoreau "to be men first, and Americans at a late and convenient hour," and to say to the Stevensons and Schlesingers about Cuba, as Thoreau said to the organization liberals of the 1840s, that "this people must cease to hold slaves, and to make war on Mexico, though it cost them their existence as a people." Early in this century Keir Hardie declared that socialism was "not a system of economics but life for a dying people." Under the nuclear shadow his statement has become more true than when first uttered. A new American socialism must begin by affirming that an American life is worth no more than any other life; that the fundamental blasphemy of the arms race is not that we bring death on ourselves, but that we make ready in cold blood to kill millions upon millions of others; that the American Revolution is an idea, not a place, and that some other people or peoples may be destined to nurture to maturity the seedling planted here in '76.

And if this be treason, make the most of it.

I had the honor of coordinating Freedom Schools during the 1964 Mississippi Summer Project. Today I want to talk about the voter registration part of the Project: the effort to send Mississippi Freedom Democratic Party delegates to the national Democratic Party convention in Atlantic City in August 1964, in the hope that they might be seated in place of the so-called regular delegates from the all-white Mississippi Democratic Party.

I took my mind with me to Mississippi but at summer's end it was filled, not with historical analysis, but with luminous memories. I began to think as a historian three years later, in June 1967, when I was walking across the New Haven Green and ran into Dave Dennis. The Lynds were leaving for Chicago the next day, but we invited Dave for breakfast, and he told us that the majority of SNCC and CORE staff had initially opposed the Summer Project. I haven't been able to stop thinking since.

## I

My first knowledge about the idea of going to Atlantic City also came about through a one-on-one encounter. Sometime during the winter of 1963-1964 I was walking along a red brick sidewalk near the Atlanta University campus and met Jack Minnis, SNCC research director. Jack and I collaborated that winter in publishing one of the first critiques of the official, single-shooter version of President Kennedy's assassination.

Jack had apparently just come from a discussion of going to Atlantic City at the SNCC headquarters nearby. He was excited about it. He imagined Dr. King, not Mrs. Hamer, addressing the delegates. It is crystal clear to me in memory that Jack Minnis did not expect the MFDP delegates to be seated, and that he thought of going to Atlantic City not as a strategy, but as a magnificent tactic.

Yet a strategy was implicit in the tactic. First, the MFDP, in order to distinguish itself from the Mississippi regulars, felt obliged to emphasize its fidelity to President Johnson and to the program of the national, as distinct from the state, Democratic Party. Organizing materials prepared by Donna Richards, Casey Hayden and other SNCC folk for MFDP precinct and county meetings accordingly called for a "loyalty pledge" to the national Party.[1]

Second, in spring 1964 Bob Moses and (I believe) Ella Baker went to the national convention of the United Automobile Workers (UAW) and arranged for UAW attorney Joseph Rauh to represent the MFDP at Atlantic City. It seemed a logical move at the time. Rauh was an influential Democrat. The National Lawyers Guild attorneys who were doing the day-to-day legal work in Mississippi were *persona non grata* to many liberals in the national Democratic Party. No one imagined that a conflict could arise between the UAW, which had contributed heavily to the 1963 March for Jobs and Freedom, and the MFDP. As late as August 6, a summer volunteer wrote home "from the floor of the State Convention of the Mississippi Freedom Democratic Party":

> Attorney Joseph Rauh . . . addressed the group. Mr. Rauh is also Walter Reuther's attorney and his appearance indicated the support of Mr. Reuther who is, of course, one of the powers of the Democratic Party.[2]

## II

Just as there was controversy within SNCC as to whether to invite hundreds of white volunteers to Mississippi, so there was a less-well-known controversy within SNCC as to whether the Atlantic City strategy was a good idea.

Going to Atlantic City was different from the Freedom Vote of November 1963. November 1963 was the creation of a political process for the marginalized and excluded "parallel" to the official electoral proceedings. Summer 1964, in contrast, expressly sought to assist Mississippi African Americans to become part of the national Democratic Party. And it looked to a trade union leader who was close to President Johnson and who would, in years to come, support the Vietnam War, for critical support.

Long before the escalation of United States involvement in Vietnam, indeed on the eve of the 1964 Summer Project, SNCC staff expressed their deep uneasiness with the idea of seeking to be seated at Atlantic City. The following are desperately brief extracts from the minutes of the SNCC staff meeting on June 9-11, 1964.[3]

Ruby Doris Smith opened a discussion on goals with the words: "We could begin with discussion of whether we're working to make basic changes within existing political and economic structure. . . . What would the seating of the delegation mean besides having Negroes in the National Democratic Party?" Here were some of the responses.

> IVANHOE DONALDSON. Disagrees with just making more Democrats and more Republicans. Perhaps the way is to create a parallel structure. . . . Our problem is that our programs don't change basic factors of exploitation. Perhaps it's better to create a third stream. . . . [W]hat is the point of working within the Democratic Party? It is not a radical tool.
>
> CHARLIE COBB. Feels there would be negligible value in merely being part of the Democratic Party structure. . . . There is a danger of Negroes being manipulated by the national parties. . . . It is bad if you make people part of a decadent structure.
>
> JOHN LEWIS. He is not sure that we can get what we want within "liberal politics." The basic things we want to achieve are equality for Negro and white, liberate the poor white as well as the Negro.
>
> JIM FORMAN. We should agitate for dignity. . . . Dignity is an umbrella concept. E.g., a man without a job has no dignity.
>
> JIM JONES. SNCC's program is limited to desegregating facilities and voter registration.
>
> LAWRENCE GUYOT. If our goal is just voter registration then we should stop. We have to organize around something.

The day after the conference ended, June 12, 1964, I wrote a letter to Howard Zinn. I wrote: "We have just finished an extremely moving staff meeting, which I was permitted to attend because of my involvement in the Summer Project." Continuing, I put in my own two cents:[4]

> I tend to feel (as I said at the SNCC conference) that it is a mistake to emphasize only a) the vote, and b) protection, without at the same time sketching out some sort of vision and program as to what sorts of measures will ultimately solve the problem. Several staff members said this week: I'm ready to die, but I need a program worth dieing for. I know Ruby Doris feels this way. I don't think either the vote or Federal protection is worth dieing for unless one can see beyond them by just what steps the society will be changed. I said this in substance to Bob, Cortland, and Tim Jenkins in March and their response was: You want us to have an ideology. But this week I heard my own question asked in substance by several field workers. Thus,

I think that both for the movement's effectiveness and for its morale there really must be more thinking as to program. Bob said this week he had never supposed that anything more than limited goals could be achieved. But there is a question as to how many people will continue to risk their lives for limited goals; and there is also a question as to whether, in fact, those limited goals can be achieved within present American society except in the context of more fundamental changes.

## III

Ten days later, of course, we all learned that three young men who had risked their lives for limited goals had in all probability been murdered. It became much more difficult to continue the discussion begun at the SNCC staff meeting in June. On the one hand, support for actually seating the MFDP delegates at the Democratic Party convention increased dramatically. On the other hand, a feeling grew that only if the delegates were seated would the sacrifice of Schwerner, Chaney, and Goodman have been worthwhile.

This was the latent or suspended state of dialogue within the movement when, at Atlantic City, Lyndon Johnson and Walter Reuther testified by conduct—as lawyers say—about where they were really coming from. Nelson Lichtenstein in his biography of Reuther and Taylor Branch in his biography of Dr. King tell the identical story:[5]

At Johnson's request, Reuther broke off negotiations with GM and flew to Atlantic City by chartered plane. Arriving at 3 a.m. Reuther went into session with Hubert Humphrey and Walter Mondale. They agreed that the MFDP would be required to accept a so-called "compromise": the Mississippi regulars would continue to be the official delegation and the MFDP would have two "at large" delegates named by the president, who, so Humphrey made clear the next day, would not include "that illiterate woman," Mrs. Hamer.

The next day exhausted MFDP delegates instructed their attorney, Joseph Rauh, to hold out for at least the same number of seats allotted to the regulars. However, Reuther told Rauh: "Here's the decision. I am telling you to take this deal." If Rauh did not do what he was told, Reuther added, he would terminate Rauh's employment with the UAW.

The same kind of strong arm tactics were used with Dr. King. Reuther told him: "Your funding is on the line. The kind of money you got from us in Birmingham is there again for Mississippi, but you've got to help us and we've got to help Johnson."

The rest is, sadly enough, history.

## *IV*

At a conference in Waveland, Mississippi, in November 1964, SNCC tried to digest the summer's experiences. Most accounts have emphasized the tension between black staff and white volunteers, exacerbated by the fact that so many volunteers stayed on in Mississippi; or the conflict between Jim Forman's desire to make SNCC into a Marxist-Leninist vanguard party and the aspiration of Casey Hayden, Bob Moses and others that SNCC continue as a decentralized network in which those who did the work made the decisions.

I suggest a third explanation for the difficulty experienced by SNCC folks in finding a way forward. Bayard Rustin and others were encouraging SNCC to look to its "coalition partners" for allies in confronting the economic and social structures that underpin racism in the United States. But precisely those allies—the national Democratic Party, and the allegedly most progressive trade union leader in the country—had just finished stabbing the MFDP delegates in the back at Atlantic City. Here is how Bob Moses put it at the Waveland conference:[6]

> Let's sum up the box we're in:
> 1) Labor unions are political organizations, now within the Establishment.
> 2) When labor is organized, it can only discuss a narrow aspect of the problem: wages. Reuther sat in the meeting with King, Humphrey and others to urge the FDP to accept the compromise, talking anti-Goldwater, keep morality out of politics, etc. . . .
> If we organize people, all should decide where to focus attention.

SNCC failed to find a way out of the box described by Bob Moses. We ought not be too hard on SNCC, however. We are still in that box.

### *ENDNOTES*

1   Casey Hayden, "Fields of Blue," in *Deep In Our Hearts: Nine White Women in the Freedom Movement* (Athens, GA: University of Georgia Press, 2000), p. 357. I believe that such maneuvering took a toll. By the Waveland conference in November 1964, Casey felt "uninterested in electoral politics." *Id.*, p. 367.

2   Quoted in *Letters From Mississippi*, edited and with a new preface by Elizabeth Sutherland Martinez (Brookline, MA: Zephyr Press, 2002), pp. 250-251.

3   Staff meeting minutes, June 9-11, 1964, SNCC Papers, Roll 3, Frames 975-992. I wish to thank Wesley Hogan for making these minutes available to me.

4   Carol Polsgrove found this letter in the Zinn Papers at the Wisconsin State Historical Society in the course of researching her book, *Divided Minds: Intellectuals and the Civil Rights Movement* (New York: W.W. Norton & Company, 2001), and quotes from it, *id.*, p. 226. She kindly made it available to me.

5   Nelson Lichtenstein, *The Most Dangerous Man in Detroit: Walter Reuther and the Fate of American Labor* (New York: Basic Books, 1995), pp. 394-395; Taylor Branch, *Pillar of Fire: America in the King Years, 1963-1965* (New York: Simon & Schuster, 1998), pp. 469-475.

6   Minutes, discussion of Nov. 9, 1964, SNCC Papers, Reel 11, Frames 935-959. Once again I have Wesley Hogan to thank for the opportunity to see these records.

G reetings, fellow teachers.
What I plan to do in the next little while is to tell you about my experience in the Mississippi Freedom Schools in Summer 1964 and to offer my thoughts about how that experience might relate to the question, What is to be done?

In my remarks, I shall try to convince you of three things:

I. Everything we know about learning instructs that people do not learn by reading Left-wing newspapers, nor by attending lectures like this one at which some learned person offers correct theory. **People learn by experience.** And that is especially true if the learning we have in mind is glimpsing the hope that Another World Is Possible. People must touch and taste an alternative way of doing things, they must however briefly live inside that hope, in order to come to believe that an alternative might really come true.

II. Capitalist society in the United States offers very few opportunities to experience another world, another way of doing things. During the transition from feudalism to capitalism in Europe it was possible to create the institutions of a new society in the interstices of feudal society: thus there came into existence free cities, guilds, Protestant congregations, banks and corporations, new styles of painting and making music. By the time an emerging bourgeoisie created parliaments, and sought to take over state power, a network of new institutions had come into being within the shell of the old. This does not seem to be possible within capitalism as the sad history of trade unions teaches us.

III. How then, are we to help young people to imagine what a new society might be like? As educators we know that we can't do it just by talking, it has to happen through experience. As organizers we know that it is very difficult to provide such experiences in these United States. The answer, therefore, is . . . but wait, this talk has to have some surprises. I'll get to that.

# I

So, first: Everything we know about learning instructs that people learn by experience.

I assume that this is a topic about which we are in agreement, and so I can be brief. Let me tell a couple of my favorite stories about Myles Horton and the Highlander Folk School.

The Highlander Folk School in Tennessee was created in the 1930s. During its early years Highlander supported the creation of trade unions and then, in the 1960s, assisted the civil rights movement. The civil rights version of "We Shall Overcome" was put together by Guy Carawan and others at Highlander, whereafter they taught it to civil rights workers who came to Highlander for retreats. Myles Horton, the principal founder of Highlander, was the Paulo Freire of the United States, and there is a wonderful book entitled *We Make The Road By Walking* in which Freire and Horton as two old men share their experiences.

One summer in the early 1930s, when Horton was more of a Christian than in his later years, he taught bible school for the YMCA in a remote Appalachian hamlet named Ozone. Midway through the summer the young teacher concluded that this impoverished community in the midst of a Depression needed something more than the Bible. He let it be known that on a certain evening there would be a meeting to address the question of what was to be done.

People walked across the mountains barefoot to get to that meeting. As the meeting was about to begin, Horton realized that he had nothing consequential to suggest. In panic and desperation he said, "Let's go around the circle and see what ideas people brought with them." They did so. A program materialized. The Highlander style of education emerged from this experience.

A second story concerns how Horton dealt with race. When the CIO began organizing in 1935, segregation, disfranchisement, and racism pervaded the South, including its fragile labor movement. As individual union organizers, black and white, arrived at Highlander for a retreat, they would be assigned to cabins in order of their arrival. Sleeping, eating, and discussing were integrated throughout the week of the retreat, but nothing was said about race. Participants experienced the overcoming of racism. At week's end, as folks made ready to disperse, Horton would say something like: "Now, we all know how silly these racial customs are. How are we going to get that across to workers we organize?"

## II

Second, and again to repeat: Capitalist society in the United States offers very few opportunities to experience another way of doing things.

When I was a teenager in New York City I rode the subway for half an hour to get to school. I gave myself a radical education. One of the books I read, by an ex-Trotskyist named James Burnham and entitled *The Managerial Revolution*, laid out the way in which the rising middle class in medieval Europe created, first, new institutions, and only second, a revolution, and concluded that nothing like this was possible in a capitalist society. Burnham particularly insisted that trade unions were not prefigurative institutions, that they would never challenge the capitalist economy comprehensively. Their role, Burnham argued, was at best to smooth a few of the rough edges and make capitalism tolerable for those it exploited.

When I got off the subway I hurried to my parents' bookshelves to find the answer to Burnham. I looked, for example, at Emile Burns' *Handbook of Marxism*. I couldn't find an answer then or for decades afterwards.

I tried to respond to Burnham's thesis in a different way at the end of the 1960s.

Those of you old enough to have lived through that time will recall that in those years there again came to the fore the Marxist idea that the working class would lead the way in creating a new society. So I briefly considered looking for a job in a steel mill. A young friend employed at U.S. Steel Gary Works told me that if I did so, after twenty years workers would still say to each other about me, "Let's see what the Professor thinks."

I decided that I might do better seeking to assist those same workers by offering a needed skill. I became a lawyer. I was a Legal Services lawyer for almost twenty years, confronting as best I could the layoffs, plant closings, and bankruptcies of that time. Unfortunately my experience confirmed rather than rebutting Burnham's conclusion that unions were not a force for fundamental social change. I often represented local unions as well as individual workers in trouble. It was the larger structures, the national unions, that repeatedly let down the rank-and-file workers they represented. Bureaucrats at some national headquarters far distant from the shop or school floor drafted contracts that gave the employer the unilateral right to make the big decisions, like closing a facility or canceling health benefits for retirees. At the same time, national unions acquiesced in a no-strike clause that took away from local unions and their members the only effective way to resist.

Critical as I am of national unions, I do not wish to romanticize the ordinary rank-and-file worker. Much depends on whether people are encouraged to stand beside their brothers and sisters, risking personal sacrifice on behalf of a shared vision, or instead to base decisions on a calculus of individual self-interest. At the end of the 1800s and the beginning of the twentieth century, the Knights of Labor and the Industrial Workers of the World popularized the phrase, "An injury to one is an injury to all." Ralph Chaplin, a member of the IWW, while imprisoned during World War I took the old tune to the Battle Hymn of the Republic and wrote the words of "Solidarity Forever." But how many fellow workers do any of us know who still believe that "In our hands there is a power greater than their hoarded gold" so that "We can bring to birth a new world from the ashes of the old"?

I don't mean to issue iron pronouncements of doom for union effort at all times and in all places. I tried for twenty years. In the end I found more solidarity among the prisoners locked in Youngstown's many new prisons than I had experienced in the steel mills that the prisons replaced.

### III

That leaves, brothers and sisters, schools. If we calculate 7 hours to the school day, 18 days to the school month, 10 months to the school year, and 12.5 years in school, that comes to 15,750 hours in which a young person who graduates from high school has been in the presence of another human being called a teacher.

I know a man sentenced to death who is writing his autobiography. He figures that despite a miserable, heart-breaking childhood, he kept it together as a youngster who got good grades and had hope for the future until his early teens. His first encounter with the criminal injustice system came when he went joy-riding in a stolen car with several older friends. The judge took note of the fact that Keith had no criminal record and asked his stepfather and mother if they wished to take him home or have him assigned to the juvenile detention facility. Keith's stepfather told the judge, "You take him."

Later, after shooting a best friend in a dispute over drugs and brief participation in a major prison riot, Keith Lamar was sentenced to death. He decided that something out of the ordinary was required and took the name Bomani Shakur, Swahili for "Thankful Mighty Warrior." He asks himself the question I am asking: When a young person experiences next to no support, encouragement, or recognition from everyday life in his community, how can we expect that young person to become anything other than a candidate for life behind bars?

And I am answering, Maybe, just maybe, in a place called "school."

You may be skeptical and, if so, I think I know how you feel. I lost my opportunity to make a living as a teacher when I tried to go all-out to stop the Vietnam War. I took account of all the rules and requirements. I went to Hanoi during Christmas vacation, and practically overturned the world Communist bureaucracy to be back in the States in time for my first scheduled class in the new year. It didn't make any difference. The president of Yale said I had "given aid and comfort to the enemy," a phrase from the law of treason.

But I don't want to exchange war stories, or display our respective scars. I don't want to have an abstract debate about education as a social force. I want to tell you about the Mississippi Freedom Schools, which I had the honor of helping to create, and which I coordinated in the summer of 1964.

Freedom Schools were improvised summer high schools. They did not offer academic credit. For the most part the schools were located in church basements, and in more than one instance the church was bombed or burned to the ground. The students were African American teenagers. The teachers were mostly from the North, mostly white, and mostly women, who lived with African American families brave enough to take them in. By attending Freedom School the youngsters deprived their families of days of much-needed labor in the fields.

As I assume you can understand, statistical exactness wasn't possible in these circumstances. All studies agree that more than 2,000 youngsters attended more than forty Freedom Schools.

The summer project began with a two-week orientation at the College for Women in Oxford, Ohio. Voter registration volunteers attended during the first week. They left as we who would try to create Freedom Schools arrived. I drove from Atlanta with three students from Spelman College who were summer volunteers like myself. The trunk of my Rambler was packed with copies of the Freedom School curriculum, laboriously reproduced on an ancient hectograph machine in the Lynds' apartment on the Spelman campus.

The day after we arrived at Oxford there came the news that Meridian project director Michael Schwerner, summer volunteer Andrew Goodman, and Mississippi resident James Chaney, had disappeared. They had driven from Ohio, had snatched a few hours sleep, and then had set out for nearby Philadelphia, Mississippi. There the deacons of a local African American church, after lengthy discussion, had voted to let the church be used for a Freedom School. Soon after the church was burned down. Schwerner, Goodman, and Chaney went to Philadelphia to find a new location for a Freedom School. Their station wagon got a flat tire. I assume you know the rest of the story. The bodies were discovered the first week of August.

Back at Oxford, every one was making long distance telephone calls to Mississippi, to the Department of Justice in Washington, D.C., to parents. I was invited to a small meeting of staff for the Student Nonviolent Coordinating Committee, or SNCC. Bob Zellner and others volunteered to travel to Philadelphia and go through the woods at night to see if there was underground knowledge in the black community about what had happened to the missing men. I was in and out of larger meetings, talking with volunteers for the Freedom Schools about whether to go home or go to Mississippi. I don't remember anyone going home.

During that week I made an arrangement with a volunteer named Tom Wahman. Tom's wife Sue was a member of the cast of Martin Duberman's play "In White America." They were going to be rehearsing in Jackson, the state capitol. Tom wondered if he too could be assigned to Jackson. I said, "Sure: you go to headquarters every day and answer telephone calls about the Freedom Schools, and I will spend the summer traveling through Mississippi, visiting the schools."

I remember going to McComb, Mississippi. It was just after the Freedom House where summer volunteers had been sleeping, and where the Freedom School had been meeting, was bombed. We gathered on the lawn next to the Freedom House. We sang "I'm on my way to the freedom land," and Bob Moses suggested the verse, "If you can't go let your children go."

One of the summer volunteers, Wally Roberts, was having a hard time getting the Freedom School started in Shaw, in the Mississippi Delta. We talked. The solution turned out to be for the youngsters to do voter registration every morning. Then in the afternoon, at Freedom School, it took on more meaning to learn that in the Reconstruction period after the Civil War there had been black representatives in the Mississippi state legislature.

Alongside my fragmentary impressions the best way I can convey what happened in those schools that summer is to read some of the letters to home written by teachers, and some of the prose and poetry by Freedom School students, and a recollection of one of my students at Spelman who went to Mississippi.

Some teachers were welcomed as heroes. Geoff wrote home:

Batesville welcomed us triumphantly—
at least Black Batesville did.
Children and adults waved from their porches and shouted hello
as we walked along the labyrinth of dirt paths and small wooden houses . . . .

In a few days scores of children knew us and called us by name.

Similarly in Ruleville, in the Delta, the summer volunteers

. . . were given the best of everything,
and housing was found for all of us.
Two people have already lost their jobs for housing us,
and yet in each case half a dozen families
begged us to stay with them.

My student Gwen Robinson was welcomed just as warmly, but much less obtrusively, in Laurel, Mississippi. She recalled:

One of the few things that I was trying to hold onto in terms of thinking **maybe I will survive this** [was] the fact that there were all these white young people going. . . . So when I was told I was being assigned to Laurel with two other people only and both of them were black men and the three of us were going to Laurel because it was too dangerous for white people, I was like, "Well, wait a minute. . . ."

We went and we did have some names of people. One of them was . . . Mrs. Euberta Sphinks.

When I got to Mrs. Sphinks' door, I knocked on her door. I introduced myself . . . . She looked at me and said, "Girl, I've been waiting [for] you all my life. Come on in."

Freedom School students in Hattiesburg wrote a Declaration of Independence that said in part:

In this course of human events,
it has become necessary for the Negro people
to break away from the customs
which have made it very difficult
for the Negro to get his God-given rights.
We, as citizens of Mississippi,
do hereby state that all people
should have the right to petition,
to assemble, and to use public places.
We also have the right to life,
liberty, and to seek happiness. . . .
We do hereby declare independence
from the unjust laws of Mississippi
which conflict with the United States constitution.

Naomi Long Nadget, Greenwood Freedom School wrote a poem:

> I've seen daylight breaking high above the bough,
> I've found my destination and I've made my vow;
> So whether you abhor me or deride me or ignore me,
> Mighty mountains loom before me and I won't stop now.

You recall that in McComb the Freedom House had been bombed
and the Freedom School had to meet on the grass outside. No local black
institution dared offer facilities for a school. Joyce Brown, 16, addressed
the problem in a poem in which she said in part:

> I asked for your churches, and you turned me down,
> But I'll do my work if I have to do it on the ground.
> You will not speak for fear of being heard,
> So crawl in your shell and say, "Do not disturb."
> You think because you've turned me away
> You've protected yourself for another day.

According to Professor Dittmer, author of a splendid book on
the Mississippi Movement, "Moved—and shamed—by Joyce Brown's
poem, local people soon made church facilities available for the
Freedom School."

At the end of the first week in August, the same week that the
three bodies were discovered and the Mississippi Freedom Democratic
Party held its state convention, there took place a so-called Freedom
School Convention. Sandra Adickes, a professional teacher from New
York, says that I suggested it. I have only a visual memory of the meeting
of Freedom School coordinators where we decided to do it. The idea was
for each Freedom School to send a couple of delegates, accompanied by
a teacher, to a ramshackle Baptist seminary on the outskirts of Meridian,
and for the assembled delegates to debate and adopt resolutions about
the future of Mississippi as they envisioned it. The "1964 Platform of
the Mississippi Freedom School Convention," adopted that weekend,
includes resolutions on Public Accommodations, Housing, Education,
Health, Foreign Affairs, Federal Aid, Job Discrimination, the Plantation
System, Civil Liberties, Law Enforcement, City Improvements, Voting,
and Direct Action.

The most consequential discussion concerned whether, at summer's
end, the Mississippi Movement should attempt to extrapolate the summer Freedom Schools into a comprehensive alternative school system, or
whether, instead, these young people should return to their segregated

schools with used textbooks handed down from the white schools, inadequately prepared teachers, not enough money, and a curriculum that prohibited African American history.

They decided that individual communities might experiment with Freedom Schools or school boycotts as desired, but as a statewide movement they would go back to their old schools. I believed then, and I believe now, that it was the correct decision. We did not have the resources to create a permanent parallel school system. Had we tried to do so, the effort would predictably have collapsed and students might have had to face the world without even a high school diploma.

But that was not quite the end of the story. To begin with, there was the experience that Freedom School students carried into the rest of their lives. John Dittmer says that he could always tell which of his students had been in Freedom Schools: they did not hesitate to challenge the professor and ask questions, they were comfortable in discussions, and they were not intimidated by white teachers. Dittmer tells the story of one such alumnus, Wayne Saddler. Saddler attended the Freedom School in Gluckstadt, Mississippi. Saddler recalled the night that the school was burned to the ground and how, after the summer ended, he continued to attend a Freedom School in nearby Canton. Little more than a decade later, Wayne Saddler was the anchor of the state's most widely watched TV news program.

The Freedom Schools also laid the basis for the Mississippi Headstart program, which in summer 1965 served 6,000 children through eighty-four centers in twenty-four counties. I believe that many of the church basements in which the pre-school children gathered had previously been used for Freedom Schools and that many of the African American women who staffed the Headstart program had previously welcomed 1964 summer volunteers into their homes.

And there was also the following. Years later I was making my way through law school. I read the decision of the United States Supreme Court in *Tinker v. Des Moines*, the case of a high school student in Iowa who wore a black arm band to school to protest the Vietnam War, and was sent home. The high Court held that what she did was protected by the First Amendment. I noticed that the Supreme Court, in its opinion, repeatedly cited a case called *Burnside v. Byars* decided by an appeals court in the South. I looked it up.

It seems that on the first day of school in Fall 1964, African American students in Philadelphia—that same Philadelphia where Schwerner, Goodman, and Chaney had been murdered a few months earlier—went to school wearing buttons that said "SNCC" and "One Man One Vote." They were sent home, but the federal appeals court held that what they did was not so disruptive as to outweigh their right to free speech. Thus the action of these black students—the single most courageous action I remember from that summer of bravery—protected the right of a young white student in a Northern state to protest the Vietnam War a few years later.

### *IV*

So my proposed solution to the dilemma I posed at the outset is, Let's try to make every school a Freedom School. 15,750 hours in which a young person who makes it through high school has been in the presence of someone called a teacher is a fair chunk of time within which to try to offer young people a glimpse of the dawning of a new day.

Am I saying, Because we did it in Mississippi under these dangerous and difficult conditions, you should be able to do it? No, I'm not saying that. Danger and difficulty gave rise to opportunities as well as obstacles. Who amongst us would not wish to teach with a program for first-time voter registration, or any other kind of popular liberation, going on—so to speak—next door?

But I *am* saying, we *did* do it. And hopefully, knowing that may make it a little easier for you when next you confront the teacher who teaches out of last year's notes but has more seniority; the Neanderthal principal and School Board; or indeed, hostile parents and students who seemingly don't give a damn.

In the face of all that, I say, Let's make every school a Freedom School.

Every school a Freedom School, because how else will young people have the experience of putting the chairs in a circle and sharing as equals?

Every school a Freedom School, because this may be the one time and place, the one island of experience when youngsters experience the possibility of taking seriously ideas and ideals.

Every school a Freedom School, because the military is raiding inner city public schools to recruit for its imperialist wars and we have a duty to help our students resist.

Every school a Freedom School, because this may be a young person's one chance to meet a person whose example will reverberate for the rest of that student's life, namely, yourself.

Every school a Freedom School, because even for those who make it through high school it is very difficult to find a decent job and young people will need whatever inner resources we can help them to develop before graduation.

Every school a Freedom School, because if that aspiration will create risks for teachers, it is a greater risk for our students to grow up in inner city America.

Every school a Freedom School because: If not now, then when? If not here, then where? If not ourselves, then who?

For some time after Students for a Democratic Society in 1962 coined the term "participatory democracy," it was received with more humor than respect by civil rights workers in the South. The concept has become important this past winter, for two reasons. First, a number of SDS leaders have left college and are seeking to apply the idea in Northern ghettoes. Second, many members of the staff of the Student Nonviolent Coordinating Committee have begun to look beyond voter registration to what SDS, in its Port Huron Statement, called its

> two central aims: that the individual share in those social decisions determining the quality and direction of his life; that society be organized to encourage independence in men and provide the media for their common participation.

A new style of work, fusing politics and direct action into radical community organization, is emerging in both SDS and SNCC.

Those in SNCC most interested in the SDS concept as a guide to their own work in the South are mainly stationed in Mississippi. This adds significance to their sense of the future, for Mississippi has been the place where the emphasis on voter registration, dominant in SNCC since 1961, has been most fruitfully developed. Why should activists who have just finished so successfully founding the Mississippi Freedom Democratic Party [MFDP or FDP] now find themselves questioning conventional politics as a desirable agency for social change?

One could see the new emphasis growing in Mississippi last summer. Bob Parris [Moses], personally, has always intensely distrusted leaders who prevent the growth of a capacity for responsibility in others: he is famous for sitting in the back of meetings, avoiding speeches, and when obliged to speak standing in his place and asking questions. His is the philosophy of the anarchist leader in the Spanish Civil War who, discovered at the rear of a long lunch line and reminded of his importance to the revolution, answered, "This is the revolution." As "freedom registration" went on in Mississippi last summer, SNCC staff workers and volunteers at many places in the state began to ask questions, in the spirit of Parris' concern, about the process of political organization they were engineering.

It was necessary, for example, to hold precinct meetings of the FDP so as to duplicate fully the steps through which the regular Democratic Party selected delegates to the Atlantic City convention. Such meetings, with perhaps ten to fifty persons in attendance, were something quite different from the mass meetings at which charismatic orators harangue an audience on the eve of direct action. The Southern mass meeting is modeled on a church service. The minister, or his functional substitute, the civil rights worker, remains firmly in control despite the vocal participation of the congregation; decisions made in advance by a small group are translated to the rank and file in an emotional setting. The FDP precinct meeting appeared to offer a setting in which members of the rank and file could be drawn into the expression of their ideas, in which the anguished back-and-forth of decision-making familiar to SNCC staff could become the experience of the Negro masses too, in which the distinction between rank and file, and leaders, could be broken down. Should not the precinct meetings be continued for other purposes? some asked. Others began to experiment with block meetings and ward meetings, conversations outside the church in a neighbor's living room, at which thinking began about local problems, programs, candidates.

Meantime the Freedom School component of the Mississippi Summer Project offered something of a model to those working in voter registration and pondering new approaches to the political process. In the schools 2,500 Mississippi Negro youngsters miraculously found voice, in poems, in plays, in newspapers, in the honest asking of questions about their society. Early in August each of the Freedom Schools sent delegates to a Freedom School Convention. The delegates brought with them political programs hammered out in every school in response to the challenge: If you could elect a Mayor, or a state legislator, or a Senator, what would you want him to do? By the second day of the convention the delegates were confidently rejecting adult participation in their workshops or plenary sessions. The convention, and the atmosphere of free and intimate discussion from which the convention was precipitated, left seeds in the minds of participants.

Then came [the national Democratic Party convention in] Atlantic City. However successful the FDP challenge may have seemed to television viewers, for those who were there the experience was traumatic. Clearly, starkly, the result of an enormous months-and-years-long labor of preparation, the Negro people of Mississippi themselves brought to the attention of the nation their political exclusion. As seen by their SNCC collaborators, what they received was a piece of public relations, the offer of a deal which would not add to their power. Hardened SNCC veterans wept. Bitterness at those national civil rights personalities who urged acceptance of the compromise on grounds of political expediency—Martin Luther King, Bayard Rustin, Joseph Rauh, as well as Walter Reuther and other erstwhile allies—was indescribable. Three months later Bob Parris told a New York audience: They told us to be responsible because the destiny of America was in our hands; we learned that it is not in our hands; we will pursue our own goals, and let the chips fall where they may.

Surely for Bob Parris and others the trauma of Atlantic City brought to the surface, not only a growing awareness of the positive possibilities of participatory politics, but also certain ambiguities embedded in the FDP challenge from the start. The challenge as a strategy had not been created by the Negro people of Mississippi, but by a handful of leaders. The strategy required the demonstration that the FDP was more loyal to the national platform of the Democratic Party, and to President Johnson personally, than the regular Democrats of the state. It led to a focus of attention on Washington which, no matter how one sought to involve local people by delegations to the Capitol, enfeebled civil rights activity at the grass roots. Precisely as the FDP succeeded, it began to develop a hierarchy of its own. Seeking to escape from issueless politics and charismatic leaders, the FDP in its own work emphasized personalities—that is, the seating of individual challengers—rather than program. In each of these ways the institutional thrust of the FDP as it developed ran counter to the new notions about people and politics which the summer had also produced.

The old politics and the new confronted each other once again in Selma. SNCC was the first civil rights group on the ground there. This winter [of 1964-1965], in step with the new thinking in the organization, it began to develop ward meetings and a youth group in which local Negroes could learn to manage their own destinies. Then, by agreement with SNCC but nonetheless traumatically for the SNCC workers in Selma, Dr. King's Southern Christian Leadership Conference moved in. SCLC's focus was the passage of national legislation, not the political maturing of persons in the Alabama Black Belt. Ward meetings, stimulated at first by the new activity, stopped as the pattern of demonstration intensified and each evening had its mass meeting as each morning had its march. SNCC had seen that pattern before, notably in Albany, Georgia, where SNCC workers Charles Sherrod and Cordell Reagan had been displaced by Dr. King and his assistants, and the upshot, for the people of Albany, had been disillusion, a great weight of court costs, and bitterness on the part of local whites.

Concerned that the obstacles to voting be torn down but concerned also that institutional progress go hand-in-hand with a quickening of the people's capacity for self-direction, SNCC could only experience Selma with mixed feelings and considerable frustration. The "march" of March 9, when Dr. King led people to a confrontation he knew would not occur and then accused the police of bad faith for exposing his hypocrisy, must have seemed to those in SNCC a symbolic summation of much that had gone before.

The concern to involve plain people in the decisions which affect their lives crops out elsewhere in SNCC's activity this winter. An educational conference in Mississippi in November threw away a prepared agenda to encourage open-ended discussion among the participants. A fear, muted last summer, lest masses of white volunteers inhibit Southern Negroes from developing their own leaders, led to scaling-down of the Black Belt project planned for summer 1965. Meeting in Atlanta in February, SNCC planned instead to organize "people's conferences" in states of the Deep South, at which new Freedom Democratic parties, directed from the beginning by local leaders, could take root.

Also in February 1965, indigenous leaders drawn from SDS ghetto projects in the North met at Cleveland with some Negroes activated by SNCC work in the South. In SDS as in SNCC, workers seek to apply the participatory philosophy to their own organizations, asking that central offices be abolished, leaders rotated, and executive committees curbed by general staff meetings. In both groups, the elite of the New Left, the theory and practice of participatory democracy grow.

# I

What is the strategy of social change implicit in the concept of participatory democracy? What is its relation to older philosophies of the Left: socialism, nonviolence, anarchism? As one distant from the scene I offer the following observations diffidently, in the hope that they will [elicit] comment from "participatory democrats," North and South.

One aspect of participatory democracy is the idea of parallel structures. The FDP is a parallel political party, prompted by the conclusion that registration of Negroes in the regular Democratic Party of Mississippi is presently impossible. Freedom Schools were parallel schools, although delegates to the Freedom School Convention decided they would return to the public schools and seek to transform them rather than continue into the winter a parallel school system. In the North, neighborhood unions organized by SDS represent parallel antipoverty agencies, challenging the legitimacy of the top-down middle-class "community organizations" sponsored by urban renewal and antipoverty administrators.

The intent of these structures is still unclear, even to those involved in organizing them. There is a spectrum of possibilities. At one end of the spectrum is the concept of using parallel institutions to transform their Establishment counterparts. Thus it would follow that when Mississippi Negroes can register and vote, the FDP would wither away. At the spectrum's other end is the conviction that in an America whose Establishment is inherently and inevitably hostile, existing institutions cannot be transformed, participation will always mean cooptation and merely token successes, hence parallel institutions must survive and grow into an anti-Establishment network, a new society.

For the moment participatory democracy cherishes the practice of parallelism as a way of saying No to organized America, and of initiating the unorganized into the experience of self-government. The SNCC or SDS worker does not build a parallel institution to impose an ideology on it. He views himself as a catalyst, helping to create an environment which will help the local people to decide what they want. Recognizing himself as a part of the society's sickness, the organizer inclines to regard the unorganized poor as purer than himself. There is an unstated assumption that the poor, when they find voice, will produce a truer, sounder radicalism than any which alienated intellectuals might prescribe. In the meantime the very existence of the parallel institution is felt to be a healthier and more genuine experience than any available alternative. It seems better to sit in the back of the room in silent protest against the bureaucrats up front than to seek to elect a man to join the executive committee.

In form, parallelism suggests a kinship between participatory democracy and Trotsky's conception of the Soviets as a "dual power," or Gandhi's concern to preserve the Indian village community. But thus far the new movement does not feel itself a part of either the Marxist or anarcho-pacifist traditions. What is most clear at the moment is the call reminiscent of the Radical Reformation to "come out of Babylon." Let the teacher leave the university and teach in Freedom Schools; let the reporter quit his job on a metropolitan daily and start a community newspaper; generally, let the intellectual make insurgency a full-time rather than a part-time occupation. As the Russian radical movement grew from Tolstoyism and the Narodnik's concern to dress simply, speak truth, and "go to the people," so participatory democracy speaks at this point most clearly to the middle-class man, daring him to forsake powerlessness and act.

I for one believe that participatory democracy, even thus vaguely conceived, offers a growing point far more alive than conventional coalition politics. At the same time, it is incumbent upon new radicals to explain how they propose to answer the problems which conventional politics purports to solve. How will participatory democracy feed and clothe the poor, as well as stimulate and involve them? If voting is a snare and a delusion, what is not? Unless in time these questions can be answered, participatory democracy could become a subtle, even if heroic, form of self-indulgence.

Employment appears to be the Achilles heel of parallelism. From time to time SNCC workers have sought to organize producers and consumers cooperatives, and the leather-working business in Haywood and Fayette counties, Tennessee, has had considerable success. The thriving toy business of the Society of Brothers (Bruderhof) proves that even in the age of monopoly a small cooperative enterprise can survive. But one cannot imagine such economic beginnings becoming, like the free cities of the Middle Ages, the "germ of a new society within the womb of the old." In Mississippi the movement has hardly been able to provide for Negroes fired as a result of civil rights activity, let alone address itself to the larger problem of cotton-picking machinery and the displacement of farm labor; and what provision there has been has come, not through the creation of a new economic base, but from charity.

It would seem, therefore, that in the area of economics participatory democracy cannot provide a full alternative to established institutions except by capturing and transforming them. By pressure it can democratize the distribution of income, as SDS does in boring-from-below against antipoverty programs, as SNCC does in demanding the participation of Negroes in local committees sponsored by the Department of Agriculture. Perhaps, like Dolci in Italy, radical community organizers can use symbolic direct action to dramatize the need for that massive public works program which the March on Washington called for (and then forgot). Thus Noel Day proposes using money collected from rent strikes to employ unemployed youngsters at a $2.00 an hour wage to repair substandard housing. But can we not agree that participatory democracy, understood as a movement building new institutions side-by-side with the old, cannot provide bread and land? Failure to face this problem realistically will result in the poor turning for help to those who can provide it at least in part, and the cooptation of protest movements by the Establishment.

A similar perspective is suggested by turning to the theorists of existential radicalism in other countries. Let us use the term "socialism" to designate the movement for a planned, publicly-owned economy which, in Europe as America, preceded the newer radicalism of "participatory democracy." If one examines carefully the formulations of the latter tendency in Europe (and I believe much the same thing would appear from a scrutiny of Africa), one finds it articulated as a partner in dialogue with socialism, as a humane affirmation constantly necessary to correct (but not to supplant entirely) bureaucratic institutions and political action. Thus in Silone's *Bread and Wine* the protagonist, like Thoreau, asserts that the social action needed above all is individual lives displaying morality and truth. But Silone adds:

> He had not forgotten that the social question is not a moral one and is not resolved by purely moral means. He knew that in the last resort the relations established among men are dictated by necessity and not by good will or bad. Moral preaching did not suffice to change them. But there came a moment when certain social relations revealed themselves as outworn and harmful. Morality then condemned what had already been condemned by history.

This is a formulation which has not yet created an impassable gulf between itself and Marxism. Silone's statement could be rendered, more woodenly to be sure, as an assertion that when "objective" conditions are "ripe" for change, the "subjective factor" becomes all-important.

To much the same effect, Martin Buber in *Paths in Utopia* takes public ownership as a matter of course, arguing that the critical question is: "what sort of Socialism is it to be?" The relation between centralization and decentralization, between bureaucracy and community, is, says Buber,

> a problem which cannot be approached in principle, but, like everything to do with the relationship between idea and reality, only with great spiritual tact, with the constant and tireless weighing and measuring of the right proportion between them.

This is to say of popular participation much [of] what Howard Zinn has insisted regarding nonviolence, that to ignore its limitations invites hypocrisy and, ultimately, a tendency for it to turn into its opposite

Even Camus—so far as I can judge the strongest intellectual influence on the thinking of Bob Parris—does not quite turn his back on the Marxist "logic of history." Rather, he writes in "Neither Victims Nor Executioners":

Since these forces are working themselves out and since it is inevitable that they continue to do so, there is no reason why some of us should not take on the job of keeping alive through the apocalyptic historical vista that stretches before us, a modest thoughtfulness which, without pretending to solve everything, will constantly be prepared to give some human meaning to everyday life.

Others of us, then, will continue to address ourselves to structural changes, to socialism. In the words of the Port Huron Statement, "a truly 'public sector' must be established," and the New Left should include socialists "for their sense of thoroughgoing reforms in the system."

## II

In itself, however, this formulation papers over a difference rather than resolving it. What could be more sterile than a movement with two predefined wings, a left one and a right one (we could argue endlessly about which was which)? If "some of us" were committed to one traditional concept and others of us to another, would it not be another version of coalition politics, frustrating and dead?

Some common ground, some underlying vision needs to be articulated which genuinely unites socialism and "participatory democracy," which challenges each to transcend itself. Here one strikes out into unexplored territory which can only be adequately clarified by experience. A helpful starting point may be the concept of "community." "Politics," affirms the Port Huron Statement, "has the function of bringing people out of isolation and into community." And A. J. Muste writes, correctly I think, of the civil rights movement:

No one can have a fairly close contact with the civil rights movement and the people in it, including the young people, without feeling that, in spite of all contrary appearances and even realities in the movement, deep near its center is this aspiration for a blessed community and the faith that this is what they are working for and already in a sense realizing now.

Community was what one Freedom School teacher meant who wrote to me: "The summer project presented itself to us as a potentially life endangering situation, and so we all worked our fears out together, which gave coherence to our group. We had temporarily put aside our human fears and were accepting a responsibility which was ours and we were doing it together."

Lest this seem maudlin utopianism, let us begin with the most hard-headed meaning of community to a new radical movement: the political. How can one build a political campaign, or a political party, without sacrificing the shared intimacy experienced in a direct action "project"? If it be true that both peace and civil rights activists must turn toward politics to cope with the economic problems which confront their movements, can it be done without losing the spiritual exaltation of the direct action years?

I think a clue here is to begin to think of politics as administration. Political representation was devised as a mechanism to obtain consent for taxation. It is an institutional process peculiarly appropriate to an economy in which production is in private hands, and the state takes money from the citizen to spend it on a separate category of public activities. In a communal economy—by which I simply mean an economy wherein men share the fruits of their labor in the spirit of a family— many functions, now centralized in private hands, would be centralized in the hands of the government; but also, many functions now locally privatized would at once become neighborly responsibilities. Consider urban renewal. If land were publicly owned and building a public function, slum clearance could really become a process in which the people of a site participated at each stage. Nation- and city-wide considerations would enter in, of course, but much that now happens in public and private offices on upper floors could then be left to the collective discretion of neighborhood meetings.

In centering its attention on grass roots participation in urban renewal and antipoverty programs, rather than on running candidates, SDS appears instinctively to recognize the communal opportunities of public economic administration. As more and more candidates begin to run for public office on a movement platform, so also new forms of direct action will be improvised to democratize administration; and as regional and national coordination takes form in the one area, so will it in the other, too. Thus entrance into politics need *not* mean an abandonment of direct action demonstration, nor of its spirit.

In conversation after the recent March on Washington, Bob Parris suggested two specific ways in which an elected "freedom candidate" could keep himself from being absorbed by conventional politics. First, if an MFDP candidate were elected to the Mississippi legislature he could act as a representative of *all* the Negroes of Mississippi rather than of a particular locality. Second, an elected candidate could simply decline to "take his seat" in a legislature and remain in his constituency as a symbol of identification with their concerns.

The local project can grow from protest into administration; if necessary it could also be the building block for resistance to more extreme forms of repression, for protest against Fascism. Like a biological cell it can take many forms, responding in a variety of appropriate ways to alternate stimuli from the environment.

But for this to be so it becomes necessary to think of a project from the beginning, not merely as a tool for social change, but as a community. The community is made up both of people from the neighborhood and of staff persons who, on a long-term basis, so far as they can become part of the neighborhood. The spirit of a community, as opposed to an organization, is not, We are together to accomplish this or that end, but, We are together to face together whatever life brings.

The experience of Utopian or "intentional" communities suggests certain ground rules which all groups seeking to live as brothers should consider. One is: It is important to be honest with each other, to carry grievances directly to those concerned, rather than to third parties. Another is: The spiritual unity of the group is more important than any external accomplishment, and time must be taken to discover and restore that unity even at the cost of short-run tangible failures.

If indeed, as Marxism affirms, mankind will one day enter a realm of freedom that will permit men to guide their behavior by more humane and immediate criteria than the minimum and maximum demands of political programs, the work of transition can begin now. The need for structural change (socialism) should neither be ignored nor overemphasized. Provided we do not deceive ourselves as to the bleakness of our society's prospects for hopeful change or the catastrophic dangers of nuclear war and domestic totalitarianism, perhaps it is not unreasonable to look for a more firm and definite strategy to develop as the collective experience of the movement unfolds.

Peculiarly difficult, I think, will be the coming-together of "staff" and "neighborhood" persons on questions of foreign policy. This was a problem which confronted the Freedom Democratic Party, obliged by its strategy to support a President just then escalating the war in Vietnam. Tentatively it would seem that staff must be honest about such questions, and surely the ideological framework of brotherhood and community should make it easier to be so than one simply oriented to pragmatic goals.

In sum, then, participatory democracy seems to be driving toward the "live-in," the building of a brotherly way of life even in the jaws of Leviathan. It is conscientious objection not just to war, but to the whole fabric of a dehumanized society. It is civil disobedience not just by individuals, but, hopefully, by broad masses of alienated Americans. Like the

conscientious objector, however, the participatory democrat has unfin-
ished business with the question: is what's intended a moral gesture only,
or a determined attempt to transform the American power structure?

In the fall of 1947 the CIO held its annual convention in Boston. The author of what is for the moment the standard history of the CIO says, "At the CIO's mid-October annual convention formal unanimity masked deep conflicts."[1] What I heard, as a student from nearby Harvard listening in on the debates, was hardly masked. I was present when George Baldanzi, vice president of the Textile Workers Union of America, delivered what remains the most hate-filled, demagogic speech I have ever heard, denouncing Communists and Communism. When he finished Baldanzi came to the back of the hall, very near to where I was standing, and threw himself into the arms of his ideological supporters with the air of a prize fighter climbing out of the ring.

Apart from this moment, I have very little firsthand knowledge of the expulsions from the labor movement. But I was thrown out of the United States Army in 1954. I offer the written allegations against me as a reminder of the existential experience of McCarthyism.

The background was that some months before April 1954, when I received an Undesirable Discharge, Senator McCarthy discovered an Army officer at Fort Dix who, he said, was a Communist. The Army panicked, and decided to rid itself of what I believe was between one and two hundred persons whom it had inducted, on the basis of information altogether in its possession at the time of our induction.

I've never shared this document with anyone outside my immediate family. Let me read to you most of the allegations against me.

> 1. Derogatory information has been received in this office which reveals the following. That you:
>    a. In 1947 and 1948, were an officer in American Youth for Democracy and John Reed Club at Harvard University. The American Youth for Democracy is cited as subversive and Communist by the Attorney General of the United States. John Reed was one of the

        earliest Communist leaders in the United States.
   b.  Were believed to be a Communist sympathizer.
   c.  Included considerable Marxist philosophy in papers submitted while a student at Harvard University.

It's possible that they got that from fellow students. But I think not. I think members of the Harvard faculty took a break from the timeless, selfless search for truth to snitch on their former students. See the articles by Sig Diamond and Robert Bellah that appeared in *The New York Review of Books* some years ago on the systematic cooperation of Harvard University with the United States government in those years, and remember that McGeorge Bundy, later of Vietnam War fame, was dean of Harvard College at the time.

   d.  Were described as "at least an idealistic Communist."
   e.  Appeared at the Russian Research Center, presumably at Harvard University, requesting interviews for the publication "Masses and Mainstream" which is cited as a successor to "New Masses," a Communist magazine.
   f.  Were believed to be a member of the Communist Party.
   g.  Were described as "a dangerous type Communist" who would be disloyal to the United States in the event of an emergency affecting this nation.
   h.  Have a father, Robert, who:
      (1) Was repeatedly closely connected with the Communist Party.
      (2) In 1944, 1946, 1947 and 1948, registered in New York City as an affiliate of the American Labor Party. The American Labor Party is cited by the House Committee on Un-American Activities as being under Communist control in New York City.

And then i., the real kicker:

   i.  Have a mother, Helen, who was described as a hypermodern educator . . . .

The shame of it! To stagger through life with such a burden! Then they went on to say, j. and k., that I was a member of the two Trotskyist parties, the Independent Socialist League and the Socialist Workers Party. If you've been keeping track, that makes three of them, each one of which passionately hated the other two.

  l.  Attended meetings of the Socialist Youth League.

I have no idea what that is, or was

> which is cited as subversive and Communist by the
> Attorney General of the United States.
>   m.  You are advised that you have thirty (30) days in which
> to make rebuttal. This letter has been classified to pre-
> vent embarrassment to you. However, should you desire
> to obtain legal advice, permission is granted to disclose
> the information contained herein to your counsel.

Having laid on me this set of amorphous allegations by nameless, faceless persons, whom I had no opportunity to confront or cross-examine, they give me permission to talk to a lawyer! They're all heart. Who can say that this was a totalitarian procedure?

Now this particular story, I hasten to add, had a happy ending. One of the affected group found a lawyer more creative than the counsel with whom I spoke, and a class action was brought. The theory of the law suit was, If the Army knew all this stuff at the time of our induction, perhaps we were moral lepers and should have been excluded from military service; but it was dirty pool to induct us and then give us undesirable discharges which we would carry around for the rest of our lives. A federal court, in the late 1950s, agreed. Our discharges were all upgraded to honorable. I got GI bill, and went to graduate school.

But on information and belief, I think that many folks were drummed out of the labor movement with about the same degree of due process that I got from the United States Army. This document should alert you to the fact that I am hardly a detached commentator. Being thus possessed of a strong bias and very little firsthand knowledge—an unpromising combination—it seemed to me that I might best contribute to this occasion by discussing something about which I know a good deal more: how we in the movement of the Sixties tried to deal with the history we inherited, where that took us, and what I think about it now.

## *I*

Todd Gitlin rightly states that the "ungainly double negative, anti-anti-Communism, was for the New Left what anti-Communism was for the postwar liberals and social democrats: the crucible of a political identity."[2]

In June 1962, several dozen students belonging to Students for a Democratic Society (SDS) met at the UAW retreat in Port Huron,

Michigan. They amended and then approved Tom Hayden's draft of what came to be known as the "Port Huron Statement." This document as amended stated in part: "As democrats we are in basic opposition to the communist system . . . . The communist movement has failed . . . to achieve its stated intention of leading a worldwide movement for human emancipation." But the Port Huron Statement expressed even more forcefully its opposition to what the Statement termed "an unreasoning anti-communism," which, according to the document, "has become a major social problem for those who want to construct a democratic America."[3]

At Port Huron there took place a celebrated confrontation between the young SDSers and a thirty-four-year-old left-wing intellectual, Michael Harrington. Harrington showed up at Port Huron with an AFL-CIO staffer named Donald Slaiman. The two young men proceeded to lecture the assembled young people that their proposed statement was too hard on the trade union movement, and too soft on Communism. A shouting match went on for several hours.

The next morning a question arose: Should a high school student from a Communist-sponsored youth group be seated as an observer? One frustrated participant remarked that, "It was [made to seem] somehow tantamount to diplomatic recognition." SDS decided, Yes.

This was not the end. At the time SDS was technically the youth arm of the League for Industrial Democracy (LID), which gave the students office space and money. SDS leaders were summoned to a sort of trial in New York City, at which Harrington, it was said, played the role of grand inquisitor. The whole experience became for the embattled anti-anti-Communists a kind of political rite of passage.[4]

Meantime the Student Nonviolent Coordinating Committee (SNCC), organized in 1960, also committed itself to non-exclusionism. As understood in SNCC, non-exclusionism meant that if you did the work, no questions were asked about your political background and ultimate political intentions.

Just as the non-exclusionism of SDS contrasted with the fanatical anti-Communism of groups like the LID and individuals like Michael Harrington, so SNCC differentiated itself from the Southern Christian Leadership Conference (SCLC) and its leader, Dr. Martin Luther King. Just before the 1963 March on Washington, Dr. King fired Jack O'Dell, a former member of the Communist Party. In the words of King biographer Taylor Branch, Dr. King "saw the purge as the price of alliance with the [Kennedy] administration."[5] I can still recall the incredulity with which I heard Dr. King's aide, Andrew Young, defend this discharge in private conversation.

SNCC's attitude was different. Let me give some examples.

The Cuban Missile Crisis occurred in the fall of 1962. The mayor of Atlanta wired President Jack Kennedy that Atlantans supported him 100 percent. The SNCC national headquarters staff in Atlanta immediately organized a picket line against United States policy, on which they were joined by Howard Zinn, myself, and others from the Spelman and Morehouse College faculties.

In June 1964, orientation sessions for the Mississippi Summer Project took place at the Western College for Women in Oxford, Ohio. The National Council of Churches, which had paid for the occasion, objected to the presence of Carl and Anne Braden. SNCC understood that the Council could hardly cancel a program that had already begun, much less a program strongly supported by the religious community. The Bradens stayed.

At about the same time, various Northern groups and individuals objected to the National Lawyers Guild as legal representative of the Summer Project. But representation of the Mississippi Freedom Democratic Party (MFDP) at the Atlantic City convention of the national Democratic Party in August 1964 was placed in the hands of Joseph Rauh. Rauh was a leading member of Americans for Democratic Action (ADA) and counsel to the UAW. Acting on direct orders from Walter Reuther, who flew from Detroit to Atlantic City to supervise the operation, Rauh scuttled the MFDP's efforts to replace the regular Mississippi Democrats.[6] For those of you think that what the labor movement needs is a return to Walter Reuther, check out Nelson Lichtenstein's biography—certainly not the work of a fellow traveler—at pages 392 to 395.

After the Summer Project I took a job at Yale. I shall never forget C. Vann Woodward asking me one day, "What are we going to do about the Communists in SNCC?" "What Communists?," I responded, and he had no answer. Later the same conversation took place with Allard Loewenstein. It was not just SNCC's turn to Black Power that caused Northern funding to dry up. It was also the drumbeat of wholly unsubstantiated Red-baiting from distinguished Northern liberals.

The same drama played itself out in the emerging movement against the war in Vietnam. SDS called for a March on Washington in April 1965. It refused to exclude from the occasion particular groups or slogans. On the eve of the march, Bayard Rustin, Robert Gilmore, Harold Taylor, Norman Thomas, H. Stuart Hughes, and to his later regret, A. J. Muste, issued a press release calling for a peace movement "independent" of totalitarian influences.[7] There followed an acerbic exchange between myself and various defenders of Bayard Rustin, who had muted his criticism of the war in order to seek new allies in the trade union movement. I said that Bayard's position amounted to "coalition with the Marines."[8]

At least through mid-1965, then, the burgeoning movement of the 1960s New Left consistently and in all its aspects disavowed the anti-Communism of the previous generation. Tom Hayden and I wrote as follows in *Studies on the Left*:

> [W]e refuse to be anti-Communist. We insist that the term has lost all the specific content it once had. Instead it serves as the key category of abstract thought which Americans use to justify a foreign policy that often is no more sophisticated than rape. It also serves as a deterrent to building an open movement for change in this country, because organizations that refuse to be anti-Communist must fight bitterly for funds and allies. Our feeling is that the anti-Communist organizations, such as the trade unions, are far less democratic than the organizations, such as SNCC and SDS, which refuse to be anti-Communist. We have confidence that movements can be built which are too strong to be "used"; the anti-Communists do not have that confidence.[9]

## II

The confidence expressed by Tom Hayden and myself in the strength of the movements of the New Left to deal with sectarian invasion proved to be misplaced.

I first experienced this in the fall of 1965. After the April 1965 March on Washington, SDS decided not to put itself at the head of the growing movement against the Vietnam War. Persons associated with *Liberation* magazine and various peace groups, myself included, decided to call a so-called Assembly of Unrepresented People in Washington, D.C. for Hiroshima and Nagasaki Days, August 6 to 9. The idea was that we did not support the undeclared war with Vietnam, and that we would show this by declaring peace with the people of Vietnam on the steps of the Capitol. As Bob Moses of SNCC, Dave Dellinger, and I led a column of demonstrators from the Washington Monument toward the Capitol, counter-demonstrators threw red paint on us. Moments later we were all arrested.

During the Assembly in August 1965 it was democratically decided that on October 15-16 there would be "international days of protest" against the war in cities across the country. Just prior to these dates, Attorney General Nicholas Katzenbach floated some trial balloons about suppressing SDS as a subversive organization, and Paul Booth and others of SDS held a press conference to announce that SDS policy was to "build not burn." Critically, just as the April march in Washington surprised everyone by drawing 25,000 participants, the decentralized protests in mid-October were attended by tens of thousands more. The federal government backed off. This was one war where protest and dissent on the home front were not going to be suppressed.

It was also decided in August that at Thanksgiving 1965 there would be a conference in Washington, D.C. of the ad hoc antiwar groups that had sprung up all over the country. Students in Madison, Wisconsin volunteered to coordinate the event.

As November neared, knowledgeable persons told me that Trotskyists organized in the Young Socialist Alliance (YSA) were going to try to take over the conference. I scoffed, assuring my informants that they were thinking of the bad old days of the 1930s, and that the New Left—decentralized, experimental, and consensual—did not lower itself to such things. You're wrong, I was told. The fact that the person running the Madison office was Frank Emspak, son of Julius Emspak of the UE, fed Trotskyist suspicions.

I asked who it was that was organizing the Trotskyist effort, and was given the name of a man in New York City named Jack Barnes. I went to speak to him. I asked him for a minimum level of civility at the impending conference, stressing the fact that young people new to politics were coming from all over the country and that we did not want to turn them off the movement by sectarian in-fighting. Barnes appeared to agree.

My naive effort was for naught. At what came to be known in movement oral history as "the crazy convention," Trotskyists and Communists contested from the opening gavel, to the bewilderment of folks who had driven from Iowa or North Carolina to try to stop the war. My most vivid memory is of a locked hotel room, where by the end of the gathering the Trotskyists were forming a new national organization.

I must add a footnote. Last month I had occasion to meet again in California one of the Trotskyist organizers at that conference. He said he hadn't seen me since 4 a.m. on a certain night in 1965, when he, Jack Barnes and I had argued about what was happening. He pointed out that there was a difference between the Communist and Trotskyist positions on the war, the former supporting some version of cease-fire and negotiations, whereas the latter insisted on immediate withdrawal. I, according to this man, had said that I agreed with Barnes and himself politically but opposed the methods used to promote our common position.

I find this plausible and important. I tended to agree with the politics that Marxist groups brought to these larger gatherings but to deplore the manipulative style—as I perceived it—in which they operated.

Exactly this pattern was repeated in 1965-1969 when the Maoist Progressive Labor Party invaded, and in the end destroyed, SDS. PLP's principal concern was that SDS was only a student movement and that unless it went off campus and made contact with the American working class, it could not change United States society. I thought that this was true, and indeed, have ever since been trying to do something about it.

But I was appalled at the ruthless way in which PLP and all the other Marxist sects operated. Here is how I put it in June 1969, very close to the time of the final convention in which SDS imploded.

> Some styles of politicking are objectionable in the movement, not because they are communist but because they are undemocratic. . . .
>
> It is hard to talk with someone in a heartfelt manner if you know he made his mind up in a caucus before the conversation began, or worse, if you only find this out when the conversation is over . . . . Whether an organization is communist or noncommunist, whether it is centralized or decentralized, whether it makes decisions by voting or consensus, manipulative relationships between people will tend to destroy it. Liberals, as we all know, can be the most accomplished manipulators. Nevertheless, in one way there is a connection between adherence to Marxism as a total world view and exclusive guide to practice, and a manipulative political style. If you believe that there is such a thing as a scientifically "correct" political strategy, you will go on believing this even if a majority disagree with you; and you may be tempted to manipulate the decision-making process to make it confirm what (you are convinced) is true.[10]

## III

I trust that the irony or tragedy of this tale is clear enough. The anti-anti-Communists were ultimately done in by Marxist-Leninist grouplets.

The disintegration of SNCC and SDS by the end of the 1960s left me with what I consider a genuine Post Traumatic Disorder. I am terrified at the thought of trying to organize another national movement, for fear that some Marxist sects would once again try to take it over.

How a disciplined radical minority should properly relate to a broader popular movement is a continuing problem for the Left. History may give us another chance at this project, and we would be well advised to learn the lessons of the Cold War years beforehand.

What are those lessons? I shall offer three.

First, to the survivors of the New Left: Another time we must recognize that when an organization grows to a certain size, consensus decision-making is no longer possible and some form of representative government becomes necessary. Consensus decision-making in a group too large or too diverse to practice it effectively invites takeover by a minority. Representative government does not necessarily mean Robert's Rules: imaginative alternatives have been attempted, for example at the Seabrook occupation, when affinity groups chose so-called "spokes" who made decisions for an entire assemblage. Nor does representative government foreclose the practice of participatory democracy and consensus decision-making in subprojects of the organization. But Lesson One is that next time around, we must do our organizational housekeeping. We must have a structure for decision-making and a written code of conduct, and we must be prepared to invite the departure of folks who violate these rules: rules not of belief, but of behavior.[11]

For the Old Left amongst us, Lesson Two: Ways must be found to be more up front, from the beginning, about who you are and what you believe. Caucusing in itself is not the problem. It is good to have small groups prepare for a larger meeting by focusing discussion in a way that only a small group can do. But somehow each small group must remember that the problems are bigger than all of us, and we all may have something to learn from our common experience. Lesson Two is that we need to discover what I can only describe as an open Left, a Left that wears its convictions on its sleeve and stretches out a hand of invitation to those who differ in good faith.

Finally, Lesson Three, for all of us: We must learn to recognize as comrades persons who belong to other Left organizations. I will quickly give three examples of the practice of this Third Lesson, and then I am done.

My first example is Karl Marx. Marx employed a polemical style against political opponents that is not, in my opinion, something we should emulate. But I recently had occasion to reread *The Civil War in France*, the pamphlet Marx wrote about the Paris Commune of 1871. (If you think I'm dragging this in by the hair, let me offer the Paris Commune as a progenitor of more recent ideas. One: like the UE, its elected officials could make no more than the wages of the workers who elected them. Two: it passed an ordinance that the workshops of Paris that had been abandoned by the employers should be organized as workers' co-operatives, the beginning of the Tri-State Conference on Steel's eminent domain strategy.)

I was struck by the fact that the Communards—the brave men and women who kept that venture alive for two months, and then were destroyed in blood—were followers of Blanqui and Proudhon. They were opponents of Marx in the politics of the First International. (Read Engels' 1891 preface to a new edition on just this point.)[12] And these are the men on whom Marx heaped praise as "plain working men" who had discovered "the political form under which the working class would work out the economic emancipation of the labor movement." That took a largeness of spirit to which we might well aspire.

My second example is Monsignor Charles Owen Rice. Had I been on the scene, I would have opposed him root and branch in the labor wars that followed World War II. But he had the courage to say publicly well *before* the end of the Cold War: "I was more of an unblinking American-style patriot than I should have been . . . . I was not only a cold war liberal, but an unforgivably naive one to boot." And: "It is tragic that there is not a strong Left in American trade unions today . . . . [T]he American trade union movement would be healthier today if Phil Murray had not purged the CIO and if a strong, broad based Communist minority had been able to survive in the trade unions. The split of the U.E. was a loss and so was the transformation of the U.A.W. into a monolith." And finally, from the same 1977 essay and most pertinent to my theme—it's interesting that he gives this highest priority—"What bothers me personally, most of all, is that, in the very bad days of the Cold War . . . I did not defend all the victims [Whatever group you belong to, or have belonged to, think of the victims from other Left groups that your group did not defend] . . . . I did not defend brave people whose careers and lives were destroyed by McCarthyism."[13] Who among us has publicly confessed error so undefensively?

Finally, I offer a recently published book by a veteran of the Abraham Lincoln Brigade, Harry Fisher's *Comrades*. In his Preface he tells us that his children persuaded him to tell about the negative incidents he witnessed, as well as the heroic ones. He does so, and in doing so names names: a commissar who reported the Jarama disaster as a victory, the shooting of a frightened deserter. Most impressive to me was Fisher's affection for Pat Reid, whom he describes as "perhaps the only anarchist in the battalion." Reid and Fisher became friends when they climbed over the Pyrenees into Spain. They worked together stringing telephone wire under fire. Reid, as his friend Fisher remembers him,

> refused to become an officer. . . . [He] was a buck private to begin with, and even though he was in charge of an important group, he remained a buck private until the day he left Spain. And true to his anarchistic philosophy, he never issued orders. He would ask his men to do a job; if they couldn't, he would

do it himself. If the job was dangerous, he wouldn't even ask; he'd just do it.[14]

May we all be such comrades one to the other.

## ENDNOTES

1 Robert H. Zieger, *The CIO 1935-1955* (Chapel Hill: University of North Carolina Press, 1995), p. 267.

2 Todd Gitlin, *The Sixties: Years of Hope, Days of Rage* (New York: Bantam, 1987), p. 122.

3 The Port Huron Statement is most conveniently available as an Appendix to James Miller, *"Democracy is in the Streets": From Port Huron to the Siege of Chicago* (New York: Simon and Schuster, 1987). The quoted passages are at pp. 350-351.

4 For Port Huron, see Gitlin, *op. cit.*, pp. 112-126; Miller, *op. cit.*, pp. 110-117; Michael Harrington, *The Long-Distance Runner: An Autobiography* (New York: Henry Holt, 1988), pp. 57-58.

5 Taylor Branch, *Parting the Waters: America in the King Years, 1954-1963* (New York: Simon and Schuster, 1988), pp. 850-851. See also David J. Garrow, *Bearing the Cross: Martin Luther King, Jr. and the Southern Christian Leadership Conference* (New York: William Morrow, 1986), p. 275.

6 Nathan Lichtenstein, *The Most Dangerous Man in Detroit: Walter Reuther and the Fate of American Labor* (New York: Basic Books, 1995), pp. 392-395.

7 Gitlin, *op. cit.*, p. 182.

8 See James Tracy, *Direct Action: Radical Pacifism from the Union Eight to the Chicago Seven* (Chicago: University of Chicago Press, 1996), pp. 128-133.

9 Quoted in Hal Draper, *Socialism from Below* (New Jersey: Humanities Press, 1992), pp. 126-127.

10 Staughton Lynd, "On 'Anti-Communism,'" *Liberation* (June 1969), pp. 3-4.

11 I have elaborated Lesson One in Staughton Lynd, "The Prospects of the New Left," in *Failure of a Dream? Essays in the History of American Socialism*, ed. John H. M. Laslett and Seymour Martin Lipset (Garden City: Anchor/Doubleday, 1974), pp. 713-739.

12 In his 1891 Introduction to a new edition of *The Civil War in France*, Engels wrote: "The members of the Commune were divided into a majority, the Blanquists . . . ; and a minority, members of the International Working Men's Association, chiefly consisting of adherents to the Proudhon school of socialism." Karl Marx and Friedrich Engels, *Writings on the Paris Commune*, ed. Hal Draper (New York: Monthly Review Press, 1971), p. 30.

13 Charles Owen Rice, "The Tragic Purge of 1948" (1977), in *Fighter with a Heart: Writings of Charles Owen Rice, Pittsburgh Labor Priest*, ed. Charles J. McCollester (Pittsburgh: University of Pittsburgh Press, 1996), pp. 97-98.

14 Harry Fisher, *Comrades: Tales of a Brigadista in the Spanish Civil War* (Lincoln: University of Nebraska Press, 1998), pp. xiv (negative incidents), 26 (crossing the Pyrenees), 67 (Reid as a buck private).

*WHAT HAPPENED AT COLUMBIA?*

Mark Rudd burst into prominence in April 1968 as the most visible leader of the insurgency at Columbia University. In the minds of many young activists the Columbia uprising then became the template for overthrowing United States imperialism and the capitalist system that engendered it. A few years later, as one of a handful of members of Students for a Democratic Society (SDS) who called themselves Weatherman, Mark Rudd went underground. In *Underground: My Life with SDS and the Weatherman* (New York: HarperCollins, 2009), he tells us what happened as he experienced it, and how he feels about it now.

In Part I of Rudd's memoir, the reader who was not present at the Columbia events (as I was not) will find a detailed narrative of what happened there.

Shortly before the Columbia confrontation Rudd had been part of an SDS delegation to revolutionary Cuba, and in this country Dr. King had been assassinated. One of Rudd's first acts of public defiance was to seize the microphone at an official Columbia memorial for Dr. King. "Trembling inside with fear" he denounced Columbia's hypocrisy for mourning a black leader when the university was fighting the unionization of black and Puerto Rican workers there, as well as starting to build an eleven-story gym on the land of a public park in nearby Harlem. He then led about forty persons out of the meeting.

A showdown with the university administration was planned for April 23. The idea was to begin with a series of speeches at an outdoor location and then march into Low Library where the Columbia president had his office. Word came that the doors to Low had been locked. Someone in the crowd yelled, "To the gym site!"

Part of the crowd streamed toward the gym site where another impasse ensued. A demonstrator had been arrested. Police were present in force. Finally someone proposed returning to the original rally site. Rudd recalls: "I was totally dejected by now. The day had been an utter disaster. . . . I, the big leader, had no notion of what to do."

There then followed a sequence of events that might have caused any participant to conclude that revolution has its own organic logic for those brave enough to ride the wave. Hamilton Hall, where the Columbia dean had his office, had not been locked. Accordingly it was occupied. A Steering Committee was elected and a six-point set of demands was drawn up, beginning with the demand that construction of the gym be stopped and ending with a demand for amnesty.

Within the next few days four more buildings were occupied. "The situation was way beyond control by 'leadership,'" Rudd writes. "Students were joining the Low occupation on their own." The joyous atmosphere inside the liberated buildings, which included performance of a marriage ceremony, led the occupiers to call them "communes." When the long-awaited police bust came on April 30, it was carried out with an indiscriminate brutality that won the arrestees considerable public sympathy.

The lesson drawn by Rudd and his colleagues at the time, then carried across the country and into Weatherman, was that "exemplary action leads to mass support and participation." "Organizing," Rudd told innumerable student audiences, was just "another word for going slow." This analysis fell short in two respects.

First, as Tom Hayden (who was at Columbia) and Cathy Wilkerson (who became a Weatherperson) stress in their own memoirs, despite its apocalyptic frenzy the Columbia revolt achieved its principal specific goal: it stopped the construction of the gym. The possibility of winning important attainable goals tended to be forgotten in subsequent confrontations with "the system."

Second, as Rudd emphasizes in hindsight, what happened in April 1968 could not have happened without years of preparatory organizing. Rudd describes how David Gilbert knocked on the door of his dormitory room one evening and drew him into the Movement at Columbia. Likewise, according to Wilkerson, Gilbert recruited Teddy Gold when Gold went to his first day of classes wearing an NLF button. April 1968, she adds, came about because antiwar and SDS activists at Columbia had "distributed materials, held rap sessions in the dorms, protested recruiters, and held referendums, first on student ranking [which determined eligibility for the draft] and then on military recruiting."

Both the importance of winning reforms and the need for preliminary organizing tended to be forgotten in the passion to create two, three, many Columbias.

## STORMY WEATHER

Parts II and III of Mark Rudd's memoir recalls how the self-described Weatherman grouping emerged, floundered, and then went underground.

I don't pretend to have mastered the entire literature on Weatherman. However, I find persuasive the fact that Rudd, a member of the initial central committee or "Weather Bureau," and Cathy Wilkerson, a rank-and-file Weatherperson who describes her experience in *Flying Close to the Sun: My Life and Times as a Weatherman* (New York: Seven Stories Press, 2007), tell essentially the same story.

In the Weatherman sub-culture there was a bizarre commitment to demonstrate one's capacity to engage in violence. This is especially striking in Rudd's case, because he apparently recognized even in early skirmishes at Columbia that "[d]eep down I knew I was no fighter." Following a demonstration at Richard Nixon's inauguration in 1969 a black acquaintance forced Rudd to admit to himself that ever since he "was a little kid," he had been and still was "afraid of violence." Nothing had changed later on that year, when after an encounter in Milwaukee with a group of about a dozen working-class youngsters he comments, "I knew I was no fighter and suspected that most of the other Weathermen were similarly incapable." Still, he continued in speech after speech to deride pacifists and "liberals," and to call on all committed persons to prove their Movement credentials by acts of violence.

Further, Weatherman's purported commitment to "criticism and self-criticism" amounted in practice to ridicule and bullying of anyone who disagreed with the current party line. Rudd gives several poignant examples.

Friends forcefully informed Rudd that the Cubans believed that Weatherman's planned "Days of Rage" in Chicago was a terrible idea. The Cubans like the Vietnamese considered it necessary to build "the broadest possible unity of as many Americans as possible against the war, not a fantasy of violent revolution in the streets." But when Rudd tried to share this information with his Weather friends Terry Robbins and Bill Ayers, they jumped on him. "How could you be so weak?" Robbins demanded.

A few months later another powerful Weatherperson, Bernardine Dohrn, went to Cuba and likewise was told that the American antiwar movement "had to become even broader." This time Rudd, along with John Jacobs (J.J.), played the part of interrogator, barraging Dohrn with unrealistic expectations about the Days of Rage until she "capitulated."

Witnessing the remorseless criticism of a gentle, thoughtful younger comrade, Rudd says he "knew the whole thing was nuts but couldn't intervene to stop it." Wilkerson recounts many similar moments. Why, one wonders, were these strong and dedicated activists, committed to criticism and self-criticism, paralyzed when it came to standing up against majority sentiment in their own in-group?

## *A Road Not Taken*

Bill Ayers, another member of the Weather Bureau, came to Weatherman after experiencing earlier phases of the Sixties more fully than had Mark Rudd. As he tells us in *Fugitive Days: A Memoir* (Boston: Beacon Press, 2001), Ayers was a "full-time freedom school teacher" in the Ann Arbor Children's Community and an organizer for the East Side Community Union in Cleveland.

The Children's Community, like the Mississippi Freedom Schools that I coordinated in summer 1964, was what we called a parallel institution created side-by-side the traditional structures it sought to replace. The East Side Community Union was one of several efforts initiated by the SDS Economic Research and Action Project (ERAP) to create in Northern cities an inter-racial movement of the poor.

Because of his previous immersion in this kinder, gentler period of the Movement, Ayers is able to describe in a remarkably precise way how the early Sixties approached the challenge of devising a strategy.

> The ascendancy of ideology among us foretold the end of what had been a genuinely new left, a left that refused received ideas and based itself, instead, on the wisdom of experience. Until now the way out of disagreements was practice—if some of us believed that knocking on doors in working-class neighborhoods and engaging people in discussions about the war was effective, then that's what we did; if others of us thought that a large mobilization in Washington was the way to go, then that was our assignment. Or we could do both, and/or a hundred other things in between. The key was to act on what our knowledge demanded of us, to experiment, and then to sum it all up in order to move forward, to link our conduct to our consciousness. Our ideas would all be the fruit of our own labor, our own experience.

In place of this process, reflecting the educational wisdom of John Dewey in an earlier generation and of Paulo Freire, the end-of-the-Sixties embraced "ideology." As Ayers says:

> Ideology became an appealing alternative . . . . Practice was uncertain and inexact; ideology cloaked itself in confidence. Practice was slow and ideology a smooth and efficient shortcut.

... I didn't know yet how domesticating and cruel and stupid ideology could become, or the inevitable dependency it would foster in all of us.

There was a danger now from inside, from ourselves. We were becoming prisoners of our own schemes, intoxicated on theory.

Neither freedom schools nor community unions seemed to be doing much to stop the Vietnam War, however. It was the unending holocaust in Vietnam that caused Rudd, Wilkerson, Ayers and many others to lose patience with early Sixties organizing and seek to "bring the war home" in some more immediately effective way. (Had they waited a little longer they would have witnessed the astonishing insurgency of United States soldiers in Vietnam, complete with their own versions of both parallel institutions and inter-racial solidarity).

Not being God, I don't presume to stand in judgment over these brilliant, passionate, committed comrades. The most devastating critique of their practice comes from themselves. Bill Ayers has returned forty years later to what he was doing in the mid-Sixties. His models, he writes, "remain civil rights champions like Ella Baker and Myles Horton and Septima Clark, each an activist community educator. They were workers in literacy and voting-rights projects, in community organizations and educational institutions."

## *Two, Three, Many Weathermen?*

Reading these admirably candid memoirs, the most troubling thought they provoke is that the new Movement may be following a romanticized image of Weatherman down the same dead-end road.

The young people who make up the new Movement by and large call themselves "anarchists." Like Rudd after Columbia, they believe in the "propaganda of the deed." And the deed, all too often, seems to consist of youthful demonstrators in black jackets breaking the nearest plate glass windows and provoking acts of violence from the police.

One such apocalyptic encounter was unexpectedly successful. In 1999, demonstrators, including delegations from the Steelworkers and Teamsters unions, prevented the World Trade Organization from holding a meeting in Seattle. Since then, however, the powers that be have been careful to gather at sites inaccessible to would-be disrupters. As a result such occasions have tended to become latter-day Days of Rage: opportunities for participants to prove themselves in the eyes of their colleagues, rather than serious political events.

The new Movement is a blessing. When Abbie Hoffman committed suicide, Tom Hayden said that we were all waiting for a new Movement and he guessed Abbie couldn't wait any longer.

But the new Movement will be a more fruitful blessing if its organizers and activists read these books and resolve to make violence a last resort rather than a badge of courage. They might even consider turning away from violence altogether.

M y father, Robert Lynd, once characterized history as a "vast wandering enterprise." That seems true enough as a description of academic history.

But movements for change need history. The Cuban Revolution that came to power in 1959 encouraged students to go into the mountains, not only to teach literacy, but also to record experiences that might otherwise be lost. In my earliest formulations of what I came to call "guerrilla history" I imagined a group of workers who threw up a picket line, and afterwards returned to the union hall or to a local bar to assess their effort. Why didn't more people come? How well did we handle our confrontation with the cops? How did we feel about fellow workers who tried to cross the picket line? This, too, is history.

"Reflections on Radical History" appeared in *Radical History Review*, Issue 79 (Winter 2001), and is reprinted with permission of the publisher, Duke University Press. In it I describe my mentors, Edward Thompson and Howard Zinn. Thompson wrote his two masterworks, a biography of William Morris and *The Making of the English Working Class*, while employed as an extra-mural lecturer in a workers' education program in the North of England. Howard Zinn, from first to last, wrote for an audience outside the academy in a forthright effort to promote needed social change.

Essay 10, "President Kennedy's Assassination," is a talk delivered at Carnegie Hall early in 1964. When John F. Kennedy was assassinated, on November 22, 1963, the Lynds did not own a TV. A day or two later I got a phone call from Jack Minnis, research director for the Student Nonviolent Coordinating Committee. He did have a TV and had been watching it non-stop. He told me among other things that the doctors at Parkland Hospital in Dallas described the wound in President Kennedy's Adam's Apple as an "entrance wound."

I hung up. A few minutes later I called Jack back and asked, "What did you say about the doctors at Parkland Hospital?" He repeated what he had said. If one of the bullets entered the president's body from in front, Lee Harvey Oswald could not have been the only shooter. Minnis and I wrote a critique of the single-shooter theory of the assassination and entitled it "Seeds of Doubt." Alice and I reproduced it on our hectograph machine and mailed it to a number of periodicals.

To our great surprise, *The New Republic* printed "Seeds of Doubt" along with a supportive comment by Richard Dudman of the *St. Louis Post Dispatch*. "President Kennedy's Assassination" assesses the state of the controversy a few months later.

I presented "De Te Fabula Narratur" ("This Story is About You") to a Chicago audience in September 1967. A version of the talk was later published under the title "Academic Freedom: Your Story and Mine" in the *Columbia University Forum*, v. X, no. 3 (Fall 1967). That talk together with later remarks in "The Two Yales" concerns the decision of the Yale History Department not to grant me tenure. A biography by Professor Carl Mirra of Adelphi University discusses the topic definitively and concludes that the Department's motivation was political.

"Intellectuals, the University and the Movement" was a keynote address to the New University Conference in 1968. It was published by the *Journal of American History*, v. 76, no. 2 (September 1989), and is reprinted with the permission of the Organization of American Historians, which holds the copyright and reserves all rights. Therein I discuss how radical intellectuals can pursue their professions outside as well as inside the university.

"Guerrilla History in Gary" marked my turn from history based solely on documents to a history that also draws on the perceptions of living protagonists. The article appeared in *Liberation* magazine in October 1969. Charlie McCollester, then teaching at a community college in northern Indiana, read the piece, got in touch with me, and thus began a friendship that has lasted more than forty years. Together we organized a community forum on "Labor History From the Standpoint of the Rank and File" at which older steelworkers shared their experience with newcomers to the labor movement.

Several of those presentations were among the accounts that my wife and I gathered into *Rank and File: Personal Histories by Working-Class Organizers*, published in 1973. The making of *Rank and File* is described in Essay 15, a chapter in the volume *Visions of History*, published by Pantheon Books in 1976. It is reprinted with permission from MARHO: The Radical Historians' Organization, Inc.

Finally, "History's Simple Truths" was a talk offered in 2003 at a conference of historians of the American Revolution. As I say at the outset, I felt like Rip Van Winkle, returning to what had been my field of specialization and to an academic audience after so many years as a lawyer, away from the university. The talk was published in *Labor: Studies in Working-Class History of the Americas*, v. 1, no. 4 (Winter 2004), and is reprinted with permission of the publisher, Duke University Press, which holds the copyright. The occasion led on to the re-issuance in 2009 of new editions by Cambridge University Press of my two books first published in the 1960s, *Class Conflict, Slavery, and the United States Constitution* and *Intellectual Origins of American Radicalism*.

I am one of the New Left historians who in the 1960s espoused "history from the bottom up." The honor of first advocating that particular set of words belongs to Jesse Lemisch. I believe he first used the phrase in a pamphlet by that title he wrote for Students for a Democratic Society (SDS). I recall that about 1969 there was an occupation of the University of Chicago administration building to protest denial of tenure to a sociologist named Marlene Dixon. Jesse and I conducted a teach-in at the sit-in. He described the project of retrieving the history of the so-called inarticulate: those who do not leave behind correspondence, public papers, and the like, whose thoughts must be teased from court records, from eyewitness accounts of street demonstrations, from the minute books of obscure popular entities like the Muggletonians or the International Order of Odd Fellows. I talked about a methodology that seems to me inevitable for historians who are serious about retrieving the insights of those who talk more than they write—namely, oral history.

There are two historians whose example has especially influenced me.

The first is Howard Zinn. The sit-ins had begun, and I had informed my teachers at Columbia University that I wanted to teach at a "Negro college" in the south. Howard recruited me at the Columbia history department's smoker in December 1960. I can still see in my mind's eye his lanky form, then topped by black hair rather than white, making its way across the floor to me.

The Zinns and Lynds spent some time together in New Hampshire during the summer of 1961. As he has described in his autobiography, *You Can't Be Neutral on a Moving Train,* "we decided to climb a mountain together and get acquainted":

> That mountain-climbing conversation was illuminating.
> Staughton came from a background completely different from

mine[,] . . . had been raised in comfortable circumstances, had gone to Harvard and Columbia. And yet, as we went back and forth on every political issue under the sun—race, class, war, violence, nationalism, justice, fascism, capitalism, socialism, and more—it was clear that our social philosophies, our values, were extraordinarily similar.

(History requires me to add that it was not Mt. Monadnock, as Howard writes, but Mt. Chocorua.)

It was when I arrived at Spelman College and began to teach with Howard that I learned most from him. Fresh out of graduate school, I asked him what scholarly papers he was writing and what academic conferences he planned to attend in the near future. He looked at me as if I were speaking a foreign language. I came to understand that although Howard Zinn was *making a living* as a college teacher, he seemed entirely indifferent to academia. That which absorbed his intellectual attention was to clarify what strategy the civil rights movement should pursue in overcoming institutional racism. We had long conversations about alternative strategies of social change: "all deliberate speed," as in school desegregation, as compared to mandated change from above, as in desegregation of the armed forces. We struggled with the role that radical intellectuals could and should ask the national government to play.

One day I walked unannounced into the Zinn apartment. (The Zinns and Lynds lived next to one another on the Spelman campus.) Howard was tape recording an interview with two African American young men, field secretaries for the Student Nonviolent Coordinating Committee (SNCC), who had just been released from jail in Albany, Georgia. A lightbulb went on behind my eyes. It was not Studs Terkel, nor was it my native genius, that led me to oral history: it was Howard Zinn.

More than anyone else I have known, Howard has a magical ability to make emotional contact with an audience. Self-evidently, this gift stays by him when he writes. I believe that those who consider themselves radical historians need to grapple with the fact that Howard Zinn's *People's History of the United States* has probably done more good, and influenced more people (especially young people), than everything the rest of us have written put together. And I believe the key to why this is so is Howard's indifference to the usual rewards and punishments of academia. He was abruptly and scandalously fired by Spelman College. He got a job at Boston University *as a political scientist*. He made tenure there.[1] On his last day of teaching, he ended class early so as to join a picket line of campus workers. Throughout, he has steadily directed what he had to say to an audience off campus, and thereby taught us all.

The other historian who has most influenced me was Edward Thompson. I met him only once. In the course of a brief conversation he administered political shock therapy. Somehow he challenged me not to give up on the political possibilities of industrial workers in the advanced capitalist nations. He set me on a path in 1966 that I have been traveling ever since.

As I have come to know Thompson better through his writings and writings about him,[2] I feel I have encountered in his life the same paradigm that I experienced closer to hand with Howard Zinn. I suspect that most radical historians in the United States who knew Thompson personally made his acquaintance at the University of Warwick, or in the years after 1965 when Thompson began teaching there. To me by far the most interesting period in his life is the seventeen previous years (1948-65) when he was a staff tutor in English and history for the Department of Extra-Mural Studies at the University of Leeds.

It is recalled about Thompson (whose background was as upper middle class as my own) that people who got to know him "admired and trusted him." Each tutor taught four or five classes and had to travel long distances. A common pattern was that an initial recruitment of fourteen or fifteen lost six or seven during the autumn but gained two or three latecomers. Colleagues did not live near each other. Obviously, as with Howard Zinn in his relation to SNCC, and I should like to think, as with myself in relation to working-class colleagues in Youngstown, during these years Thompson drew emotional sustenance less from fellow professionals than from his students, with whom he often joined in political demonstrations.

Accounts of Thompson in these years make clear that then, as in his posthumously published book on William Blake, he was preoccupied with two different notions of workers' education. One was the idea of workers laboriously bringing themselves up to middle-class standards so that they might participate effectively in a capitalist society. In this pedagogy, the emphasis was not on "what students bring to their classes, but on what the tutor had to do for them."

Of course, Thompson's approach was entirely different. He stressed how much he learned from his students. "Within living memory, it seems, miners have worked lying down in eighteen inch seams, children have been in the mills at the age of nine." One assignment—thirty or forty years before this assignment became commonplace in the United States—was to find an older person to talk about their younger days. Of one literature class, Thompson wrote that it had learned to work "in the spirit so desirable in the Workers' Education Association—not as tutor and passive audience, but as a group combining various talents and pooling different knowledge and experience for a common end." Sheila Rowbotham recalls a class on the history of mining when one student finally told the instructor: "Give me the chalk, Mr. Thompson."

The bottom line was expressed by Dorothy Greenald. She came from a miner's home where there was only one book. Edward Thompson, she later recalled, "brought it out that your background wasn't anything to be ashamed of . . . that changed me really."

The Himalayan fact is that *The Making of the English Working Class* was written in those years of teaching extramurally, "outside the walls." Somehow, defying the idea that intellectual work and political engagement are at war with each other, Thompson did his greatest scholarly work during the period of his fullest immersion in working-class life. *The Making* was initially envisioned as a survey text for workers' education classes. As he came upon original sources, Thompson shared them with his students and asked them to comment in class. The book is dedicated to Dorothy and Joseph Greenald.

In describing these exemplars I have run out of space to say more. What Zinn and Thompson model for me is the idea of a radical intellectual who is only incidentally an academic; who is an "organic intellectual" in the sense that, whatever his or her personal background, he or she lives out a professional life in the midst of social struggle; who "accompanies" the poor and oppressed, not only by thinking and writing about them, but by living near them and being available to them day-by-day.

### ENDNOTES

1   On pages 184-185 of *You Can't Be Neutral on a Moving Train*, Howard tells the story of how he got tenure. The BU trustees were to meet to consider, among other things, tenure for Howard Zinn. On the same day, outside the same place, students decided to hold a rally to protest the presence of Secretary of State Dean Rusk. They asked Howard to speak. He accepted with fear and trembling, believing he would be only one of many speakers. Arriving at the rally, he discovered he was the only speaker. He spoke and learned a few days later that the trustees had voted him tenure earlier in the day!

2   What follows is based on Peter Searby and the editors, "Edward Thompson as a Teacher," in *Protest and Survive: Essays for E. P. Thompson* (London: Merlin Press, 1993), pp. 1-17, and on Bryan D. Palmer, *E. P. Thompson: Objections and Oppositions* (London: Verso, 1994), chapters 2-3.

I believe that what most needs to be said about what happened in Dallas is that there has been something wrong with the "feel" of this affair from the very beginning. Three people are dead, and that is real enough. But these horrible tragedies have been enveloped in an atmosphere of artificiality, of manufactured information, of insubstantial and changing facts, so that occasionally the sequence of events seems a production of Madison Avenue or Hollywood . . . .

Is it not strange that when radio, TV, magazines, newspapers are absolutely sure of what happened, when the Warren Commission seems to have lost interest in how the president was killed, when even poor Marina Oswald is brought forth to say that she is sure her husband did it—isn't it strange that when these things are so, you, and I, and so many more Americans, still have an uneasy feeling about the whole production from one end to the other?

One of the things that makes me uneasy about the Warren Commission is that it apparently does not intend to investigate how President Kennedy was killed. I had assumed, and I imagine you assumed, that the Commission was set up primarily to answer the many questions that have nagged so many people as to how three bullets could have been fired so rapidly and accurately from one gun, how the president could have been shot from behind with a bullet that entered his throat from in front, and so forth and so on. But according to Mr. Rankin's statement on January 11 President Kennedy's murder is not among the six areas of inquiry which the Commission has set itself. Mr. Rankin says the Commission will investigate (1) every detail of Lee Oswald's activities on the day of the assassination, (2) the life and background of Oswald, (3) Oswald's career in the Marine Corps and his stay in the Soviet Union, (4) the murder of Oswald in the Dallas police station, (5) the story of Jack Ruby, and (6) the procedures used to protect President Kennedy. He does not include the murder of the president. That would seem to mean that the Warren Commission intends to accept without question the F.B.I. report on the details of the murder. And that makes me profoundly uneasy.

It makes me uneasy because the F.B.I. is so obviously an interested party. Mrs. Paine, with whom Marina Oswald was living last fall, has stated that the F.B.I. knew early in October that Lee Oswald was employed at the Texas Schoolbook Depository building. Dallas Chief of Police Curry stated on November 23, and then abruptly withdrew, the information that the F.B.I. had interviewed Lee Oswald himself a matter of days prior to November 22. Since the assassination *The Nation* magazine, and newspapers in Philadelphia and Houston, have suggested that Lee Oswald may have been an F.B.I. agent. Certain facts, such as the ease with which he repaid a large government loan and the fact that he obtained a passport last summer in one day, do seem to point in that direction. Given these circumstances, for the Warren Commission to accept at face value the F.B.I. version of an event in which the Bureau was so intimately involved, strikes me as a flagrant dereliction of duty.

One may say, doesn't the autopsy at Bethesda clear up all doubts as to how the president was killed?

The first question that raises about the autopsy is why its contents were leaked no earlier than December 17, almost a month after the assassination. The apparent answer is that "Seeds of Doubt" was published in *The New Republic* a day or two before. Now, this does not mean that the autopsy was forged or false. Yet it is strange that the authorities permitted statement after statement by the Dallas doctors about an unquestionable wound of entry in the front of the president's throat to go unchallenged until Jack Minnis, Richard Dudman and I pointed out that if there were an entry wound in the throat the bullet could not have been fired by Lee Harvey Oswald.

Further, newspaper accounts of the alleged autopsy report have the same confused, contradictory aspect as newspaper accounts about every other facet of this case. Some stories (e.g., *New York Times*, Dec. 17) said that the first bullet did not hit the president's throat but entered his back "where the right shoulder joins the neck." Others (e.g., *Washington Post*, Dec. 18) placed the bullet's entry five to seven inches below the collar line.

Moreover, the alleged back wound—which no one at Parkland Hospital noticed as the president's coat, shirt, undershirt and braces were being removed—is said to have been only two or three inches deep, with no injury to vital organs. This raises other questions. If the first bullet was not fatal, why did the president make no sound in the five seconds before another, fatal bullet struck him? If the first bullet entered the president's back, why did his hand move convulsively to his throat? And if no vital organ was injured, how is it that the Dallas surgeons were convinced that the first bullet to hit the president entered his lung? On November 30, the *New York Times* described the scene in the emergency room, stating: "Then one of the doctors noticed a frothing of blood at the neck wound. 'He's bubbling air,' the doctor said. This means a hole in the lung." That description was consistent with Dr. Kemp Clark's statement (*New York Times*, Nov. 27) that the first bullet struck the president at the Adam's apple, ranged downward into his body and did not exit. Another of the Dallas surgeons, Dr. Robert Shaw, went so far as to specify that the first bullet had entered the throat and coursed downward to puncture the right lung (*New York Herald Tribune*, Dec. 1). Thus, if one believes the leak about the alleged autopsy, one is required to reject not only the testimony of the Dallas surgeons as to the nature of the wound in the president's throat. One must also disqualify their repeated, explicit statements that the bullet which entered the throat coursed downward, puncturing a lung.

The most serious contradiction in press reports of the autopsy involves the bullets. As Minnis and I stated in "Seeds of Doubt," the identification of the gun allegedly belonging to Oswald with the president's death was made on the basis of a bullet supposedly found on a stretcher by a Secret Service man. Now, if we accept the autopsy leak, that bullet must have been the bullet which entered the president's back, for, according to the leak, both bullets two and three fragmented. Bullet two, the bullet which struck Governor Connally, is said to have fragmented in such a way that a splinter passed out through the windshield of the limousine. Bullet three, which struck President Kennedy's head, is said to have fragmented in such a way that a splinter passed down through his neck and out at the Adam's apple. By this explanation the hole in the windshield and wound in the throat are accounted for after a fashion.

But what thereby becomes impossible is the story of the bullet on the stretcher. Since bullets two and three fragmented—bullet three, according to *Time* magazine (Dec. 30), "literally exploded in Kennedy's head"—then the only bullet which could have remained intact to be found on the stretcher was bullet one. This was the bullet which, according to the autopsy, entered the president's back. But, also according to the autopsy, "that bullet was found deep in his [the president's] shoulder" (*Washington Post*, Dec. 18). *U.S. News and World Report* likewise affirmed that the first bullet "struck President Kennedy in the back . . . and lodged in his body." Seemingly, after the first report of the autopsy leak somebody noticed that this new version of the assassination made the earlier story about the bullet found on a stretcher impossible. For on Dec. 30 *Newsweek* had this to say of the bullet which, according to the *Washington*

*Post*, had been found deep in the president's shoulder: "This bullet, the Navy doctors believe, probably dropped out of the President's body and was the one reported found on his body at Parkland Hospital in Dallas."

I have been trying to demonstrate to you that the autopsy leak, far from settling all problems as to how the president was killed, only adds further complications. Consider how much more economical an hypothesis results if one supposes that the first bullet came from in front. It travels from the viaduct at a slight downward angle; it passes through the windshield at a point (as Mr. Dudman has described the hole to me) about mid-way between the two sides of the windshield and mid-way between bottom and top; still traveling at a slight downward angle, it enters President Kennedy's throat at the Adam's apple. If one chooses to believe that there was a back wound, one can go on to suggest that the bullet, after entering the throat, traveled through the body at a slight downward angle and exited—not entered—about six inches below the collar line. The hypothesis of a shot from in front restores credibility to a number of witnesses. It would even make believable, for the first time, the story of the bullet found on the stretcher. But of course it also requires giving up the idea that the bullet found on the stretcher was fired by Lee Oswald.

In conclusion with regard to the alleged autopsy, I think the public is justified in saying flatly to the Warren Commission that any report from the Commission which does not include the full text of the F.B.I. report, the full text of the Bethesda autopsy, and the Commission's evaluation of these documents, is thereby disqualified as an adequate answer to the questions which the nation is asking.

You may be thinking: Can one really suppose that here, in these United States, there may have been a conspiracy to kill the president? Or that, if there was a conspiracy, parts of the federal government may desire to conceal it?

Let me, as a historian, suggest an answer to these questions by a historical analogy.

There was once a man accused of treason on the basis of circumstantial evidence. He was convicted because a secret dossier was sent to his judges by the counter-espionage agency of his government with the consent of the Minister of War, but without the knowledge of the rest of the cabinet. The prosecution was unable to suggest a motive for the alleged crime of the defendant, and the defendant himself steadfastly affirmed his innocence. Yet the defendant was declared guilty. No one in public life questioned the judgment of the court. Only the family of the condemned man protested the decision and were determined to bring about a revision of the trial by working to find evidence pointing to the real traitor. Eighteen months later a new head of the secret service accidentally discovered that the condemned traitor was, in fact, innocent. When he attempted to have the case re-opened he was broken in rank and given a job outside the country. Not until twelve years later did a court finally clear the name of—Alfred Dreyfus.

The Dreyfus Case suggests to us how a conspiracy might have worked in Dallas. Only a very few persons need have been part of the actual conspiracy to kill the president. After the crime, one or more of these persons would have directed the investigation away from the couple who so many people saw running away from the viaduct, and toward the killer whom nobody saw, Lee Oswald. The historian Mercel Thomas has said that no one suggested Dreyfus was guilty because he was a Jew, but that "because he was a Jew, the idea of his guilt was accepted more easily than it would have been for another." Similarly with Oswald: once it was clear that a man who had been to the Soviet Union and who, so it was said, had worked for Fair Play for Cuba, was a possible culprit, public opinion would consider no one else. Then, on this hypothesis, Federal agents who may well have known better closed ranks behind the theory of Oswald's guilt. To quote another historian of the Dreyfus affair, it was "not that the leaders of all those forces deliberately meant to invent a charge against an innocent man, but once it had been levied, and its solidity assumed, the innocence of the accused became really unthinkable." Still later, when it was realized that the original trial of Dreyfus had gone astray because of evidence concocted by the French secret service, a military court of review—comparable to the Warren Commission—nonetheless once more declared Dreyfus guilty, in the belief (to quote Prof. Thomas) that "the counter-espionage service would have been disorganized, to the great cost of national security, if its methods had been divulged."

Actually, I don't believe the conspiracy theory is unbelievable to persons close to this story. I would be prepared to wager that a majority of high officials in Washington privately have their doubts about the received version of this crime. The real problem is what they do about their doubts. For I think most of them go on to say to themselves: Even if Oswald is not guilty, isn't it better that things be left as they are? Lee Harvey Oswald and John Fitzgerald Kennedy are dead, we can't help them now; so isn't it wiser to keep silent rather than challenge the prestige and authority of those agencies and individuals in government who are committed to the theory of Oswald's guilt?

No, it is not better. The fundamental issue in this case is whether truth and the welfare of individuals should be sacrificed to the supposed national interest. And I say, No. There was a time when Americans were convinced, with Milton, that let winds of doctrine blow, so long as truth be in the field, then there is nothing to fear. There was a time when Americans could say, with Thoreau in *Walden*, that finally, we want only the truth. Now we seem to have become a society in which, when push comes to shove and the blue chips go down, we fall back on a previously-prepared cover story. And so we lied about the U-2, we lied about the Bay of Pigs, and now, in my judgment, we are lying about the assassination of a president. Surely at some point we should stop and ask ourselves why our society has become so fearful of the truth.

The answer to those who plead for silence in the national interest was long ago phrased by the French intellectual Charles Peguy. Peguy, commenting on the Dreyfus case, put the case of the pseudo-patriot as strongly as it can be put, and then refuted it. "A nation," said Peguy, paraphrasing the condemners of Dreyfus,

> is something unique, a gigantic assemblage of the most legitimate, the most sacred, rights and interests. Thousands and millions of lives depend on it in the present, the past and the future. . . . It is all of infinite price because it can only be made once, be realized once; it cannot be made or begun over again. . . . The first duty of so unique an achievement is not to let itself be jeopardized for one man, whoever he be, however legitimate his interests; that is a right no nation possesses. That is the language of wisdom, of reason. Dreyfus had to sacrifice himself, and to be sacrificed against his will, if needs be, for the repose, the safety of France.

Thus Peguy put the case of his opponents. And then he said, and I would like to lay these words on the conscience of each person here tonight:

> But we answered that a single injustice, a single crime, a single illegality, especially if it be officially confirmed and registered, a single insult offered to justice and to right, especially if it be universally, legally, nationally, conveniently accepted, a single crime, is enough to break the whole social pact; a single breach of honour, a single disgraceful act, is enough to dishonour and disgrace a whole nation. It is a gangrenous spot, which soon spreads over the whole body. What we defend is not our honour only, not only the honour of our nation now, but the historic honour of our nation, the honour of our ancestors, the honour of our children.

"Our adversaries," Peguy concluded, "were concerned with the temporal salvation of our country; we were concerned with the salvation of its eternal soul."

I would like to conclude with a quotation from an American. In 1735 the New York printer John Peter Zenger was charged with seditious libel. Defending him, attorney Andrew Hamilton used words which I think might be the motto of all of us concerned about the case of Lee Oswald: "And all the high things that are said . . . upon the side of power will not be able to stop the people's mouths."

## 11. DE TE FABULA NARRATUR [THIS STORY IS ABOUT YOU]

There is a Latin proverb, *de te fabula narratur.* Roughly translated it means: Just at first what I'm going to say may seem to be no concern of yours, but don't go to sleep, brother, this story is about you, too.

I am a thirty-seven-year-old white middle-class Quaker professor who has traveled to North Vietnam and refuses to pay part of his income taxes in protest against the war in Vietnam. Most of you are young and students; some of you are Negroes; very few of you are Quakers, and none, I venture to say, have recently traveled to North Vietnam. But watch out, brothers and sisters. This story is about you, too.

This story is about you because what has happened to me as a professor happens day in and day out to elementary and high-school teachers in public school systems across the country. Here in Chicago, for example, I have been told on good authority of a teacher who was fired when he invited an aide of Dr. King's to speak in his classroom; of a teacher who was fired from one school when she picketed another school which her small son attended; and of a teacher who, when he decided to run for political office, was warned by his district supervisor that this would jeopardize his promotion.

A professor, presently teaching at a Chicago-area college, who once served on a committee of the Chicago Board of Education which orally examines would-be teachers seeking accreditation, described for me the questions often asked at these examinations (which, incidentally, are tape recorded), questions such as: What political groups have you joined? What magazines did you subscribe to when you were an undergraduate? What would you do if you were an adviser to the school newspaper and a student submitted an article critical of the war in Vietnam? The professor recalled one girl who did a superb job on national teacher examinations. She failed her oral examination when asked: What would you do if a teacher made a prejudiced remark or an unfair judgment of a child in your presence? The candidate failed to give the correct answer: Support the authority of the other teacher under all circumstances.

Or consider the case of Father Peter O'Reilly, whom I met for the first time a few days ago. Father O'Reilly is fifty years old, a Catholic priest and a professor of philosophy. Father O'Reilly has not been to North Vietnam nor, so far as I know, does he advocate nonviolent civil disobedience. But he is having as much difficulty in finding academic employment as am I.

Father O'Reilly's transgression was to help organize a teachers' union at St. John's College in New York City. For this he and thirty-two other professors were dismissed from their jobs in the middle of an academic year, without explanation, without advance notice, and without the opportunity of a hearing. Like myself, they are contesting this arbitrary action in the courts. But in the meantime one must eat. Father O'Reilly was fired in December 1965. In spring 1966 he was offered a position at Chicago State College which he accepted. However, Archbishop Cody of the Chicago diocese forbade Father O'Reilly to take up the position and the latter bowed to the instruction of his religious superior. In spring 1967 Father O'Reilly was offered a position at Southern Illinois University. He accepted and signed a contract. But when the Board of Governors of that institution met late in June, the president of Southern Illinois refused to submit the appointment to the Board for confirmation. Father O'Reilly has been without academic employment for almost two years.

Writing in the magazine *Continuum* about what he called "St. John's: A Chronicle of Folly," Father O'Reilly makes the argument for academic freedom which Jefferson made for religious toleration: that a man truly believes only that which he "freely embraces." He who attempts to prescribe what should be taught or what should be believed is "at that point dominating that which should never be dominated by others, namely the personal commitments of teachers and students," and therefore "subverting education." Education, Father O'Reilly continues,

is not the handing over of one's grasp of what is—is not the handing over of truth. If this were the case, the student's personal acceptance of something as true would be imposed on him by his professor's acceptance communicated in the teaching. This, of course, is precisely the aim of educational authoritarians. Parents who conceive education this way expect a college or university to guarantee their offspring will be returned to them unchanged as to value commitments, that their son or daughter will have, on graduation and thereafter, the same basic views as to what is true and good and beautiful as their parents have. And, what is more important, college and university administrators and trustees who share this view of the

educational process attempt to guarantee this by seeing to it
that the faculty hold those same values.

Father O'Reilly arrives at the following definition: "Academic freedom is
that property of man's search for knowledge which renders him intolerant
of the arbitrary coercion from other men (through threats and punishments,
through enticements and bribes) that would impede the search . . . ."

Of course these are abstractions, and like all other abstractions only
become a part of what one knows through experience. Like yourselves, I
first became acquainted with "academic freedom" as a story which concerned other people, not myself. Let me tell you a little about the experience which made me realize that the story was about me, too.

My first teaching job was at Spelman College, a Negro women's
college in Atlanta, where I came in the fall of 1961.

I soon learned that many of the elementary freedoms which my
Negro students sought downtown by sitting-in were not available to
them on their own campus. There were understandable historical reasons
for the protective, paternalistic attitude of the college administrators. But
this was 1961, not 1895, and the students felt increasing resentment of
the sandbox politics of the student government, the high wall topped by
barbed wire which surrounded the campus, the censorship of the student
paper (which at the height of our controversies appeared with pages 1,
2, 5 and 6, [pages] 3 and 4 having been found objectionable), and other
indignities. The upshot was that my friend and department head Howard
Zinn was dismissed very much in the manner that St. John's disposed of
Father O'Reilly, except that Zinn was fired the day after commencement,
when the students had gone home and so could not protest.

What I learned from this episode was how poorly I responded.
A colleague of mine, in a weaker financial position than I myself was,
resigned at once. It was the only appropriate action; but in situations,
and there are many of them, where resignation *is* the only appropriate
action, human nature finds a thousand ways to rationalize delay. I waited
to resign until I had been offered a better job elsewhere.

That job was at Yale. I have never before spoken about what happened to me at Yale and I do so now with mixed feelings. Despite the
fact that it has at no time been my wish to stay at Yale permanently, I
suppose—human nature again—that I would like to be offered tenure and
then decline. This being the case any complaint I may have as to Yale's
treatment of me can easily be written off as sour grapes. Nevertheless,
I have an increasingly clear impression that Yale and its president have
acquired from their handling of my situation a reputation for academic

freedom which is undeserved. I believe that if I explain why I feel this, and if academic public opinion sustains my judgment, it may prevent similar mistreatment of someone else in the future.

The facts, as I perceive them, are as follows:

Yale sought my services with some persistence. I was first offered a job in 1962. I declined (the man who interviewed me managed, in the course of a few hours' conversation, to advise me not to leave my briefcase in his car because of the proximity of "darktown" and not to live in a certain suburb because so many of "the sons of Abraham" resided there.) In 1964 Yale again offered me a job, proposing this time that my work be divided between teaching and recruiting Negro students for Yale in the capacity of assistant dean. (In view of all that has transpired there is something droll about the idea of myself as a Yale dean.) The offer came not long after Howard Zinn's dismissal at Spelman, and I accepted a five-year appointment as an assistant professor of history at Yale, the term of my appointment to begin in fall 1964 and end in spring 1969.

Adjustment to Yale was not easy for me. I came there directly from teaching in the Freedom Schools of the 1964 Mississippi Summer Project and experienced what I suppose should be called culture shock. My students preferred John Adams to Tom Paine because Adams was "more balanced"; it seemed to me that they were growing old without ever being young. I also concluded with astonishment that Yale was a no less authoritarian institution than Spelman. Students called teachers "sir," just as at Spelman; there was no student government at all; it was next to impossible for undergraduates to get permission to live off campus; a grade-point system of evaluation required grown men solemnly to pretend that they knew when to give a "77" rather than a "75"; students took five courses, and typically finished their undergraduate careers with a comprehensive examination rather than a major research project in an area of personal concern.

The unspoken premise of the system was that college undergraduates are unprepared for real scholarship, hence the purpose of college is to select the brightest students for real scholarship later on. This meant an emphasis on appearance rather than content and it meant, too, that students had to be kept at tasks which could be quantitatively compared. Those students who survived this obstacle course for three years reassured each other in senior secret societies that they were still human beings, and girded their loins for the next laps at law school, Wall Street and Washington. Both at Spelman and Yale education was oriented to the manufacture of a standard product rather than to the reexamination of basic premises or to the encouragement of individual self-discovery.

At the end of my first year the annual *Course Critique* of the student newspaper pronounced "the always-controversial Staughton Lynd" to be "quite objective in his classroom," and was even kind enough to say that "it may very well be that a star was born last year." More to the point, since students do not participate in decisions about promotion, the chairman of the History Department frequently praised my teaching, more than once told me that the department would not have asked me to Yale had it not expected to give me tenure, and emphasized the fact that there was a gap in Yale's history offerings for the period between the Revolution and the Civil War in which I specialized. Thus matters stood when I left for Hanoi.

While I was out of the country my wife was told by the wife of an important officer of the university that President Brewster [of Yale] was very angry, that until my trip to Hanoi none of my political activities had raised any question about my eventual promotion but the trip definitely had.

When I returned there were no decisive developments for three months. President Brewster issued a statement in which he termed my Christmas journey "naive and misguided," condemned a speech I had made in Hanoi for giving "aid and comfort" to the enemy (a phrase from the law of treason), but implied that the university would take no punitive action. The Yale chaplain introduced me to a mass meeting of the university community at which I reported on my trip, as "Yale's beloved professor." For the moment I was part cad-beyond-the-pale, part Mr. Chips. (I note parenthetically that when Arthur Schlesinger, Jr. revealed that he had told deliberate untruths about the impending Bay of Pigs invasion while serving as adviser to President Kennedy, the president of Harvard felt no need to apologize, condemn, or defend. Apparently trying to tell the truth in Hanoi is conduct unbecoming to a scholar but telling lies in Washington is not.)

Then in April the chairman of the History Department asked to see me. He told me he wished to discuss "two entirely unrelated matters."

The first was my activity against the war. The chairman asked me whether I had missed any classes. I said, No. (I had practically overturned the world Communist bureaucracy to be back for my first class in January.)

The chairman then handed me a clipping from a Canadian newspaper containing a hopelessly garbled account of a speech I had made in Toronto, and asked me to make written corrections of anything that was false. This request surprised me. President Brewster had twice asked me to correct newspaper accounts so that he might better respond to irate alumni. Professor Blum, however, had up to that point maintained that whatever I might do or say when off the campus was not his proper concern, as indeed it was not. Finally the chairman told me that, speaking as a friend, he wanted me to know that he considered my mode of protest "strident."

Now, nothing I am about to say is intended to detract from the fact that Professor Blum and other members of the History Department have shown me considerable decency and kindness. But I believe they have also been under much institutional pressure and that, when push came to shove, they have chosen to protect Yale rather than me. After the first talk I gave at Yale protesting the bombing of North Vietnam, Professor Blum met me on the street the next morning and casually congratulated me. After I returned from Hanoi, Professor Blum (so he told me) did not attend the meeting at which I reported on my trip and did not even listen to my talk on the radio, so that (he told me) if anyone asked him what he thought of it he would be able to say he had not heard it. The defect of this method of ensuring objectivity was, of course, that the chairman in fact made up his mind on the basis of second-hand accounts. Now in April, having already retreated from support to neutrality, Professor Blum moved with the institution from neutrality to condemnation.

The chairman then proceeded to the "entirely unrelated" second point on the agenda: he told me that I should not expect to receive tenure when my appointment as an assistant professor ended. I was on the eve of a year's research as Morse Fellow during which, ordinarily, a junior professor does that work on the basis of which (at least in part) his candidacy for tenure is evaluated. The date was April 1966; my contract ran to 1969, and the department would not formally make its decision on tenure until 1968. Nevertheless, Professor Blum chose this moment to tell me not to expect promotion. The next fall he confirmed his oral statement in a letter which said that my chance of promotion was "minuscule."

Naturally I inquired whether any inadequacies in my teaching or scholarship contributed to the decision. Not in the least, the chairman responded, the problem was purely financial. At my request the chairman met with me again a few days later together with the senior professor who had asked me to come to Yale. Again I asked whether my academic performance had been in any way unsatisfactory. The senior professor responded that he had wanted me at Yale because I was "the most promising scholar of my generation in my field."

A columnist of the *Yale Daily News* has asked "whether the narrow-mindedness displayed by the Illinois Board of Governors of State Colleges and Universities [in breaking a written contract and denying me a job]—so easily dismissed as Midwestern provincialism—does not find its counterpart here under the guise of a smoothly-run establishment." I share this question. During the spring of 1965 President Brewster was quoted in the *News* to the effect that the question of my promotion would be decided on academic grounds alone. I believe he has reneged on that promise. It is hard for me to avoid the conclusion that the university has sought to place me in a position such that I will decide to leave voluntarily, counting on me to cooperate in maintaining that fiction because resignation looks better than dismissal on a man's record.

Well, I decline to resign. No matter how little I may wish to return to Yale—and I trust I have made it clear that it is not the place I would choose to pursue light and truth—I intend to oblige Yale, if it wants to get rid of me, to fire me and say why.

I want to mention one more academic freedom experience . . . . This concerns the University of Chicago. I want to mention it because I believe persons associated with universities like Yale and Chicago tend to assume too quickly that, in contrast to institutions such as Chicago State College, Northern Illinois University, or the Circle Campus of the University of Illinois [at all of which I was denied employment by administrators after the History Department offered me a job], they have academic freedom. From my standpoint the truth is almost the reverse: first, that Chicago State College had the courage to carry my appointment to a final stage where it became public knowledge; second, that the Board of Governors, much as I resent their action, at least had the candor to say that they rejected me for political reasons and had no questions about my record as a teacher and scholar. The University of Chicago in my experience was both more timid and less honest.

Shortly after the Board of Governors declined to confirm my appointment at Chicago State I was approached by the chairman of one of the social science departments at the University of Chicago about the possibility of a job there. From mid-July through mid-August there ensued a series of conversations and small meetings with University of Chicago personnel. Finally on August 19 the chairman who had been good enough to approach me in the first place telephoned to say that he was giving up. According to notes I made soon after our telephone conversation, the chairman stated that while many factors were involved in a decision to hire or not to hire, certain persons in the appointing process on whose support he had counted declined to give that support after reading in the University of Chicago student newspaper a comment I had made about the case of Professor Jesse Lemisch. The chairman said that some felt my comment showed such "bad judgment" that my appointment would be inappropriate. After the story in *The Chicago Maroon* became general knowledge, the chairman said, it became apparent that his effort to secure my appointment would not be successful.

Professor Jesse Lemisch is a junior professor in American history. He was hired by the University of Chicago for the three-year period 1964-1967. The University makes its decision about tenure, ordinarily, toward the end of a second successive three-year appointment. As one appointing officer explained the University's practice to me, a second three-year appointment presupposes a more than 50 percent likelihood that the junior professor will eventually receive tenure.

Last fall Professor Lemisch was informed that he would not be reappointed to a second three-year term. I happen to specialize in the social history of the period of the American Revolution, just as Professor Lemisch does. I consider his work on the seamen and, more generally, the common man during that period to be the most brilliant and original research yet done by an American specializing in the eighteenth century on what in Europe has been termed the "history of the inarticulate." I was a panelist at the meeting of the Organization of American Historians in Cincinnati in the spring of 1966 when Professor Lemisch read a paper summarizing his results, and I know at first hand the excitement with which his paper was received by other specialists.

When I learned that Professor Lemisch would not receive the second three-year appointment which ought certainly to have been expected for a scholar as promising as Professor Lemisch, I could only wonder what other factor was involved. The obvious answer was that Professor Lemisch had taken part in a student sit-in in the spring of 1966 directed against the practice of sending students' class ranks to draft boards; moreover, in contrast to certain other professors involved, he had supported the more radical students who wished to prolong the sit-in rather than leave the university's administration building. My supposition that this factor had indeed been critical was strengthened when I read a fact sheet distributed by Students for a Democratic Society at the university which quoted, for example, a letter from Professor Soia Menschikoff, a senior professor of Law, which said in part: "I consider any member of the faculty, junior or otherwise, who urged students to participate in the sit-in in the Administration Building as lacking in judgment . . . . Certainly in connection with any appointment, this evidence of lack of judgment would be a factor that I personally would weigh."

Accordingly, when after my nonconfirmation at Chicago State College I was asked by a community organizers' newsletter to write a piece on "Why I Was Fired," I stated that I considered the Board of Governors' action not an isolated incident, but part of a pattern of harassment of opponents of the Vietnam War. One of the illustrations of that pattern, I suggested, was the University of Chicago's failure to reappoint Professor Lemisch "because he took part in the sit-in against sending college grades to draft boards in the spring of 1966." This was the quotation picked up by the *Maroon* in its July 28 issue which, apparently, became decisive in the university's failure to appoint me.

I have one further comment about this incident. After the *Maroon* article appeared, I talked with three different men in the social sciences at the University of Chicago who were interviewing me in connection with the possibility of my own appointment. Each brought up the *Maroon* quotation before discussing any other matter with me. Each had a different reason as to why Lemisch was not being reappointed: one said his scholarship was bad, the second said his scholarship had been good before coming to the university but he had done nothing since, the third said the reason was not scholarship at all but had to do with "citizenship" in the university community. Logic—something which I understand to be highly valued at the University of Chicago—suggests that a phenomenon so variously over explained may have a different cause altogether. And the more so for this reason: I have it on excellent authority that when the Department of History at the University of Chicago decided not to reappoint Lemisch, and notified the university bureaucracy to that effect, the man whose job then was to pass on such decisions and has since become president of the University of Chicago, sent the decision back to the department with the comment that he saw no reason why Lemisch should not be promoted.

Now what is the connection between this tedious catalogue of examples of academic unfreedom, and the responsibility of the educator? Simply this. We do not fulfill our responsibility to the life of the mind by just any variety of intellectual busywork. The intellectual is indeed guilty of treason to the truth if he fails to concern himself with clarification of those problems which are central to the experience of his generation. Whether as a teacher who chooses inner-city teaching or a scholar who goes outside the boundaries of his specialty to deal with war, race, and class conflict, the job of the intellectual is to be at that place where the critical questions of direction for his society are fought out.

Yale has not been able to put to rest its encounter with the Vietnam War. Two members of Skull and Bones [George W. Bush and John Kerry] recently sought the Presidency, one anxious to conceal the details of his military service, the other afraid to take credit for his finest hour: his testimony before the Senate Foreign Relations Committee in 1971. The place in which we gather tells the same story of uncertainty about the contrasting claims of God, country, and Yale. In 1967, the 450th anniversary of the Reformation, student deacons voted to nail a proclamation to the door of Battell Chapel declaring it a sanctuary for young men refusing military service. President Kingman Brewster told Chaplain Coffin that Battell was university property, Bill was a university employee, and the answer was No. Both men then appealed to the faculty deacons, who backed Brewster. Coffin concluded that "[t]here was nothing to be done except to change the constitution of the church so that in the future students could have more say in its decisions."[1]

There are two Yales, and the Vietnam War is only one of the unresolved issues between them. The unresolved issue of most ancient origin appears to be unionization. When David Dellinger arrived here in the fall of 1933 for the first week of his freshman year, he "saw a sign in Dwight Hall inviting students to join a campaign to help the nonacademic employees improve their wages and working conditions by joining a union." He enlisted. David was then summoned to a meeting with the Dean. "The Dean [I am quoting Dellinger's autobiography] said that the campaign was organized by Communists and that, once I knew this, he was sure I wouldn't have anything to do with it . . . ."[2]

Sadly, the dialogue between the two Yales has not changed that much since 1933. I arrived here in the fall of 1964, fresh from a summer in which I was coordinator of Freedom Schools in the Mississippi Summer Project. A few weeks later an extremely distinguished senior professor said to me, "Staughton, what are we going to do about the Communists

in SNCC [the Student Nonviolent Coordinating Committee]?" I knew
at the time on the basis of first-hand experience, what I believe has
since been confirmed by forty years of scholarship, that there were no
Communists in SNCC.[3]

So how may we define the two Yales? The easier of the two subcul-
tures to understand is that represented by Dellinger. In the 1960s, many
of those at Yale who came to oppose the Vietnam War had previously
worked for civil rights in the South. It was true of Bill Coffin and myself.
It was also true of Jonathan Steele, presently editor of *The Guardian*, a
British newspaper strongly opposed to the war in Iraq. Another figure
concerned with both civil rights and the war was a Yale undergraduate
and student of mine named John Wilhelm, or as we called him back then,
"Farmer," persistent organizer of trade unions at Yale who now helps to
lead one of the largest unions in the country, HERE-UNITE. At a meeting in New Haven in July 1966, eight young men pledged to return their
draft cards and called on others to do the same. Three of the eight had
been in Mississippi.[4]

Many of those at Yale who came to work against the Vietnam War
shared a certain ecumenical religiosity: Unitarian for Michael Ferber,
Quaker for myself, Presbyterian for Bill Coffin. The song most often sung
at draft resistance gatherings all over the country was "Amazing Grace."

The folks in the other subculture who represent the "other Yale"
are more difficult for me to describe, because I was not and am not now
part of their world. It goes without saying that Yale alumni constitute a
network of persons in leadership positions in law, finance, academia, and
government, including the CIA. According to Russell Jacoby, writing in
*The Nation*, in 1951 when William Buckley published *God and Man at
Yale* "he worked for the CIA."[5] I remember distinctly a moment of discovery in May 1965. I had taken my son on a birthday expedition up Mt.
Tom in Massachusetts. After my son fell asleep I read a paperback book
by flashlight, and discovered that the man who managed the Bay of Pigs
invasion was yet another Yalie in the CIA, Richard Bissell.

I want to make it clear that while I accuse these men—Bissell, the
Bundys, the Rostows, and so on—of a misguided ideological commitment to free markets and to the opportunity of unregulated investment
of private capital all over the world, I do not accuse them of greed. In
their own way they were and are every bit as idealistic as the Dellingers,
Ferbers, Lynds and Coffins. And that is the single thing—the decency of
the human beings on both sides of the divide—that makes it most difficult for Yale to bring the Vietnam War to closure.

One way we can describe the interaction of the two Yales at the
time of the Vietnam War is to imagine a time line. In the mid-1960s, Bill

Coffin and I used to trade impressions as to which of us was taking the most far-out and vulnerable positions. I distinctly remember Bill asking me one day, in the doorway of this building, whether I supported burning draft cards. I hemmed and hawed, and allowed as how I did. But in the end it was he, not I, who was indicted by the federal government.

Most spokespersons for the other Yale eventually came to condemn the Vietnam War. In 1966, after Coffin had not only been indicted but had been found guilty in the trial court, the Yale Corporation voted to give Reverend Coffin "administrative tenure, that is, an indefinite [contract] extension."[6] In October 1969, President Brewster stated publicly: "we cannot tolerate . . . continuation of the killing and the dying . . . the perpetuation of terror and death."[7] In 1971 John Kerry, who as an influential Yale undergraduate deplored antiwar demonstrations, told the Senate Foreign Relations Committee about rape, mutilation, torture by electric shock to the genitals, random killing, destruction of villages "in [a] fashion reminiscent of Genghis Khan," poisoning food stocks, and the "very particular ravaging which is done by the applied bombing power of this country."[8] I recall a letter to the *New York Times* by the history professor who had recruited me, denouncing the massacre at My Lai in language I found indistinguishable from that used by myself and others in the antiwar movement three or four years earlier.[9]

The problem with leaving the matter there is the following. In an intellectual community, one likes to think of ground gained as permanently possessed. Darwin propounded the theory of evolution. Leaving aside occasional tremors in the Red States, evolution appears established and one moves on. Watson and Crick discovered DNA. It does not need to be periodically rediscovered.

In the matter of wars between the United States and the developing world, however, with each new war we seem to need to begin the argument all over again. The positions are always the same. There is talk of "neo-conservatism" as if it were a new thing under the sun, but I think the other Yale has been neo-conservative since the extermination of the Pequot Indians. Former Yale professor Paul Wolfowitz broadcasts the same mistaken platitudes that Yale graduate Walt Whitman Rostow offered forty years ago.

To my mind the key to the neo-conservative mindset is that God, country, and Yale appear inextricably connected, in a matrix or Gestalt called "freedom," with capitalism. I suggest that this devotion to capitalism is the reason that the ideological war over Third World revolutions has constantly to be refought, as it were from Go.

Be honest: it is not the absence of democracy that offends our governing class. It is the interference with private capital, which that class considers the indispensable precondition for democracy. Mossadegh in Iran, Arbenz in Guatemala, Allende in Chile, Aristide in Haiti, were all democratically elected, but to one degree or another, each had taken into public control resources desired by United States corporations. The United States government therefore overthrew them. In Vietnam there was not very much to be nationalized or privatized, but Vietnam was wrongly believed to be a client state of Communist China and Ho Chi Minh was rightly believed to be likely to win any free election, and so, as President Eisenhower confessed in his memoirs, the United States deliberately sabotaged the nationwide democratic election planned at the 1954 Geneva conference. Saddam Hussein was not democratically elected but neither were the rulers of Kuwait or Saudi Arabia: since it was Saddam who had nationalized oil it was he, not they, who had to be removed. Chávez in Venezuela, Lula in Brazil, perhaps the next president of Mexico, await their turns.

What can be done to separate a commitment to capitalism from the devotion to God, country, and Yale? That is a question we should take away from this gathering and to which we should direct our best attention.

I stand where I did forty years ago. Just as I then traveled to Hanoi and saw first hand the effect of United States bombing, so I have met with the mothers of young Sandinista soldiers killed in Nicaragua, with Palestinians whose children are held in indefinite administrative detention and whose homes are demolished as a form of "collective punishment," with Mexican farmers who can no longer make a living because they are undersold by corn and beef from Iowa. I am not just critical of United States foreign policy. I oppose it. And I support the brave servicemen who after seeing service in Iraq, refuse to redeploy because they would be required to commit more war crimes.

### ENDNOTES

1 William Sloan Coffin, *Once to Every Man* (Cambridge, MA: Athenaeum Press, 1977), pp. 257-58.

2 David Dellinger, *From Yale to Jail: The Life Story of a Moral Dissenter* (New York: Pantheon Books, 1993), p. 24.

3 There was a former Communist named Jack O'Dell who worked for Dr. King's Southern Christian Leadership Conference. Mr. O'Dell was fired a few weeks before the 1963 March on Washington under pressure from the Kennedy Administration.

4 Michael Ferber and Staughton Lynd, *The Resistance* (Boston: Beacon Press, 1971), pp. 51-52.

5    Russell Jacoby, "The New PC," *The Nation*, Apr. 4, 2005.

6    *Once to Every Man*, pp. 269, 277.

7    Anthony Lewis, "A Thoughtful Answer to Hard Questions," *New York Times*, Oct. 17, 1969.

8    "Legislative Proposals Relating to the War in Southeast Asia," http://www.truthout.org/article/transcript-john-kerry-1971-senate-testimony,    last visited Mar. 20, 2009.

9    Robin Winks, the then chair of the Yale History Department, stated a few years ago: "Staughton Lynd . . . had much more courage than I did. . . . He put his money where his mouth was." Thrity Umrigar, "A Quaker Warrior," *Akron Beacon Journal*, Nov. 22, 1968.

I ask that we consider carefully whether the American university is realistically likely to become, in the words of the conference call, a place where "we may freely express the radical content of our lives" and a "base" which will export "humane values" to other institutions in the society. Asking that question also means not accepting unthinkingly the equation of radical intellectual and full-time academic. Even in America this equation is inaccurate: surely we have had as much to learn from Paul Sweezy, who was thrown out of the academic world, and Herbert Aptheker, who was never permitted to enter it, and Isaac Deutscher, who first taught at a university the last year of his life, as from, say, C. Wright Mills and William Appleman Williams. What is far more striking is that of the principal luminaries of the intellectual tradition to which most of us in some degree are drawn, namely Marxism, no one—not Marx, not Engels, not Plekhanov, not Lenin, not Trotsky, not Bukharin, not Rosa Luxemburg (who had a particular contempt for professors), not Antonio Gramsci, not Mao Tse-tung—put bread on the table by university teaching. Please observe that I am not quoting the eleventh thesis on Feuerbach. I am not arguing (for the moment) that we should act rather than think. My point is that without exception the most significant contributions to Marxist thought have come from men and women who were not academics, who passed through the university but did not remain there.

An exceedingly modest inference from that momentous fact is that whatever else it means to be a radical intellectual in America today, one thing requisite is an experimental attitude with respect to life-styles. Conferences all over the country this past year have explored the possibilities of radical vocations and radicalism in the professions. Just as some of us in years past chose to teach in southern Negro colleges, so now adventurous souls are seeking out junior colleges and public high schools in white working-class neighborhoods. Are they not also radical intellectuals who are sweating out inner-city teaching, or researching police brutality and local power structures, or attempting to clarify current tactical dilemmas in the Movement, or painstakingly documenting trends in American imperialism at some local equivalent of the British Museum? If we believe in what Marx called "praxis," or practical, critical activity, and in a future society in which the barriers between manual and intellectual labor will be broken down, we should at least not permit our present society narrowly to define what the life of the mind, or better, the use of the mind, must mean.

We ought to take very seriously the fact that the university corrupts radicals more often than it destroys them. Whatever our social origins, the university is a marvelously effective instrument for making us middle-class men. First it sets us in competition one with another. As undergraduate, graduate, and very often as professor, we are not working together on a common task, not—like children in a Soviet kindergarten—rolling a ball too large for any one of us to roll alone. We are competing in the performance of tasks little significant in themselves to see which ones of us will be permitted to realize the upwardly-mobile fantasies which the university requires us to entertain. You cannot work at a university as a factory worker labors at the bench. In the university it is up or out; hence, simultaneously scornful of tenure and attracted to it, we are unable matter-of-factly to conceive of the university as a source of livelihood, a kind of work in which (like baseball umpiring) "you can't beat the hours"; no, we become emotionally engaged in the upward scramble and whatever our rhetoric, in fact let the university become the emotional center of our lives. Neither the first nor the second halves of the academic career curve—the frenzied struggle for position, the economic assurance which follows—seem exactly the contexts from which radicalism may be expected to emerge. It is a very peculiar sort of radicalism which permits one only to be arrested in summertime, or obliges one to hurry home from Hanoi to be on time for a seminar. But that is the kind of radical one has to be so long as one's first commitment is to university life. If it is symbolic, one-shot, moral-gesture radicalism, that may be not so much because of our ideological orientation as because of the academic schedule. The point is that whatever we may think, or think we think, university life requires us to act as if our radicalism were episodic and of secondary importance. The conference call says: "We are committed to the struggle for a democratic university." We are unlikely to do much in the direction even of that objective, let alone make an American revolution, so long as we are not prepared to be fired at any moment. The most hopeful recent happening in American intellectual life is that last fall so many graduate students and professors were arrested along with undergraduates in demonstrations against Dow.

But what is required to stand up against the blandishments and threats of academia is not merely courage, but clarity. If I am not mistaken, most of us simultaneously half-believe in two contradictory images of the university and the teacher. On the one hand, we are inclined to conceive of the university as an oasis of pure thought where Veblenian intellectuals set their idle curiosities at work. Together with this image goes the notion of the university as a privileged corporation, governed by laws different from those applicable to society at large, immune from kinds of harassment which the off-campus citizen must expect. On the other hand, however, we are attracted to the vision of the university as a power house for social transformation, a counter-society dedicated to the *Aufhebung* of its institutional environment. The first projection leads to socialist scholars conferences which seem to wish to convey the implicit message: We too have panels with speakers and discussants; we too meet in expensive downtown hotels; we too, whatever the content of our papers, are scholars. The second projection finds Martin Duberman writing *In White America*, Staughton Lynd directing Freedom Schools, Howard Zinn freeing pilots in Hanoi, Noam Chomsky arrested at the Pentagon.

From such intellectual confusion springs tactical inconsistency. Which of us objected when SNCC was the "institutional client," when intense young men in blue jeans walked onto college campuses, scorned debate as bullshitting, and recruited students for illegal activities in the larger society? Is it not the case that before we sought to get the military off the campus we did our darnedest to get the civil rights movement on it? It would seem that, intellectuals though we may be, we change our definition of the university every year or two, just as we change our attitudes toward decentralization or the Supreme Court. We should be able to do better than that. We need to recognize, if we cannot resolve, the tension between the rhetoric of truth-seeking and the rhetoric of ethical commitment.

Consider the position of the American Association of University Professors toward obstructive demonstrations on campus. The association states: "Action by individuals or groups to prevent speakers invited to the campus from speaking, to disrupt the operations of the institution in the course of demonstrations or to obstruct and restrain other members of the academic community and campus visitors by physical force is destructive of the pursuit of learning and of a free society." This is not an illogical position if the university is conceptualized as an oasis of freedom in a hostile environment, a conception we often espouse. However, the position of many Dow demonstrators was that they were obstructing that portion of the Dow Chemical Company's activity most accessible to them. They obstructed Dow not because it invaded the campus sanctuary but because its off-campus activities are nefarious. Dow does not cleanse itself, in the eyes of these demonstrators, if, while on campus, it observes academic decorum and agrees to debate its views. Were it in the power of these demonstrators, they would put Dow out of business.

This too is a stance many of us have adopted. But where does it leave us when right-wing demonstrators seek by non-violent obstructive means to interfere with projects ethical in our eyes but nefarious in theirs?

The tension between the rhetoric of truth-seeking and the rhetoric of ethical commitment was exhibited during the recent contretemps between myself and the Board of Governors of Chicago State College. Among the professors who formed an ad hoc defense committee there were three positions. One was that a teacher necessarily teaches the whole of what he thinks and is, and therefore should have the right to say anything he wishes in the classroom.

A second position held that whatever considerations of academic appropriateness might apply to on-campus utterances, off-campus a teacher should be free to advocate like any other citizen.

My own attitude was different from both the foregoing. In contrast to the first position, it seemed to me there was a difference between the low-keyed presentation of intellectual alternatives and the attempt to kindle in an audience an awareness of some indignity. Both seemed to me important things for the man of intellect to do; yet they are different; and my instinct was to accept the proposition that a classroom is a place where one's purpose should not be persuasion, but an opening up of possible new ways of seeing things.

In contrast to the second position, I felt that a teacher should be free not only to talk as he wishes outside the classroom but to act as he wishes. It seemed and seems to me that when and if a teacher is arrested, prosecuted, convicted, sentenced, and put in jail, he will be unable to meet his classes, and at that point his academic employer may with some justice put him on leave or, if uncharitably inclined, dismiss him. Until that point is reached, I believe, a teacher should not be penalized, nor obliged to answer questions concerning his public life. Like any other citizen he should be considered innocent until proven guilty. Academic employers should eschew appointing themselves as judges and convicting a man before the courts have acted.

Perhaps many of you experience moments when such questions seem real. One characteristic answer to which we turn in such moments is: "Yes, but I am less a scholar than a teacher. The college has shown itself an instrument not only of bourgeoisifying those who stay there permanently, but of radicalizing those who pass through it for four years. As a radical faculty member I can at least protect, perhaps in part produce, radical students. I too am in one sense an organizer, dealing with a constituency, less concerned with paper than with the eager, frightened young human beings whom the campus, like the factory as Marx described it, brings together and subjects to common experience."

The fundamental problem for the full-time teacher is that he sends his students forth to confront problems which he himself has not encountered. Whether as drop-out or graduate, the student leaves the campus but the teacher does not. The teacher's life does not speak to the problem of how to "make it" as a radical off the campus. I suspect our students learn this lesson well. We may imagine that we are contributing to the revolution by teaching Marxism or socialism or radicalism to a new generation of activists. We may overlook the possibility that those whom we thus indoctrinate will become teachers in their turn, justifying their existence as radicals with the argument that they are readying for action a new generation of radicals—namely their students—who, however, are all too likely also to become teachers, speaking, just as we do, of the splendid young people to whom they lecture who need only a solid intellectual grounding—and so on.

The fact that we ourselves as full-time academics cannot provide models of off-campus radical vocation is the more frustrating this spring because the draft has forced so many of our students, as we have not been forced, to say Yes or No to the demands of the larger society.

After all these distressingly negative and essentially preliminary words, let me briefly attempt to answer the questions: What is a university? And what is a radical intellectual? The purpose of the foregoing has been to insist that, as radicals, we should take neither the institution nor the role for granted but attempt to approach them with fresh eyes. The way to do that, I think, is to begin with the reality of the Movement and observe how an intellectual function crystallizes out from its activity, or alternatively, how in the midst of the Movement's so-called mindless activism, obviously necessary intellectual tasks fail to be performed.

By now we have a certain stock of experience. SNCC, for instance, established an educational institute in Waveland, Mississippi, in the fall of 1964. The Free University of New York has existed almost three years. SDS attempted last summer to run three schools for campus organizers in Boston, Chicago, and San Francisco. Teach-ins, educational conferences, at least two new national newspapers and three nationally-circulated periodicals, all testify to the seriousness with which the Movement, charges of mindless activism notwithstanding, has tackled the function of internal education.

Different observers will assess this experience differently. Some feel that what is lacking is a systematic body of general theory. My own conclusion, perhaps predictably, is about the reverse. Having been personally involved in several of these experiments, my impression is that their characteristic weakness has been remoteness from action. At Waveland, for example, the most educational experience for the SNCC people assembled there was to travel into a New Orleans courtroom where, I believe, the precedent-establishing Dombrowski case was being argued, and then return to Waveland to discuss its implications with the lawyer, Arthur Kinoy; almost everything else in the program presented at Waveland by distinguished guest speakers passed the students by, because not linked to their immediate experience. Similarly, the Free University of New York struck me as different from the usual bull session of campus radicals mainly in locale. Those who talked together were not acting together. What was exhilarating about Vietnam teach-ins, it seems to me, was that students and teachers together addressed a problem in relation to which all were amateurs. Although action was not always explicitly projected, in the atmosphere of such occasions was a serious search for means of protest. Subsequent teach-ins at which this element was lacking, as at Ann Arbor last September, appear to me to have been sterile by comparison.

Remoteness from action in such educational ventures reflects the fact that those commonly called in as teachers, namely ourselves, are ourselves thus remote. There is no getting away from the fact that universities combining theory and practice, like the University of Havana whose students work together in the cane fields or the University of Yenan where students grew their own food, wove their own clothes, and graduated together to fight the Japanese, can only be created by individuals who combine theory and practice personally. I have been at too many embarrassing occasions when full-time activists and full-time intellectuals were brought together in the naive hope, on the part of the activists, that the intellectuals could give them a magical something which they somehow lacked. A more hopeful model in my own experience was the Mississippi Freedom Schools. There Northern white college students and Southern black teen-agers had first to encounter one another as whole human beings, to establish trust. This happened in the process of finding a church basement together, deciding on a curriculum together, improvising materials together, that is, in a context of common work; and it matured in that context, too, as those who talked together in the morning registered voters together in the afternoon. Please note I am not advocating a narrow pragmatism. What was read together in the mornings was often James Joyce, what was talked about may have been French or algebra as well as Negro history. But I must simply testify that the context of shared experience (which meant, too, that teachers characteristically boarded in their students' homes) made all the difference.

Do I mean, then, that in the protesting words of the rector of Charles University in Prague, the social sciences must become a "mere tool of propaganda and agitation"? No. My point is that if we take Marx, or Freud, or Veblen, seriously we must understand that a man's view of the world grows out of—I did not say "reflects"—his socially-conditioned experience. You and I as intellectuals do not merely observe this phenomenon. It is exhibited in our lives, too. Many intellectuals will not and should not become activists. The intellectual's first responsibility is, as Noam Chomsky says, "to insist upon the truth," "to speak the truth and to expose lies." But what truth we discover will be affected by the lives we lead. There is no such thing as "working-class truth" or "bourgeois truth" or "truth of the anal personality." Yet that portion of the truth to which we are led, the truth which seems to us significant, is not independent of our experience as whole human beings. Moreover, to hope that we can understandingly interpret matters of which we have no first-hand knowledge, things utterly unproved upon the pulses—to hope, for instance, that upper-middle-class white professors can have much illumination to shed upon black power—is intellectual hubris. Another way to phrase what I am saying is the following. It is easy for us to see that the factory does more than oppress the worker, it also assimilates him to its hectic pace, its system of material rewards, its hierarchical decision-making. Similarly we are not merely oppressed by the university but conditioned, too. The grotesquerie of this university (University of Chicago), elucidating Acquinas with the left hand while with the right hand it uproots poor Negro families in Hyde Park and Woodlawn, is too much the grotesquerie of our own lives as well.

Again, it is easy for us to see that liberal intellectuals tacitly assume a division of labor between themselves and democratic politicians. They can restrict themselves to cloistered thought because, in their view of things, somewhere out there in the world of action is a democratic political process which in the long run will assimilate their thinking and be guided by it. But does it not affect us that, as Professor Morgenthau wrote last fall in the *New Republic*, "the great national decisions of life and death are rendered by technological elites, and both the Congress and the people at large retain little more than the illusion of making the decisions which the theory of democracy supposes them to make"? Do we not also justify our intellectual labors by assuming the existence of a political deus ex machina, whether that be the Party, or the proletariat, or the youth? I think the times no longer permit this indulgence, and ask us, at the very least, to venture into the arena where political parties, and workingmen, and young people do their things, seeking to clarify that experience which becomes ours as well, speaking truth to power from the vantage-point of that process of struggle.

To do this, we ourselves must have a foot solidly off the campus. More of us, like Joe Tuchinsky at Roosevelt, should teach part-time and supervise the training of draft counselors with the remainder; or like Sid Peck and Bob Greenblatt of the National Mobilization Committee, alternate years of full-time intellectual work with years of full-time work for the Movement. The economic problems of living thus more adventurously are not insuperable. Nothing in the Communist Manifesto, or for that matter the New Testament, assures us that at age thirty-five or forty we should expect to achieve economic security for the rest of our lives. Disgorge the bait of tenure, and the problem of making a living can solve itself year-by-year. Face the problem of livelihood as husband and wife, accepting the possibility that sometimes one of you, sometimes the other, will be the main breadwinner, and you will have taken a long step toward the solution of the so-called woman question. Face the problem of livelihood together with your friends in the Movement, recognizing that at some times you may support them, at others they you, and that you can all take greater risks because of this assurance, and you will have taken a long step toward the overcoming of alienation. The great hindrance is not in the objective world but in our heads. The hindrance is the notion that real intellectuals—unlike Thucydides, Machiavelli, Milton, Locke, Hamilton, Jefferson, Trotsky, Lenin, and unlike what Marx would have been if he could—do nothing but think. The first constituency we need to radicalize is ourselves. Our path of honor is to live so as to be able to tell the truth about the hopes and sufferings of mankind in our generation.

The history that "has the most influence on . . . the course of events . . . is the history that common men carry around in their heads." Carl Becker wrote this in 1955, repeating his long-standing argument that "everyman [should be] his own historian."

Recently this same idea has appeared in many places. For instance, in his magnificent account of the revolution from below which took place during the Spanish Civil War, Noam Chomsky advises the scholar who wants to tell the truth about that popular movement to talk with the republican exiles still living in southern France.

For labor history the memories which "common men carry around in their heads" are indispensable. They are the primary sources which written records of any kind can only supplement and, when necessary, correct.

The editor of a forthcoming collection of documents on labor history puts it this way:

> American workers have long been invisible men. Long working hours, aborted formal education, fatigue . . . militated against the accumulation of documents so dear to every researcher. The historian of organized labor has the best opportunity to surmount these obstacles, for the existence of a union virtually compels record-keeping. Union files, newspapers, membership records, and minutes provide necessary tangible evidence for a scholar. But reliance upon institutional sources reinforces the tendency to write institutional history. This is precisely why unions have fared so well in the writing of labor history—and why union members are ignored and the overwhelming majority of unorganized workers is barely acknowledged and rarely examined. In fact, if comprehensive efforts are not made now to interview and gather data from this generation of workers, whether union members or not, future historians will continue to write labor history under the same handicaps that impeded their predecessors.

In view of the current interest in the technique of oral history, it might be thought that the memories of rank-and-file workers were being systematically taped and preserved. Not at all. Oral history like every other form of American history proceeds from elitist assumptions. The oral history project at Columbia University had accumulated more than 8500 hours of taped memories by the end of 1965, but almost entirely from famous individuals. The only significant collection of tapes of the organization of the C.I.O. appears to be 150 interviews with persons who played important roles in the development of the United Automobile Workers, conducted by the Institute of Labor and Industrial Relations at Wayne State University. Ironically, while the incomparable Slave Narrative Collection was being compiled by the Federal Writers' Project, the contemporaneous self-organization of four million industrial workers went unrecorded.

As a result, existing histories of the recent labor movement tend to be both thin and misleading. In an article on "Working-Class Self-Activity," George Rawick comments: "Doubters should listen to the sit-down stories of workers from Flint, Michigan, and compare them to the official UAW history which emphasized the strikes' leadership (none other than the present national officers and executive board of the UAW). Radical scholars should begin to collect materials while there is still time."

Oral history from the bottom up, or as I prefer to call it, "guerrilla history," is of interest to more than radical scholars. Rank-and-file trade unionists want to know the history of the 1930s so that they can respond to the present upsurge of labor militancy armed with an analysis of why the CIO unions so rapidly grew bureaucratic and conservative. (I will present a concrete example of such analysis in a moment.) A second constituency for guerrilla history is the children of working-class families who are going to college so as to avoid going into the mill. Exploration of their own memories and the memories of their parents and parents' friends can provide, in the words of John McDermott, "the opportunity to discover the reasons for their attitudes on a score of moral and social questions, the reality of their social lives, and the possibility of rebuilding a more humane culture . . . for their own advantage." These young men and women may come to feel, through learning experiences like guerrilla history, that they need not be ashamed of their parents' failure to "make it" out of the factory. Perhaps they will perceive that as teachers or secretaries or health technicians they will still be wage-earners, heirs to a tradition of collective struggle, with roles to play relative to their parents, cousins, brothers and sisters employed at manual labor.

Finally, there are the radical students and ex-students taking jobs in factories, moving into working-class communities, teaching at junior and community colleges. They need to avoid the missionary attitude so well described by McDermott in his "The Laying on of Culture." For them guerrilla history can be a means of learning at the same time that they teach. As the New Left turns toward labor, guerrilla history becomes a valuable tool.

### THE WISDOM OF "SMITH" AND "BROWN"

This summer I have interviewed perhaps a dozen steelworkers in Gary, East Chicago and Hammond who helped to organize the first CIO locals in Lake County, Indiana. One man worked on the railroads in Mexico for $22.50 every two weeks before going to work at Inland Steel in 1920. (By the mid-1920s, according to David Brody, more than 10 percent of the steelworkers in the Chicago area were Mexican-Americans.) He can remember when steelworkers worked twelve hours a day and a twenty-four hour "double turn" every other Sunday. When he first came to East Chicago he was housed in barracks which had been used by the National Guardsmen who crushed the great steel strike of 1919. The way the CIO purged Communists who helped to organize it reminds this old man of the way the Mexican Revolution, after its success, killed Villa and Zapata.

Another man with whom I talked is the son of an activist who was fired after the 1919 strike and never was able to get another job in the mills. My informant's first political act was to join the Gary contingent of the 1931 hunger march. Later he was chairman of the Gary unemployed council. He is an apparently inexhaustible source of stories about street-corner meetings broken up by the police and evicted tenants restored to their homes by popular action.

With every one I have raised the question: What happened to the militancy of 1936-1937, when two years of rank-and-file pressure from below finally produced the Steel Workers' Organizing Committee, when half a million workers around the country sat down in their factories, when ten men were shot in the back and killed at the Republic Steel plant near the Indiana-Illinois state line?

The most interesting response thus far has come from two men with a combined experience in their local of more than fifty years. Both belong to the local's rank-and-file caucus and from time to time have held important offices in the local.

The two men, whom I will call John Smith and Jim Brown, made me aware of the fact that between the failure of the Little Steel strike of 1937 and formal recognition of the United Steelworkers in 1942, Little Steel labor bargained with management without written contracts. In the plant employing Smith and Brown the Steel Workers' Organizing

Committee met monthly with the plant superintendent. The workers were represented by grievers in each department, just as they would be after the signing of a contract. (Monthly meetings continued after union recognition until 1950. One of the men to whom I spoke had a complete set of the minutes of these meetings from 1938 to 1950.) But until 1942, as the superintendent himself remarked in the meeting for July 1941, "we have no contract."

Further research revealed that it was just this issue of a written contract which kept labor and Little Steel management apart for these five years. The understanding signed between U.S. Steel and the Steel Workers' Organizing Committee on March 6, 1937 obligated both sides to meet no later than March 10 to effectuate "a written agreement." According to Tom Girdler, president of Republic Steel and leader of Little Steel management forces, SWOC then demanded that Republic and other Little Steel corporations sign an identical understanding. Republic's refusal to do so initiated the bloody industrial warfare of the following half decade. "The sole remaining issue was that of a signed contract," Girdler states. "The union demanded that we sign the contract and we refused."

Now, what one might term the received version of these events casts SWOC as the unequivocal good guy and Girdler, with his munition stocks and scabs and company police, as indisputably wrong. (In his account of union organization in steel, *As Steel Goes*, Robert R.R. Brooks states: "It was perfectly clear that the issue was not written agreements or signed contracts, but unionism vs. antiunionism." But Brooks goes on to provide evidence undercutting his own statement and corroborating Smith and Brown. The Little Steel corporations in the Chicago area were Inland, Youngstown Sheet and Tube, and Republic. Brooks writes of the Youngstown Sheet and Tube plants in the Mahoning Valley: "[By January 1940] S.W.O.C. claimed a majority of employees as members, had set up grievance adjustment machinery which was informally recognized by the company and frequently conferred with plant officials in the settlement of individual grievances. In some respects the union was better off than in many U.S. Steel plants since it was not bound by a contract to confine its grievance claims to matters covered by the contract. It was able, therefore, to press and sometimes win grievance claims which under the standard contract would be thrown out in the early stages of adjustment." And Brooks states of union-management relations in Republic Steel at the same time: "Since there are not contractual provisions to the contrary, national officers of the S.W.O.C. may and do take individual grievances over the heads of foremen to the plant managers. . . ." Brooks' authority for both of these statements is Jack Mayo, a SWOC sub-regional director. As for Inland, a Master's essay by Jack Stein of the University of

Chicago on "A History of Unionization In The Steel Industry In The Chicago Area" states of the pre-contract period: "At the Inland plant in Indiana Harbor . . . the workers claimed that they had a better setup than in many of the plants of the United States Steel Corporation.")

Young radical scholars have begun to question this assumption. Mark Naison observes in his study of the Southern Tenant Farmers' Union:

> The CIO built its organizing drive around the recognition of vast industrial unions as the sole bargaining agents of workers in American industries; the great majority of its strikes were fought around the issues of union recognition rather than wages or working conditions. . . . In every instance in which the CIO had extended funds for organization, its goal was to win signed contracts and to institutionalize bargaining on an industry wide level, a basis upon which the CIO could 1) extend its control of wage levels and productive conditions in the American economy and 2) extract a steady income for new organizing.

Not only was the CIO model inappropriate for workers like the Southern tenants who were outside the industrial system and driven by their situation to challenge capitalism politically. In Naison's view, even for industrial workers like those in steel, CIO organizing was a mixed blessing, because it sought to assure "a disciplined response by the work force" and "to rationalize a capitalist economy."

My informants, Smith and Brown, emphatically agree. They go farther. As they see it, the critical difference between the years before 1942 and those which followed was that before signing a contract the workers retained the freedom to strike at any time. In each department, before 1942, the workers had an unwritten understanding with management backed up by the threat of striking. If management was recalcitrant a department would "go down," and in this way, according to John Smith, the 15,000 steelworkers in the plant won things, including wage increases. Both these veteran militants believe that the workers were in a stronger position before a contract was signed. If you must have a contract, adds Smith, it should be as vague as possible and interpreted by the rank-and-file through their enforcing action.

## *A WOBBLY PERSPECTIVE*
What these men advocate on the basis of their long CIO experience is nothing else than the no-contract position of the IWW. They derive

this lesson from the years after the contract was signed as well as from the years before it. Now, says Smith, "you have a pretty good company union." After the signing of a contract the union found itself obligated to police the contract by disciplining members resistant to the pledge "that there shall be no interruptions or impeding of work, work stoppages, slowdowns, strikes, lockouts or other interferences with production and maintenance of the Company's plants during the term thereof." I asked Smith what he thought of the Communist Party's advocacy of a no-strike pledge during World War II. He responded that he was critical of the Communist Party for failing to demand a more democratic structure in the international union, but that, so far as the no-strike pledge was concerned, the fundamental no-strike pledge was that in the contract itself. For instance, in 1948 when Smith was president of the local, 7,000-8,000 members of a department undergoing automation struck to ensure the retention of their jobs at undiminished pay. Over Smith's head the district director of the international union agreed with the company that sixty-five men who had led the wildcat should be fired.

Signing a contract meant not only surrender of the right to strike between contract negotiations, but institutionalization of the dues' check-off, which made possible the multiplication of salaried pork-choppers. Before 1942 stewards and grievers were unpaid. They collected dues on the shop floor at the risk of their jobs. Sometimes the local threw dues' picket lines around the mill. Smith and Brown wryly mention a member of "the opposition" in their local who in those days climbed over the fence rather than pay his union dues. Brown himself was fired while dues-collecting, and subsequently blacklisted by four other mills in the area before he got his job back in 1950. Yet he thinks it was better for the local when it had to prove its worth to its members in order to get their dues.

To discover this Wobbly period in the history of one of the more centralized CIO unions, and especially to find that experienced activists look back to that period as the time when they most effectively served their members, seems full of suggestions for organizers seeking to create, or respond to, a new surge of rank-and-file militancy. The Left has not had an effective answer to labor historians who contend that institutional hardening of the arteries is inevitable in any trade union once it begins to demand specific improvements in wages, hours, and working conditions. "Business unionism," it is argued, brings with it a business spirit and a form of organization patterned on the business corporation. For examples of unions which resisted this process we have had to point to unions in marginal sectors of the labor market. Thus one can instance the STFU which won significant strikes against the cotton growers but, according to its founder H.L. Mitchell, never negotiated with them. But

Smith and Brown remember a stretch of about five years when in steel itself a local won concessions from management without surrendering its independence.

Insight spills over into action. Smith and Brown are doubtful whether they can accomplish significant change within the limits set by the structure of the international union and the no-strike clause of the contract But they are trying, through the rank-and-file caucus. The *Voice of the Rank and File*, the caucus newspaper, proposed the following resolution to a recent convention of the union: "Resolution to Eliminate No-Strike Clause in Contract. The no-strike clause would become inapplicable under the following conditions: (a) If the Company does not abide by the arbitrator's decisions. (b) If the Company delays grievance procedure unduly. (c) If the Company makes arbitrary rules that cause harm to the members." (Clauses (b) and (c) would appear to illustrate what Smith means by a vague contract!)

In seeking change, Smith and Brown explicitly hark back to the period before the signed contract. Running for chairman of the grievance committee of the local, Smith put out a leaflet which began:

> Used to be a time when if you had a gripe you could get your grievance man, see a foreman and usually get it straightened out. That's out now. The foreman can't settle grievances. The super isn't allowed to settle grievances. Labor Relations (these relations are tougher to get along with than your in-laws) is in the hands of a small group of people who seem to have nothing else to do but figure out ways to skin you out of your rights.

These militants seem to feel a kinship not only with the early days of the CIO but with the IWW. One issue of the *Voice* borrowed language from the Wobblies in urging "that everything possible must be done to settle grievances 'at the point of production.'"

*H*ow *did you get involved in the project that led to* Rank and File*?*

LYND: I found myself more and more frustrated by the fact that a historian is not supposed to attach values to his or her conclusions. A historian is not supposed to say at the end of the book, "Now this means we should all go out and do so and so." And I felt that, as a person with an activist orientation to life, I had trapped myself into a discipline that was inherently schizophrenic for a person such as myself. If you try to infuse your objective work with your values, to comment on it, then, of course, you are "presentist." If, on the other hand, you bend over backward not to do that, you run a danger of losing track of who you are, of disassociating yourself from your own values. I wasn't happy with that dilemma, and I don't believe that radical historians have adequately resolved it. I sense a strong tendency among radical historians to project their own sublimated activism on whatever group they happen to be studying. I remember one radical historian who referred to the lower-class group he was research-ing as "my boys." And yet, as I say, when you see a person consciously take himself or herself in hand and surmount that, the result is almost as distressing because you tend to find a person who will then laboriously try to convince you that it is really valuable to try to study some obscure thirteenth-century group for its own sake. Why? Other than as art?

So in any case, I—no doubt because of, as I say, my own penchant for action—struggled with that a lot. I wasn't happy editorializing. It seemed a violation of the limits of the craft and I wanted to be a good craftsman. But I sure wasn't going to do that other thing, which was score brownie points with senior conservative historians for the rest of my life to prove that, even though I was a radical, I could be a good historian, too.

In addition, I was very conscious that the student movement had wound up cutting itself off from ordinary working people, that the worker looked at what was happening on the campus and felt, "Who are these crazy kids who are lucky enough to be able to go to college and spend their time tearing it up?" Whatever I was able to come up with methodological-ly, I wanted it to be in the direction of working-class studies and, specifi-cally, of seeking an answer to the question of whether there was something that history, since that was the thing I was doing, could do to be of help to all the young people who were again trying to take jobs in factories, take teaching jobs in working-class community colleges, and so on.

And then, of course, I was in the process of being blacklisted just at this same time. This was not insignificant in that while I was very much discontented at Yale, maybe I wasn't discontented enough to have turned my back on it and looked in new directions unless they pushed me out.

This yeast was bubbling within me, and it's funny, but one of the occasions when I can remember trying to discuss it most systematically was during a sit-in at the University of Chicago. In the first days of the sit-in they attempted to offer an intellectual program for professors who weren't quite prepared simply to "sit in" as such, but nevertheless would show up in the occupied buildings and manifest their solidarity with the students. So Jesse Lemisch and I spent a whole afternoon talking about, on the one hand, history from the bottom up and, on the other hand, what at the time I was calling guerrilla history—that is, a way to break through the methodological impasse of being an observer, a way of ceas-ing to be an eye and becoming also a hand.[1]

Thereafter, my wife Alice and I began the process that became *Rank and File*, seeking out older union organizers and having a tape-recorded conversation with them in the hope that somehow the material could be made available to younger people who were again trying the same sort of thing. Chronologically, we were located halfway between these folks in their sixties, who very often had just retired or were on the verge of retir-ing and had been active during the 1930s, and people in their twenties, who were "colonizing" with roughly the same perspective of those older people a generation ago, but often knowing very little in a practical way about what the older people felt they had learned from that experience.

After we had done that a while we got what to me was a very exciting insight. Usually when you do oral history the idea is that you are gathering material for Your Book, in capital letters, and then lots of peo-ple will read Your Book and, incidentally, you will become a hot-shot. It occurred to us that the middle link was basically unnecessary—the book part—and that the way the process should be envisioned is the older per-son directly telling younger people about the older person's experience.

If the historian wants to be there with a tape recorder and make the results available to a wider audience, that's fine, but basically the historian is only a catalyst, an organizer, the one who creates the occasion for the older people to share their experiences. If you look at *Rank and File*, at least 50 percent of the book was a community forum at St. Joseph's College or a presentation at the Gary Writers' Workshop or whatever. They were speeches, not tape-recorded interviews, although they were speeches in which the speakers had been encouraged to feel that their own lives were significant and to talk about their experiences.

There are all kinds of criticisms of *Rank and File*, of which I think the most important is that the people in the book are not really rank and filers at all, but radical organizers. Now the rebuttal is that, by and large, they are people who became radicals in the course of their experience as rank-and-file workers—that is to say, they were not by and large people who became radicals on a college campus or inherited their radicalism from their parents and applied it in a workplace. The good thing about the book is the description of the experience of becoming a radical; people would tell you how they became disillusioned with the church, and so on. But they are not ordinary people.

*Rank and File* as a product is just a tiny beginning, one variant among many others that could be imagined, but I felt that the process of doing that book was serving the people. From time to time, it would encourage me to hear about historians in Cuba or other revolutionary societies who were doing exactly the same thing, that is, who felt that their first task as historians was to gather up the collective wisdom that was already there, the history that already existed but happened to be in people's heads and not to have been set forth in a permanent medium.

I think of the kind of oral history that I am interested in as a subset of history from the bottom up. It's like history from the bottom up carried a step further because it's people at the bottom doing their own history. But all the criticisms of (1) history from the bottom up , and (2) oral history, apply: if you look at the situation from only one side, if you believe everything you are told and don't use written sources as well, etc., etc., then your product as history will be imperfect. Sure. But all of that is easy. All of that is just what a good historian would do anyway: look at the situation from the top down as well as from the bottom up, check out all available written sources as well as talk to people. We're talking—or we ought to be talking—about something that you don't do *instead* of doing all the other things, but that you do *in addition* to all the other things because, let's face it, all the other things added together very often leave you looking through a telescope from a great distance at what ordinary people were supposed to have been doing in whatever period you are talking about.

One of the strong arguments, I think, for oral history as a specialization for radical historians is that it's so difficult to know what's going on

with ordinary people unless you ask them. I have very mixed feelings looking at a study of, say, the seventeenth century from the bottom up. Scholars
perform Herculean feats: they dig up the records at the municipal court,
they figure out that a lot of people were arrested for poaching, or whatever,
and they make interesting conclusions on the basis of much more innova-
tive use of evidence, much more assiduous digging than historians who
just go to the nearest library and read some great man's manuscript collection. Nevertheless, when you consider the product, how much do you
really know about those people, especially what went on inside their heads,
how they felt about things?

That is why I say that even from the standpoint of knowledge, just
knowledge—the historian's traditional standpoint—I question how much
about the bottom really can be derived from the fragmentary documentary sources that we're perforce driven to use. Just from the standpoint
of knowledge I think that a much more satisfactory, three-dimensional
feeling about your product is possible if you are able to use both oral and
written sources. Then, when you add to that the dimension of talking to
people still alive, you have an opportunity to assist them in making their
lives useful to younger comrades, it seems to me the method has very
strong claims.

I think of the three women in *Union Maids*, what it's meant to
each of their lives to have had this opportunity to sum up and share with
younger people.[2] And, of course, they do it not only through the film, but
by going to places where the film is being shown and adding a new layer
of oral history to a film that was originally inspired by oral history, so that
it becomes quite a dense process.

So I think there are strong, strong arguments for oral history from
the bottom up as a methodology of specific interest to radical historians.
But only if they remain radical historians—I mean, only if they remain
*historians* in the doing of it, which is to say only if they look at the situation from the viewpoints of all the protagonists, only if they use written
as well as oral sources and so on. To whatever extent I failed in that, and
I think it is probably true I have failed, that I didn't adequately check out
the written sources available for each and every episode mentioned by
narrators in *Rank and File*, which was a criticism made of the work, then
that's my fault, not the fault of the method. If I was limited, or if I was
lazy, or if I was pressed by other things in my life, it doesn't mean that
the method is invalidated thereby, it just means I didn't carry it as far as
it should have been carried.

*So you really saw* Rank and File *as a way out of the methodological impasse,
as a contribution to creating or elaborating on a new method more than as the*

*expression of any particular historiographical interest in, say, the 1930s or the creation of the CIO?*

Absolutely, the original idea was helping older people to share their experience with younger people, and it wasn't so much that I had a subject matter interest in the 1930s; it was because of an interest in helping younger people to benefit from the experience of those who had tried the same thing before so they wouldn't have to go through all the same things again.

Two kinds of younger people: middle-class students leaving the campus to colonize, but also a group that Alice and I became more and more aware of, the younger generation in working-class communities, many of whom, we noticed in Gary, were trying very courageously to find ways to live as what they were—people who had been away to college and gotten radical ideas, people who didn't want to spend their whole lives working in a mill in order to buy a home but who nevertheless wanted to live in that community and make a contribution to it. And we felt that maybe they were the most important audience. In the end, of course, even that definition of being a historian wound up not being entirely satisfying, so now I am a lawyer—and yet I am very enamored with what I was trying to do with history.

*Do you feel a strong continuity between being a historian and a lawyer? Or are you embarked on a new career?*

Law is like history with dessert. For instance, I'm working on a case that involves a company moving away from Youngstown after allegedly promising to the union, during collective bargaining negotiations five years ago, that it would stay. Maybe it's called law instead of history, but I'm doing exactly what I used to do as a historian. I'm ferreting out documents. I'm talking to people. I'm trying to understand why the policy changed from one point in time to another. But as a historian when you get to the last chapter, that's it, whereas the lawyer has the chance of going a little further.

I have all the questions that anybody else does about the law and whether it misleads people more than it helps them to hold out a sense that maybe you can accomplish something in the courts. But at least for me there's the satisfaction that after you get done analyzing the situation, you can have a shot at trying to do something about it. I find that very satisfying. And another thing, I noticed in looking at the E. P. Thompson interview his comment on *Whigs and Hunters* where, in the last chapter, he suddenly bursts forth and says, in effect, "You know, the law is not such a bad thing. Marxists have gone overboard with the idea that everything is relative. There's something about the law as a society's encapsulation of its sense of right and wrong that's extremely important." I suppose it's very obvious that he also spoke for me in saying that.

That certainly is a continuity in my own life. I can remember as a Harvard undergraduate sitting in Cronin's, the local pub, with the rest of the Harvard John Reed Society and they were pounding away at my ridiculous bourgeois notion that there were certain concepts of right and wrong that didn't change from one period of class rule to another, that were more or less the same throughout human history because human beings were human.

Sometimes I feel I spend my life having that argument. One year it's with the John Reed Society, the next year it's with Eugene Genovese. But it's the same argument and it helps to explain, I suppose, how someone like myself is a sucker for the law in the sense that I really do have the notion that there's something called Justice with a capital "J," that there's something you can appeal to even in people whose experiences wouldn't ordinarily lead them to understand what you're trying to say. Of course, when I put it that way you can see the connection to notions of nonviolence as well. I'm afraid the continuities become so overwhelming the question is whether there is really any change.

*Could you describe how you decided to go into law?*

Alice and I decided together about going into law. In doing *Rank and File* we were increasingly struck by the number of working people whom we met who felt messed over by both the company and the union. Often their problems had a legal aspect. They didn't know where to turn. We put a lot of energy into finding legal help for these friends. It turned out that the available movement lawyers were not into labor law, and the labor lawyers were working either for unions or companies and were unavailable. Finally, Alice and I decided that it would save time for one of us to go to law school.

I felt Alice would very likely make a better lawyer than I because of her draft counseling experience. However, she has a reading problem and dreaded law school, so in the end I became a lawyer and she a paralegal. Alice's experience as a draft counselor remains a model for us as to how professionals can relate as co-workers to those they serve. The idea is that both the professional and the client are experts: the professional in a technique, such as interpreting Selective Service regulations, or law, and the nonprofessional in the problem. This is obvious in labor law where the worker is the expert on the nature of his or her work, the history of the particular workplace, the contract and its interpretation. As Alice and I see it, professionals and non-professionals are equals, each contributing expert knowledge.

*Do you think the law can be used as a tool for radical change?*

I think of trying to use the law as a shield rather than a sword. For instance, John Barbero[3] and I were involved in a suit to challenge ENA [Experimental Negotiating Agreement] when it was first adopted. I don't think either of us feels bad about that. As a matter of fact, I now find everybody, Ed Sadlowski included, refers to that suit almost as if they had a part in it.[4] At the time, Sadlowski very definitely stood aloof.

In any case, the weakness of it was that we were trying to use a lawsuit to do something that only a social movement could have done. I don't believe, by and large, in the Ralph Nader idea of changing society by means of the law. I believe in trying to use the law to protect people as best you can as they try to change society in other ways. Which really has been my own personal experience with the law. I've had five or six fairly serious encounters with the law and I don't think I've ever paid a lawyer a penny. The ACLU was always there to defend me.

But there's yet another aspect of the law that intrigues me. One of the problems with a radical movement or a socialist movement attempting to speak to American working people is that it's as if we just haven't found the language. I almost feel that it's not essentially a problem of ideas, but somehow the language isn't a natural language. As the son of two professors who grew up on the eighth floor of an apartment house in New York City, I am very unlikely to be able to make much of a contribution to the discovery of that language. But yet and still I'm intrigued by the precision the law can give you in talking about, for example, the idea of being innocent until proven guilty. By the time Sadlowski and McBride came down to the wire they were both advocating the concept that if the worker in the shop is disciplined, accused of something, he or she gets full pay until the thing is finally adjudicated.

I had the experience in the antiwar movement that I could get up in front of thousands of people and talk about what I personally was feeling at that moment and people out there would feel I had found the words to express their feelings, too. That was because they were people like me, college students, etc. It's a sadness to me but I don't anticipate that happening before a local union audience or in a strike situation.

But that doesn't mean I can't make some contribution toward the discovery of the language that I think needs to be discovered. I do have the basic conviction that there are, as it were, two express trains passing each other in American factories. Here are all the former student radicals of the sixties adopting very heavy Marxist vocabularies in order to communicate with the working class, and here are working people who are increasingly interested in participatory democracy and helping to make the decisions that affect their lives and all the things that the student radicals used to believe in.

*You have written important analytic pieces about the 1930s. What issues there presently concern you?*

There is a historiographical debate about the 1930s, which, as far as I am concerned, is still completely up for grabs. Where did the initiatives from above come from, who was really responsible for the Wagner Act?[5] It is all very well to say—and I think it is the best we can say for the moment—that there were two kinds of motivations. There was a motivation from below to get a little help from the government in trying to organize. There surely was also a motivation from above to give these crazy workers something so they would get off the streets. Senator Wagner felt that; Heber Blankenhorn, who did Wagner's drafting, felt that; John L. Lewis appears to have felt that. The big question, it seems to me, the big unanswered question, is whether there was any industry input in the genesis of the Wagner Act or whether it was only after the fact that the Thomas Lamonts and J. P. Morgans decided, as U.S. Steel did decide after the General Motors sit-down, "Hey, let's live with this thing." That, it seems to me, is the unanswered question about where all of that came from. I don't know the answer, but what I do know is that when the ACLU and the Communist party initially opposed the Wagner Act, they weren't as screwy as people have thought for the last forty years. When they said that this could lead to an American fascism they may have been right; look at the way labor is tied hand and foot by legal regulations today. If you set the end product beside what the Communist party and the ACLU predicted forty years ago, they weren't so off base. Now, it took a lot of backtracking by the Supreme Court to get there, but maybe that was part of the prediction, at least in its more sophisticated form: no matter how the law was written, once you had the government that far into controlling the labor movement, given the nature of power in American society it was going to wind up controlling the labor movement for the sake of business.

Just to add one little historical footnote for the benefit of anyone who wants to work on this problem: there is a very important difference between the Wagner Act as it was introduced in 1934 and as it was passed in 1935, and the difference is that the 1934 draft of the Wagner Act provides for compulsory arbitration. Now, why is that important? Number one, it helps to explain the reaction of groups such as the ACLU and the Communist party. Number two, the reaction of groups such as the ACLU and the Communist party may explain why that feature was dropped in 1935. And it's a riot to read the report of the Senate Committee on Labor in recommending the 1934 version of the Wagner Act—or the United States Supreme Court in the Jones and Laughlin case holding the Act constitutional—because both piously say, "Of course, we're not telling business and labor what to agree to, we're only telling them to sit down together and bargain—that's the American way." In 1934, they wanted to put compulsory arbitration into the law.

This is a kind of value-free observation. I don't know if it was good or bad that the bill was changed. Maybe it should have been left in its original form and rejected. Maybe it was a people's victory that it was modified. All I'm saying, as stimulus for some historian who wants to figure all this out, is that it happened. And it is a very important thing that it happened because the whole thrust of labor law under the Wagner Act is a double whammy: "We're not going to tell you what to do, but once you've agreed on what to do, we're going to enforce it." Since the people who do the agreeing are not the rank and file but the union bureaucrats and business, the upshot has tended to be the present legal apparatus enforcing collective bargaining agreements against workers who try to wildcat or whatever. To understand it you have to go all the way back and realize that, originally, at least some of the forces behind the Wagner Act wanted arbitration, they wanted to stop strikes. They didn't want a sophisticated system of free collective bargaining; they wanted to put a hammer on working people and get them to stop all this uproar.

*What about the role of the Communist party in the 1930s?*

I think we've all sort of shot from the hip on that question, and maybe there should be a moratorium on one-sentence summaries until someone has done a little more work. There probably has been a good deal of work in the last year or two that I am not entirely caught up with. But if I had to make a one-sentence summary, I would say you have a feeling of a tragedy that is very different from melodrama.

I think both the Third Period and the Popular Front periods were extremely creative, significant episodes. If you compare what the Communist party did between 1929 and 1935—let's call that the Third Period—and what it did between 1935 and the beginning of the war, if you compare what the [Communist party] did in those two five-year spans with everything it's done before and since, then the rest is just dust in the balance, the rest is inner-party squabbles and the international Communist banquet circuit. Nothing is really happening in this country compared with either of those periods.

Now the tragedy comes in that I think there was a certain exaggeration in each of those episodes that probably had to do with taking cues from abroad. It's a complicated question. I think Al Richmond is probably right in criticizing me, in saying I underemphasize the degree to which these lines grew out of the experience of the American party.[6] Maybe you have to make a more sophisticated, a more complex statement about the fact of overseas direction, and say that it lent a certain quality of artificiality and exaggeration to each of these initiatives. What is for sure is that the extremely militant, creative, courageous, never-to-be-forgotten Third Period conduct of the Communist party went overboard in the direction of calling socialists "social fascists." No question of that. And not just in the attitude toward the Socialist party, but in the attitude toward indigenous working-class organizations, toward AF of L locals, toward independent locals where the working class in response to the NRA founded their own unions. The Communist party was, for a period, out in left field in saying that the only important thing was the CP-sponsored Trade Union Unity League. So that there *were* tremendous missed opportunities.

As another element of complexity, I think there was a kind of golden age, maybe occurring at different times in different parts of the country but generally in 1934-35, when the Communist party in practice revised its Third Period orientation. And the word hadn't come down from the Seventh Party Congress yet, so it could be done creatively, and humanly, and with tactical flexibility. That was the period when the socialists and the Communists all over the country initiated local labor parties. That was the period when Norman Thomas and Earl Browder appeared together in Madison Square Garden—a forgotten time, a time that, in a *Radical America* article, I tried to call the period of the "united front from below" intervening between the sectarian Third Period and the [opportunist] Popular Front.[7]

Even in the Popular Front period, as David Montgomery was reminding me recently, there were tremendous missed opportunities. George Powers, who was in the Communist Party in the Monongahela Valley, told me that there was a certain period of time in the late 1930s where every important steel union president in the valley was a Communist. Now it was also the case that in every one of those little towns—Ambridge, Clairton, McKeesport, all those places, venerable places—the local Republican administration was thrown out by the steelworkers, by the CIO, and replaced by Democrats. Now, my question is why? Did it have to be that way? The steelworkers were so strong in every one of those places that they could have done anything they wanted to do. And in fact, of course—complexities again—even though they called themselves Democrats, I suspect that if one could really dig out the history of each of those little towns you'd find that there were steelworkers elected to office, that they had pretty tough programs in terms of rent control, things of this kind; in other words, they tried—and not for the last time—working within the Democratic party to give it an independent politics, a working-class content. But still, suppose instead of doing that, say from 1935 to 1945, the Communist party had had the insight to say, "We're going to support Roosevelt *nationally*, he's earned it; it is necessary in order to present some kind of united resistance to fascism"—all the things that they did say—but also that *locally* they would try to build independent labor parties. There would have been nothing inconsistent between critical support for Roosevelt and saying after the Memorial Day Massacre in Chicago that Mayor Kelley, who ordered the police to fire, had to go.[8] Whereas the Communists, to the best of my knowledge, supported Mayor Kelley in the election after the Memorial Day Massacre. And I just say that that is asinine. So that, there again, I think the Popular Front impulse was an extremely creative, interesting thing, and even the idea of communism as twentieth-century Americanism—that's not such a bad idea. If it isn't twentieth-century Americanism what is it? Russian subversion? There's nothing wrong with being twentieth-century American, but they overdid it. They did it mechanically, they did it artificially, they did it in such a way as to give up their own independent voice.

For those who do additional primary research on the 1930s I would like to say, "Don't go looking for scapegoats." There were giants in that era. We should be so lucky if we should ever in our lives do anything as significant as the Communist party did in the 1930s. But that doesn't mean we can't think about it, learn from it, and discuss it analytically and critically.

*You've spoken of rank and file as the fundamental reality. Not the crowd and not the party. Could you encapsulate the essence of that reality, that rank and file?*

That's interesting. I've been thinking about that because there is a screwy notion of the rank and file loose in the land, two screwy notions really.

One is that the rank and file is an electoral organization. Most of the so-called rank-and-file groups that people get excited about are nothing but electoral organizations that happen to be electoral organizations for union politics, which greatly resembles Democratic party politics and in which most of the candidates bear a striking resemblance to liberal

Democrats. It doesn't mean that it is wicked; it just means that it is what it is, and I would say for instance that the Sadlowski campaign, the Fight Back organization, had no independent reality other than that election and, if it continues, continues for the purpose of the next election. He didn't put out a newspaper in District 31 as he promised to do. To the best of my knowledge Fight Back, as Fight Back, has no autonomous activities other than his electoral campaign. Certainly the organization doesn't exist to criticize the candidate, you can be sure of that. And as a matter of fact, the universal complaint of rank-and-file groups in steel from California to Youngstown to Canada is that Sadlowski didn't approach them, didn't work with them, didn't use them. Why? He figured he had their votes anyway, and he wanted to keep the apparatus tightly under his control.

Another form of rank and file that I would think of as a pseudo form is the little group of former radical students who get together and call themselves—and I've done this—the concerned this or the rank-and-file that and put out their little newspaper. Which is fine and makes a certain contribution; it really does make a contribution. But it is not the self-activity of the working class. It just isn't. And it tends not to become that because it is very difficult for workers with different backgrounds to become a part of such a group. The nucleus of such a group is made up of former students. When an ordinary worker comes into the group he or she is in the minority. The atmosphere of the group is already set. If workers become a part of it, they do it in such a way as to give up their own identity, take on a foreign lingo.

A much more difficult question is what could a [more genuine] rank and file do? It would have to involve forms of day-to-day activity. It would have to be more than, on the one hand, election campaigns and, on the other hand, passing out radical literature, which are the two main things that rank-and-file groups do these days. And it's understandable that that is all they do because of the tremendous legal restrictions on doing anything else.

But that is just not enough. A rank-and-file group ought to be present, day to day, in working-class communities and workplaces—a group that acts differently, a group that you can turn to when you have a problem, a group that creates change. I don't sense that anywhere. Now, that may be my own limitation, but I just don't sense that kind of a rank-and-file presence in any union or the places where members of a union live.

Another missing dimension in most rank-and-file movements is, I think, a cultural dimension, and I'm not even quite sure what I mean by that. But someone was telling me that at the St. Therese General Motors plant what became a sit-down had its origins in an insistence of French-speaking workers that their language be respected; that is, the group that formed around that demand became the group that sparked the sit-down. And, of course, in the short-lived Black Revolutionary Union movement in Detroit, one sensed that extra dimension.

It was the dimension that the church contributed to the southern civil rights movement. One just took it for granted that freedom meetings were in churches, and there was an entire rhetoric—not just "We Shall Overcome" but "Solidarity Forever," and how many others that were originally hymns—because people shared a common religious background. Somehow, after [the organizers became] atheists, that still continued to matter in the cultural forms that they found to express themselves. I sense the absence of that in movements that call themselves rank and file, and I think it is absolutely critical. We are talking about something that gives people the courage to say, "Hey! I have two kids and I'm going to risk my job for this." That has got to come from somewhere. That has got to have deep roots.

Another thing I sense lacking in most rank-and-file movements is something I sense in the activity of someone like John Barbero. He has a personal relationship with everyone, and oftentimes it may be two candidates for the same office or people on opposite sides of a question, but somehow the way John conducts himself, he's entered into that other person's life, but without surrendering his own identity or integrity. That other person considers him a friend, and John thinks of this other person as a friend. Now that quality—maybe that's just what all human beings should have in the way they live their lives. There's not going to be any rank and file, or any other Left movement in this country, until the people in it have the knack of constantly reaching out beyond the movement to establish contact with those who are not in it.

*Do you see rank-and-file organizers, and your work with them as a lawyer, as part of the American tradition of radicalism that you tried to delineate in* Intellectual Origins?[9]

Yes, I do. My approach to labor law is right out of that book in the sense that the only way to free up rank-and-file people is to take the position that prior to the creation of unions, prior to the initiation of collective bargaining, they have rights, and that the institutional apparatus exists to protect and enhance those rights.

But if [the institutional apparatus] betrays those rights, power returns to the rank and file to do as it wishes. The funny thing is that you can argue that point of view much more credibly in the area of labor law than in the area of the creation of government. Because if you are going to talk about the creation of government you are driven to talk about natural rights, and about 95 percent of the Left goes up the wall. However, if you're talking about the labor movement you can make the same argument by saying, "Hey, honest, fellows, I'm not talking about natural rights. These are statutory rights. This is Section 7 of the National Labor Relations Act. This talks about the right to engage in concerted activity. It doesn't say 'after you have a union' or 'so that you can be part of a union.' It's just there. And if, in the course of engaging in concerted activity, you want to create a union, great. And if having created it you want to destroy it, great. You have the right to do that under the NLRA." So that, as I say, for better or worse I find myself using the same intellectual approach that I tried to work out in that book, perhaps more credibly in the area of labor law and rank and file.

## POSTSCRIPT

During the five years since Len Calabrese and I had the foregoing conversation, I have continually been involved in a popular movement against the closing of Youngstown's steel mills. In a forthcoming book, *The Fight Against Shutdowns: Youngstown's Steel Mill Closings* (San Pedro, Calif.: Singlejack Books), I try to tell the history of that movement. The experience has enriched my appreciation of the possibilities of "oral history from the bottom up."

I participated as a lawyer in the Youngstown struggle to save the mills. I represented an inter-denominational church coalition that sought to reopen the Campbell Works under employee-community ownership; the local union of production and maintenance workers at the Brier Hill Works; and six local unions, unemployed steelworkers, and others, who attempted to stop U. S. Steel from closing its Youngstown Works.

The following struck me when, as a participant-observer, I wrote the story of what happened:

1. It seems more true to me than ever that *unless the experience of working-class participants in popular struggles is recorded promptly, important pieces of history may be lost forever.* For instance, employee-community ownership in Youngstown was first suggested by a local union officer named Gerald Dickey in September 1977. I interviewed Dickey in the spring of 1981. He was at first unable to remember how the idea of employee-community ownership had come to him. Only after he had been talking for half an hour, and started the second side of the tape, did Dickey suddenly exclaim, "*Now* I remember," and proceed to tell the story. I felt that had I interviewed Dickey even a week later it might have been too late.

2. There is a patronizing assumption in the doing of much history, including oral history, that the participant provides the experience and the historian provides the interpretation. I found this not to be true in Youngstown. Rather, *the participants themselves interpreted their own struggle more and more profoundly as the struggle unfolded.*

When the first mill closed there was a general tendency to blame what happened on foreign imports and environmental laws. This view soon gave way to a view that the Campbell Works had been closed by a conglomerate that used the cash flow generated by its steel facilities for corporate empire-building rather than to modernize the mills. At that stage, Youngstown steelworkers blamed mill closings on the acquisition of steel companies like Youngstown Sheet & Tube and Jones & Laughlin by conglomerates such as Lykes and Ling-Temco-Vought.

But then came the closing of U. S. Steel's Youngstown mills, and this explanation no longer was adequate. A consensus emerged that the problem was not *who* made investment decisions but the *basis* on which they were made. The mills were closed because companies like U. S. Steel insisted not just on making a profit but on making as much profit as possible.

In opposition to the concept of profit maximization, Youngstown steelworkers said that modernization of industries like steel should (in the words of a favorite Youngstown picket sign) put "People First, Profits Second." John Barbero, like Dickey a local union officer, was the first person in the area to popularize the idea that modernization should take place in communities where the industry already existed rather than in new, "greenfield" sites. This "brownfield" strategy for modernization tapped sentiments with deep roots in Youngstown's working-class community. Rather than labor following capital, Barbero and others called for capital investment where workers already lived. They emphasized the value of several generations of a family living near to one another; as Ed Mann, another spokesperson, put it, "We're not gypsies." It came to be felt in Youngstown that when an enterprise has induced a community to depend on its presence, then the enterprise has an obligation to stay in the community as long as it can make *some* profit there.

Gerald Dickey's vision of employee-community ownership and John Barbero's concept of brownfield modernization became the principal ideas both of the Youngstown movement and of my history. Strictly speaking, Dickey and Barbero did not create these ideas. Dickey heard a school board candidate at a mass meeting throw out the notion, "Why don't we buy the damn place?" Barbero read about brownfield modernization in a newspaper account of a speech by Stewart Udall. What these participants did was to recognize the importance of an idea, seize it, and organize their fellow workers around it.

3. A common criticism of oral history is that it tells what happens only from one point of view, that of the inarticulate. In Youngstown, however, *the struggle drove us to probe the reasoning of corporate and government decision makers by unearthing existing documents and to generate data that would not otherwise have existed.*

When the Lykes Corporation closed the Campbell Works I filed a suit, on behalf of the local congressman, requesting Justice Department documents concerning the merger of Lykes and Youngstown Sheet & Tube several years before. Later, when the Department of Commerce denied the loan guarantees necessary to reopen the Campbell Works, another suit under the Freedom of Information Act obtained documents exposing the bias against worker-ownership on the part of the men who made the decision.

U. S. Steel's decision to close its local mills prompted a lawsuit that obtained a twenty-two-day injunction restraining the company from shutting down. In the course of preparation for trial we deposed (questioned under oath) a variety of corporate actors, including the superintendent of the mills, and the two top officers of the corporation and required the company to produce (make available for inspection) their profit data for the Youngstown mills. All this information would not otherwise have been available either to the public at the time or, in good part, to a subsequent historian.

In practice, therefore, chronicling the experience of the inarticulate and probing the experience of the mighty were not mutually exclusive, but parts of the same process.

## ENDNOTES

1 Jesse Lemisch is a radical historian who coined the phrase "history from the bottom up" in his essay "American Revolution Seen from the Bottom Up" in *Towards a New Past: Dissenting Essays in American History*, Barton J. Bernstein, ed. (New York: Pantheon Books, 1970).

2 *Union Maids* is a film about three of the women in *Rank and File*. It is distributed by New Day Films, P.O. Box 315, Franklin Lakes, NJ 07417.

3 John Barbero was a rank-and-file steelworker, peace activist, and socialist from Youngstown, Ohio. He died in 1981. Barbero described his personal history in *Rank and File*, pp. 264-84.

4 The ENA was an agreement entered into between the major steel companies and the steelworkers union in 1973 that forbade strikes at the expiration of the Basic Steel Contract. Ed Sadlowski is a United Steelworkers union dissident who challenged union leadership and Lloyd McBride for the

presidency of the union in 1977. He received 40 percent of the vote. McBride subsequently led a successful move to prohibit outside funding in union elections thereby limiting dissidents' access to financial support for their campaigns. Sadlowski has been director of the union's Chicago-Gary district.

5   The Wagner Act (National Labor Relations Act) was passed by Congress in 1935. It created the National Labor Relations Board (NLRB) with the power to recognize collective bargaining units and define unfair labor practices. Section 7 upheld the right of employees to join labor organizations and bargain collectively through representatives of their own choosing.

6   Al Richmond is the author of *A Long View from the Left: Memoirs of an American Revolutionary* (Boston: Houghton Mifflin, 1973). At pages 238 and 245-46 he comments on Lynd's writing about the 1930s.

7   Norman Thomas (1884-1968) became leader of the Socialist party in 1926. He was codirector of the League for Industrial Democracy, the educational arm of the Socialist party, from 1922 to 1937. Earl Browder (1891-1973) was general secretary of the Communist party of the United States during the years of its largest membership and greatest influence, 1930-46. He was expelled from the Party in 1946 after acrimonious debate over his leadership. The article referred to in the text is "The United Front in America: A Note," *Radical America* 8 (July-August 1974), pp. 29-37. See also Lynd's "The Possibility of Radicalism in the Early 1930s: The Case of Steel," *Radical America* 6 (November-December 1972), pp. 37-64.

8   On May 30, 1937, Chicago police fired on a group of demonstrators before the gates of Republic Steel in south Chicago leaving ten dead and eighty-four injured. "Little Steel," under the leadership of Republic Steel, refused to recognize the Steelworkers Organizing Committee as the bargaining agent for its employees though SWOC had secured recognition from U. S. Steel. By 1941 virtually all independent steel companies signed agreements with the CIO. The suggestion in the text that the Left in the late 1930s could have founded independent local labor parties is developed in Eric Leif Davin and Staughton Lynd, "Picket Line and Ballot Box: The Forgotten Legacy of the Local Labor Party Movement, 1932-1936," *Radical History Review*, no. 12 (Winter 1979-80), pp. 43-63.

9   Staughton Lynd, *Intellectual Origins of American Radicalism* (New York: Pantheon Books, 1968).

I feel like Rip Van Winkle. After a thirty-five year absence, I return to the world of manuscript tax returns, the practice of deference, and the struggle over who should rule at home.

You will recall that when Meinheer Van Winkle awoke, the well-oiled firearm at his side when he dozed off had disappeared. Its barrel had become rusty, its wooden stock decayed. I wonder, How is it with my weaponry? Especially in view of the wonderful burrowing in obscure sources that all of you have done, and that I have no practical way to assimilate, what can I contribute? What can I add to what you already know?

I shall discuss, first, my graduate research on tenant farmers and artisans in revolutionary New York, and second, the present status of the project of viewing history from below and seeking to be a voice for the voiceless.

## I

Having looked at Tom Humphrey's dissertation on tenant farmers[1] and the work of Gary Nash on city artisans,[2] I don't believe I can add much to your specific knowledge of the period of the American Revolution. When I was in graduate school the Lynds had two small children, Alice worked, and I was able to do research one morning every other week. Tom and Gary found all sorts of manuscript sources that I did not.

However, there are certain implications of my conclusions that as best I can tell have not entered into general scholarly conversation. I can't be sure whether I made these notions crystal clear in 1961 and they have been unaccountably ignored, or, what is a good deal more likely, they have become more and more clear to me as I have pondered them over the years. In any event I want to talk about this.

I studied farm tenants in Dutchess County and artisans in New York City because I wanted to prove or disprove what Carl Becker and Charles Beard had to say about the political choices made by these two groups.

What I learned about tenants was that in southern Dutchess County and neighboring Westchester County tenant farmers supported the Revolution. I held in my hands the petitions of these folks to the revolutionary New York legislature in which they asked for confiscation of Loyalist estates.

Thus far, the model of a struggle over who should rule at home worked well. While a coalition of classes struggled for independence, little people at the bottom demanded more: economic independence in the form of freehold ownership of the land that they tilled.

But in Columbia County, just to the north in the approximate present site of Bard College, tenant farmers were Loyalists. They made their way out into the Hudson River where the Continental Congress had strung nets to obstruct the junction of British forces from New York and Albany, stole the lead used to weight the nets, and made bullets out of it. In 1777 they staged a tenant uprising on Livingston Manor.[3]

So what is the explanation of this ideological diversity? Why were the tenants who rented from Beverly Robinson in southern Dutchess County ardent patriots, whereas the tenants on the land of Robert Livingston only a few miles away became Tories?

There is a simple answer, I suggest. It all depended on the politics of your landlord. If you rented from a Tory like Beverly Robinson, who sheltered Benedict Arnold when the latter fled across the Hudson, you supported the Revolution in the hope that if Robinson and his friends were defeated, you might get fee simple ownership of your farm.

But if you rented from Robert Livingston, an ardent Whig, your calculus was just the opposite. You sought victory for the King of England because if he won, Livingston might be deprived of his lands, and in this way you too might realize the American dream and become the owner of the land that you cultivated.

So it was not ideology that determined the political choices of Hudson Valley tenant farmers. It was economic interest.

When I finished my Master's essay on Dutchess County, fellow students expected me to expand my work on tenants to take in other manors in other counties, like Rensselaerswyck. My reaction was, "No, I've got the tenant farmers figured out. What about the artisans?"

Whereas the politics of Hudson Valley landlords may be an exotic kind of information known only to Tom Humphrey and myself, it is otherwise with city artisans. These are the Sons of Liberty. These are the folks who erected liberty poles, enforced non-importation agreements, dumped tea into Boston Harbor, and carried the news that the British were coming. These were Paul Revere and friends in Boston who met at the Green Dragon tavern, and comparable groups in New York City,

Philadelphia and Charleston. Carl Becker said they were the heart and soul of both the struggle for home rule and the struggle over who should rule at home. And he was right.

There is only one problem. As Charles Beard noted in passing but did not explain, these same artisans enthusiastically supported the Federalists' constitution in 1787. They did so not only at the ballot box, but as we all know, in elaborate parades in every major seacoast city.

So how did the artisan radicals of 1763-1776 become Hamiltonians in 1787? And what does this ideological transformation tell us about the relationship of economic interest and ideology?

Again, there is a simple answer. What preoccupied these folks before the Revolution was the danger that imported British manufactured goods might destroy their livelihoods. Hence they supported all things anti-British, especially non-importation agreements. And what preoccupied them in the mid-1780s as British manufactures once again began to pour into American seaports was . . . exactly the same thing. Hence they supported the project of a strong national government that could impose an effective tariff on imported manufactured goods.[4]

Artisans were altogether consistent. There only appears to have been an inconsistency because we have supposed their politics to be driven, not by economic interest, but by ideology.

These findings called for some correction in the hypotheses of Carl Becker and Charles Beard, but not for their abandonment. In the event, however, Becker and Beard appear to have been forgotten in the general excitement over E. P. Thompson's *Making of the English Working Class* and Jesse Lemisch's proposal for a Brechtian history written "from below." This brings me to my second topic.

## II

Tom Humphrey says more clearly than I have been able to what concerns me about the Thompsonian revolution. Tom ascribes to a "they" what I will bring home to roost with a "we": "[We] have succeeded only in pressing the authors of the master narrative to alter their stories slightly, or to add another box for 'the poor' on the side of the page."[5]

In other words: Yes, we may talk to our heart's content about (quoting David Brion Davis) "romanticized pirates as well as prostitutes, religious zealots, bandits, highwaymen, and criminals of all sorts." But we must stay away from overall interpretation, leaving that to Bernard Bailyn, Pauline Maier, Edmund Morgan, Gordon Wood, David Brion Davis and—you would know better than I—whoever now fills those chairs. To seek to thrust the people we write about into the foreground is, in Professor Davis' marvelously contemptuous turn of phrase, to become tiresome. We who accompany the poor in their tribulations, like those we study, must remember our proper place.

I want to emphasize that I am talking about myself as much as, perhaps even more than, about you. My wife and I have edited two books of oral histories by rank-and-file workers, and one by embattled Palestinians. I am just now preparing a manuscript in collaboration with six men on Death Row: the five alleged leaders of the Lucasville uprising and Mumia Abu-Jamal. I can hear the conversation over sherry: "It seems Staughton has run out of workers so he is taking up prisoners." It is not a case of "De te fabula narratur": This story is about you. It is about me, too.

Like you, I believe in truth. Like each of you, I die a thousand deaths over a footnote that may not be quite right. But I am convinced that we need, not just truth in the form of accurate footnotes, or even truth in the form of evocative oral histories, but also truth in the form of structural understanding. We confront a big system whose advocates think in the large and have a long-term trajectory. We too need a big picture analysis. And the way to construct it, I suggest, is by framing what we think we know as specific hypotheses to be tested by future research.

Carl Becker, Charles Beard, even Richard Hofstadter in *The American Political Tradition* and Arthur Schlesinger, Jr. in *The Age of Jackson*, proposed big ideas that could be tested, as I tried to test Becker and Beard in my own graduate work.

When did we get away from this style of doing history?

I think the answer has to do with the British Communist and ex-Communist historians of the period after 1956: with E. P. Thompson, Christopher Hill, Eric Hobsbawm, and their colleagues.

I have written about Thompson elsewhere. I yield to no one in admiring the man who wrote *The Making* for the workers in his extension classes in the North of England. I treasure the images of Thompson casting his pearls before classes whose composition changed from week to week, coming into the room with newly-discovered manuscripts and loaning his only copies to his grimy students, standing aside when a miner undertook to correct the professor's account of how to dig coal.

As for Hill, how can I not embrace the man who found that Quakers were once revolutionary? These were giants. We were right to sit at their feet.

But what exactly, other than mellifluous Oxbridge prose, did these luminaries add to what Marxism had already taught us . . . and them? Everyone refers to Thompson's definition of class in the opening pages of *The Making*. I can never remember it. I don't know exactly how it is thought to have improved the discussion of class in *The Manifesto, The Eighteenth Brumaire* and elsewhere.

Jesse Lemisch and I have talked about Thompson's idea of "agency." I still don't understand how it is supposed to differ from the concept of "self-activity" proposed by C. L. R. James; and before James, by Trotsky and Alexandra Kollontai, who used the Russian word *samodeyatelnost*, which means "self-activity," in polemics that go back to the turn of the last century. In 1904, Trotsky warned that Lenin's centralism would lead to the central committee substituting itself for the party, and a dictator substituting himself for the central committee, whereas the proper task for revolutionaries was "the development of the self-activity [*samodeyatelnost*] of the proletariat." Alexandra Kollontai used the same word both on behalf of the Workers' Opposition at the 1921 congress of the Bolshevik Party and, fascinatingly, to characterize the sense of independence needed by Russian working women.[6]

For that matter, I don't know what either of these terms—"agency" or "self-activity"—adds to Marx. I have not been able to determine whether Marx used the German word for "self-activity," presumably *Selbsttätigkeit*. If he did not, he awkwardly expressed the same idea in the concepts of class "in itself" and class "for itself." It will not do, I think, to take away from Marx what was in fact one of his central proposals: that the philosophers have interpreted the world, but the thing is, to change it; that every step in the real movement is worth a dozen programs; that in the beginning was the act, not the word. What Marx, Trotsky, Kollontai, James and Thompson all wanted, and what Lemisch and Lynd desire as well, is that human beings who are objectively oppressed find the passion and imagination to believe that another world is possible, and act to make that vision real.

Marcus Rediker tells me that he and Peter Linebaugh have rejected the Marxist idea of "stadialism," that is, stages in historical development. And yes, anyone would wish to reject heavy-handed Victorian triumphalism, whether offered by establishment historians or by the Marx who tried to tell us which capitalist country to support in various nineteenth-century wars.

But to speak for myself, I cannot imagine hope for the future without something like the Marxist understanding of how each successive economic system develops out of the structural contradictions of the system that went before. And what I find in *The Many-Headed Hydra* is not a departure from periodization, but a magnificent portrait of the underside of the developmental stage that Marx called primitive capital accumulation.

Finally, regarding the relationship of economic interest and ideology: What, in general, is the relationship between ideas—the world turned upside down, Pope's Day, William Widger's dream, the intellectual origins of American radicalism, the antinomian visions of Atlantic proletarians—and economic interests?

Here I am much more sympathetic to Thompsonian notions, provided structural economic issues are not neglected. I have lately been transfixed by the realization that in twentieth-century revolutions, students and intellectuals often acted first, autonomously, and only thereafter did workers, by their massive intervention, make possible the transformation of protest into revolution. It was so in Russia in 1905, in Hungary in 1956, in France in 1968, in Serbia just yesterday. Indeed it was so in the movement against the Vietnam war.

And I agree that it would seem to follow that ideas have their own history. Ideas are conditioned and stimulated by economics, but they are something more than mere reflections. A metaphor that I find useful is sowing (with an "o" not an "e"). The Old Testament speaks of "precious seeds," a good way to talk about ideas. The New Testament offers the parable of the sower. Ideas are like seed cast on different kinds of soil, which will determine whether or not they grow. Some seeds fall by the wayside and are devoured by fowls. Some fall on stony soil and have "no deepness of earth." Others fall among thorns. Then and now, one cannot know in advance. One must sow regardless, hoping for good ground that will bring forth an abundant harvest.[7]

### III

My concern is not so much with the specific answers we may find to these great questions about economic interest and ideology, about class, about objective oppression and subjective desire. My hope, rather, is that we take these questions seriously as integral to the historian's craft. These are matters on which we must focus, matters to be carefully explored and discussed. We should oppose the expungement of these issues from manuscripts by publishers, or from scholarship by gatherings at Colonial Williamsburg.

To my mind Marxism remains the most useful source of structural hypotheses. Consider, for example, the period of the American Revolution. A colonial governing class was frustrated by its relationship to the British empire. Southern planters were up to their ears in debt. Leaving aside the large firms that imported from Great Britain, Northern merchants felt hemmed in by mercantilist restrictions and often took to smuggling. Colonial capitalists generally were unwilling to confine their land speculation to the area east of the Appalachian crest. The rhetoric sent forth to justify rebellion by this colonial upper class found echoes among lesser folk, who sought their own places at the welcome table. And after independence, of course there were splits among the governing class, compromises beginning with the compromise of 1787, and ultimately a second revolutionary war between the planters and their dependents on one side, and Northern capitalists, farmers and workers on the other.

Simplistic? Yes, but what if it is the simple truth? I submit that some such understanding needs to be set out as a cluster of radical hypotheses about the American Revolution to be proven or disproven as we go forward. Howard Zinn's *People's History* has sold a million copies, I suggest, because other radical historians have failed to address central questions of interpretation in all periods of American history.

In sum, I am not asking that we abandon our indispensable role as chroniclers of those who are themselves abandoned. But I think we have a responsibility to do *more than* tell the story of "the inarticulate." I believe that the historical Establishment is delighted to give us the franchise for chimney sweeps who get cancer, and seamstresses who may be burned alive when their employers lock the doors, so long as we leave to our more conservative colleagues issues of overall interpretation and prediction. And I respond that we must not—speaking of deference—consent to be thus marginalized.

My plea is for a style of work that addresses major problems of interpretation, sets up results as hypotheses for further testing, and over time accrues the components of a structural analysis: of what went on then, as in the American Revolution, and also what, in Iraq and elsewhere, is going on now.

## ENDNOTES

1  Thomas J. Humphrey, "Agrarian Rioting in Albany County, New York: Tenants, Markets and Revolution in the Hudson Valley, 1751-1801," Ph.D. dissertation, Northern Illinois University: 1996.

2  Gary B. Nash, *The Urban Crucible: Social Change, Political Consciousness, and the Origins of the American Revolution* (Cambridge: Harvard University Press, 1979).

3  "The Tenant Rising at Livingston Manor, May 1777," in Staughton Lynd, *Class Conflict, Slavery, and the United States Constitution* (Indianapolis: Bobbs-Merrill, 1967), pp. 63-77.

4  "Imported manufactures brought the menace of British economic power directly home to the New York City artisans. . . . [A]fter, as before, the Revolution, the encouragement of native manufactures seemed a part of the

struggle for independence." "A Governing Class on the Defensive," in Lynd, *Class Conflict*, p. 125. This would appear to be the conclusion of every student of artisan politics in the 1780s. At the end of the Revolutionary War "Great Britain flooded American markets with manufactured goods." Billy G. Smith, *The "Lower Sort": Philadelphia's Laboring People, 1750-1800* (Ithaca: Cornell University Press, 1990), p. 75. In Philadelphia, for example, the state tariff enacted by the Pennsylvania legislature in the mid-1780s "did not solve the problem of English competition for Philadelphia's laboring classes. By 1787 they would follow their collective interests and support the federal Constitution, which promised full and effective tariffs on a national level." Ronald Schultz, *The Republic of Labor: Philadelphia Artisans and the Politics of Class, 1720-1830* (New York: Oxford University Press, 1993), p. 99. "From the mechanics' point of view, everything hung on the single question of a tariff. . . . Ratification of the 1787 Constitution was considered by mechanics to be a logical and satisfying culmination of the Revolutionary movement, not a thermidorian reaction." Charles S. Olton, *Artisans for Independence: Philadelphia Mechanics and the American Revolution* (Syracuse: Syracuse University Press, 1975), pp. 101, 117-18.

5   Thomas J. Humphrey, "Leases and Revolution in New York's Hudson Valley," p. 2.

6   "The Webbs, Lenin, Rosa Luxemburg," in Staughton Lynd, *Living Inside Our Hope: A Steadfast Radical's Thoughts on Rebuilding the Movement* (Ithaca, NY: Cornell University Press, 1997), pp. 206-231.

7   Psalm 126, v. 6; the Gospel According to St. Matthew, ch. 13, v. 3-8; the Gospel According to St. Luke, ch. 8, v. 5-8.

S o, believing that "another world is possible," how exactly and by what strategies do we get from Here to There?

Our movement objectives in the Sixties—the vote for all adults in the South, an end to the Vietnam War—were difficult and dangerous to achieve, but the strategy for achieving them was relatively straightforward. In the South, you "went down to the court house" to try to register to vote. Everywhere in the United States, and as the war dragged on, even in Vietnam, young men organized around the idea that "we won't go."

The 1970s and succeeding decades posed more complex challenges. How do you fight a plant shutdown if the collective bargaining agreement gives the company the "management prerogative" to make unilateral investment decisions? Historically, racism has been particularly virulent among white workers. How, then, can workers create class solidarity across racial barriers? How can the movement in the United States unite in struggle with overseas insurgencies without romanticizing the governments of the Soviet Union, Cuba, Nicaragua, or Vietnam, and later counterparts? Are students or workers the group destined to be the vanguard of revolutionary change, or just possibly might it be both, and if so, how?

"Nonviolence As Solidarity" was a talk at a 1999 gathering in Minneapolis. The conference styled itself "Committing to Peace: Generation to Generation." Having immersed myself for more than twenty years in labor struggles in Youngstown and Pittsburgh, I explored what "nonviolence" might mean to striking workers who see other workers crossing the picket line to take their jobs. In this matter, as in so much else, I found inspiration in the Zapatista movement of Chiapas, Mexico.

In "Overcoming Racism" I drew on the experience of particular white workers. Alice I had interviewed truck driver George Sullivan for our book *Rank and File*. Much later we came to know George Skatzes, sentenced to death after a 1993 prison uprising, and then transferred to Ohio's first supermaximum security prison, half an hour's drive from our home. The essay appeared in *Monthly Review*, v. 51, no. 9 (February 2000), at pages 16-23.

"From Globalization to Resistance" was a speech at McMaster University in Canada in February 2001. It shows me beginning to rely on, and define, Archbishop Romero's conception of "accompaniment," and to consider the relationship of students and workers in revolutionary social change. The latter topic is further developed in "Students and Workers in the Transition to Socialism," which won an essay contest named for the late Daniel Singer and was published in *Monthly Review*, v. 54, no. 10 (March 2003), pages 32-42. Therein I argued that in Russia in 1905, Hungary in 1956, and France in 1968, we see the same pattern: students acted first, workers then massively intervened in support.

The title of "Edward Thompson's Warrens" may seem mysterious. Warrens? Don't they have something to do with rabbits? Warrens, I try to show, are Thompson's metaphor for local working-class institutions that proliferate under the surface of capitalist society and prepare the way for something new and better. This essay was originally published in the Canadian journal *Labour/Le Travail*, no. 50 (Fall 2002), pages 175-186, and appears with the permission of that journal.

In 2005 I was privileged to make the keynote address to a gathering in Chicago of the Industrial Workers of the World, or IWW. Celebrating one hundred years of IWW struggle, I paid homage to the departed workers from whom I had learned whatever I may know about the working class: John Sargent, John Barbero, Ed Mann, Stan Weir, and Marty Glaberman. All of us, I concluded, must try to be on the picket line where "you'll find Joe Hill." The IWW newspaper, *The Industrial Worker*, printed my remarks in v. 102, no. 7 (July-August 2005).

My subject will be movements since the Sixties that have forced those of us immersed in the traditional culture of nonviolence to confront the reality of class. I shall examine movements of poor and working people in which individual commitment to nonviolence as a matter of principle is rare and in which defensive violence has historically been honored and accepted, namely, the rank-and-file labor movement and the resistance movement inside prisons. I will suggest that these movements require us to deepen our understanding of nonviolence by viewing it as the practice of solidarity. And in closing I shall glance at the movement of Mayan resistance in Chiapas, Mexico, which appears to have many of the same characteristics.

### THE LABOR MOVEMENT

From a distance, one might suppose that the labor movement is inherently nonviolent. It is a movement seemingly defined by nonviolent direct action: by millions of workers laying down their tools, folding their arms, withdrawing their labor. Think of the P-9 strike; the strike at International Paper in Jay, Maine; the Staley lockout; the Detroit newspaper strike. Clearly labor nonviolence is as American as coffee and doughnuts.

But so is labor violence. Anyone who has spent time on a picket line knows that when strike replacements—"scabs"—appear at the plant gate, they are likely to be received with cries of "get out the baseball bats." Indeed the labor history of the United States is sometimes said to have been the most violent in the world.

There have been two especially dramatic examples of labor nonviolence in the past thirty years. They are the Farm Workers movement, led by César Chávez, and the 1989 strike against the Pittston Coal Company.

According to Marshall Ganz, who was present, Chávez introduced the idea of nonviolence at a meeting held at Our Lady of Guadalupe

Hall in Delano, California on September 16, 1965, the anniversary of Mexican Independence Day. Chávez "put out three conditions. One was nonviolence. That was a new thing. Nobody had ever heard of that before. It was a condition that people had to accept, or the Farm Workers would not lead the strike."

In the case of the Pittston strike it appears that Cecil Roberts, then vice president of the United Mine Workers, is an admirer of Martin Luther King. Roberts quoted Dr. King at length, from memory, at strike rallies. When UMW organizers were jailed, Roberts is reputed to have said: "Good, now you will have time to read"—and provided copies of *Parting the Waters,* the massive first volume of the King biography by Taylor Branch. Appalachian men dressed in camouflage uniforms left over from military service sat down in front of company trucks, together with their families, and were hauled away to jail. When one hundred striking miners occupied Pittston's Moss 3 coal preparation plant, they were instructed that if fired upon, they should kneel and wait for further orders. Their wives and relatives surrounded the occupied facility in a giant protective circle memorably described by Jim Sessions, who was inside, and his wife Fran Ansley. All this in a part of our country where young men seem to learn to shoot at or before the time they learn to walk.

How shall we understand the curious mixture of violence and non-violence in the labor movement of the United States? One approach is psychological. When workers opt for violence some blame it on the supposed macho personality of the white working-class male. Nonviolence, it is suggested, is a wimpy middle-class affectation sought to be imposed from the outside on naturally violent hairy-chested he-men on the picket line.

I propose a different analysis. The practice of nonviolent solidarity, I suggest, has been deliberately targeted and repressed by the trade union bureaucracy, the United States Congress, and the courts. We should blame working-class violence not so much on the personality structure of blue-collar males as on the upper-middle-class males in three-piece suits who have deliberately left outside the law's protection the characteristic forms of working-class nonviolence. We should also blame the trade union bureaucrats who, from the very first collective bargaining agreements with U. S. Steel and General Motors, made the no-strike clause a standard part of the typical CIO contract and thereby made union representatives in effect cops for the boss.

The law and the typical labor contract make successful nonviolent action by working people incredibly difficult. The so-called secondary boycott, that is, refusal to do business with the companies that do business with your employer, is outlawed. Sympathy strikes [that is, action by one group of workers in support of action by other workers of the same employer] are illegal: it is unlawful to act on the belief that an injury to one is an injury to all, and, with rare exceptions, you are legally protected in striking only when the strike is in your immediate economic self-interest and takes place, predictably, at the expiration of your contract. The National Labor Relations Act purports to protect "concerted activity for mutual aid or protection," but the slowdown—concerted direct action on the shop floor, without leaving the workplace—is illegal. Why? Harvard labor law professor Archibald Cox once confessed that if the slowdown were legally protected it would give workers too much power.

Similarly, while the text of the National Labor Relations Act directs that the law should be interpreted so as to protect the right to strike, within five years of the passage of the NLRA the Supreme Court of the United States held that it was lawful for an employer to hire permanent replacements during a strike. State courts, acting on the basis of visceral class interest, routinely enjoin mass picketing as a threat to the peace. Again the stage is set for working-class violence. A handful of strikers are expected to watch passively as carloads of strike replacements are escorted by the police into their place of work, to labor at their machines or desks, and take bread from the mouths of their children. When workers decline such institutionally choreographed masochism, they are discharged by their employer and hustled off to jail by the authorities. They may also be denigrated by middle-class supporters as "impatient" and "impulsive" persons, who "ill-advisedly" took matters into their own hands, rather than trusting their lawyers to produce victory through the Labor Board and the courts.

All these prohibitions cut off possibilities of nonviolent action and channel workers toward a choice between violence and surrender. Given such constraints, how was it possible to be nonviolent at Delano and Moss 3? Farm workers successfully boycotted not just products, California grapes and wine, but the stores that sold them. They could engage in such secondary activity only because they were *not* covered by—were outside the jurisdiction of—the supposed protections of the National Labor Relations Act. Typically, as in the PATCO strike, union representatives fearful for their treasuries counsel obedience to the orders of the judge. Pittston miners were successful only because they persevered in the face of hundreds of thousands of dollars in contempt fines imposed for disobeying court injunctions.

To the many young people who are considering a commitment to the labor movement I want to say: Don't feel that this commitment requires you to stop being yourself. The moral authority of the labor movement—the way in which the labor movement *is* the seed of a new society within the shell of the old—has to do with its practice of solidarity, with the fact that even labor bureaucrats sign their letters "fraternally yours," with the words of the song that even conservative trade unions still consider to be their anthem. Be fraternal. Build solidarity. Practice nonviolence.

Fraternity, solidarity, and nonviolence are needed, first of all, to keep our own movement together. By and large, the social change organizations in which I have taken part have not been destroyed by COINTELPRO or other government repression: they have destroyed themselves. The single most important source of the Left's failure to change this society more fundamentally during the second half of the twentieth century has been our inability to practice comradeship sufficiently to keep our own organizations in being. SNCC, SDS, and the FSLN in Nicaragua were all founded in or about 1961. SNCC and SDS failed to make it through the Sixties. The FSLN, despite deep internal divisions, held together and made a revolution in 1979.

The same problem exists in labor organizations. Over the past twenty-five years I have been closely associated with three local unions in which reformers came to power: Local 1397, United Steelworkers of America, at the Homestead Works near Pittsburgh; Steelworkers Local 1462 at the Brier Hill Works in Youngstown; and Local 377 of the Teamsters, also in Youngstown. In all three instances, the reform cause came to grief because within a year or two of their election success, different members of the reform slate were no longer speaking to one another.

So don't tell me that the tendency for reform organizations to splinter and disintegrate is essentially middle-class. It affects working-class organizations, also. Patience, direct speaking (as opposed to gossip), empathy for the other person's point of view, the willingness to compromise, are all needed just as much in unions as in any other kind of organization for social change.

Finally, let me push the logic of nonviolence two steps further: let me talk about scabs and cops. Everyone knows Jack London's description of the scab as the lowest form of organism to crawl on its belly through the mud and slime. But scabs are workers, too. I know a local union president in Youngstown who led a bitter eleven-month strike at a Buick dealership. Bill would not settle without the guarantee of a union shop, but when he finally got it most of the strikers had long since retired or gone on to other jobs. Bill, when he went back to work, found himself president of a union of former scabs. To the astonishment of the boss he stuck up for these former scabs when the company tried to fire them. The erstwhile scabs were duly impressed and began to attend union meetings. Several months later, Bill confessed that the local union after the strike was stronger than it had been before it.

In my opinion, the same practice of solidarity recommends itself when dealing with police officers and prison guards. There is a habit lingering from the late Sixties of calling such persons "pigs." To do so not only offends the values to which we should attest, but does not make sense strategically. Look at it this way. The government will always have more weapons than we can ever hope to possess. Whatever may be our beliefs about violence and nonviolence, the only practical way for a people's movement to succeed is if the human beings carrying guns for the government come over to our side, or at least refuse to use those guns against us. So it was in the Russian Revolution of February 1917, when women demonstrating on the streets of Petrograd confronted soldiers on horseback, the dreaded Cossacks. The women appealed to the mounted soldiers. They said that the Cossacks were no different from the women's husbands, brothers, sons. "We need bread," the women said. "We need peace. So do you." In the most famous such confrontation, the Cossacks were three times ordered to ride the women down, and three times refused. And the Czar fell.

We have been close to a moment of this kind in Youngstown. In winter 1979-1980, U. S. Steel announced the closing of all its Youngstown facilities and angry workers occupied the company's administration building. The police called out to surround the building were their high-school classmates. We did not come to the point of discovering whether they would have followed orders to bust heads. I don't believe they would have. Again in spring 1997, management at the largest area employer—a Delphi Packard plant that makes parts for General Motors—derailed local negotiations when it insisted on the right to move equipment to Mexico at will. The union walked. As I pursued strike support tasks the next morning I listened to local radio talk shows. The whole Mahoning Valley, it seemed, understood what was at stake. Had the walkout lasted, I believe there might have been a local general strike, like those of the early 1930s in Minneapolis and elsewhere. But the company feared a repetition of a strike at two brake plants in Dayton, Ohio a year earlier that had shut down GM assembly plants worldwide. [Delphi] settled in twenty-four hours. In that short space of time, the police brought coffee and firewood to the picket line. I personally heard a honk come from a police car as it drove past striking workers.

In summary: We should honor the nonviolent solidarity that has been close to the heart and soul of the historic labor movement, accompany those workers who seek to practice it, and struggle to exemplify it ourselves. We should avoid cheap condemnation of workers who turn to violence as the only way they see to have a chance to win. And we should preserve the hope that even scabs and cops will recognize themselves as fellow workers and join us at the welcome table.

### RESISTANCE IN PRISONS

In the prison world, too, nonviolence makes itself known in the *practice of solidarity*. We who come from the traditional culture of nonviolence have a unique way of understanding this, I believe. During World War II a number of pacifists were imprisoned for opposing the war and refusing to cooperate with the conscription system. They included David Dellinger (who was imprisoned twice), Bayard Rustin, Jim Peck, and Larry Gara. These heroic resisters engaged in nonviolent civil disobedience against racial segregation and other abusive prison practices, such as censorship of mail. They fasted for weeks at a time. In doing so, they won the respect and admiration of their fellow prisoners notwithstanding the fact that these prisoners were not pacifists, often differed passionately with their pacifist colleagues about the war, and in general, came out of a different world. When pacifists at Danbury walked across the yard and into the chow hall after a fast that brought about the first desegregation of dining facilities at a federal prison, prisoners erupted in applause. At Lewisburg, Dave Dellinger received the highest honor the prison population could bestow: he was invited to eat at the murderers' table.

This immensely important experience in the history of nonviolence in the United States still teaches us how solidarity can be built on the basis of practice, of action that is in the common interest, rather than on the basis of shared ideas.

In the traditional culture of nonviolence, talk usually precedes action. The war resister fills out an application for Conscientious Objector status before refusing induction. Brian Willson wrote many position statements before sitting down on the track where a munitions train cut off his legs. Practice follows principle, and practitioners of the traditional culture of nonviolence are careful to articulate why the action they undertake expresses concepts they have previously come to affirm.

In the world of poor and working-class resistance, on the other hand, action often comes before talk, and may be in apparent contradiction to words that the actor has used, or even continues to use in the midst of action. The experience of struggle gives rise to new understandings that may be put into words much later or never put into words at all. Let me give an example.

[*Here the talk narrated the experience of black and white prisoners at the Southern Ohio Correctional Facility in Lucasville, Ohio when they joined forces during an 11-day uprising in April 1993. The talk focused on George Skatzes, a Caucasian who at the time belonged to the Aryan Brotherhood. See the next essay, "Overcoming Racism."*]

You see the point. The things that Skatzes *did*, in calming racial antagonisms, in working cooperatively with blacks, in characterizing the rebellion publicly as the work of "one strong unit," both black and white, hardly expressed the world view of the Aryan Brotherhood. In part Skatzes' actions expressed his personal decency, in part they responded to a practical situation that called for racial cooperation. Experience ran ahead of ideology. Actions spoke louder than organizational labels.

As in the case of the labor movement, the authorities make the practice of nonviolence in prison extremely difficult. The Supreme Court of the United States has declared that prisoners do not have a First Amendment right to form labor unions. The rights to associate, to petition, to be free of warrantless searches, and to receive meaningful due process, are barely alive behind bars. In an Oberlin College honors thesis, Daniel Burton-Rose argues that prison authorities responded to the spread of prisoner unions in the 1970s by inventing the super-max: that is, a prison in which all prisoners are locked in single cells at least 23 hours a day. In Youngstown, where the first Ohio supermax opened in 1998, whenever a prisoner leaves his cell he is shackled and escorted by at least two guards. During visits the prisoner's hands are painfully re-strained by an immobile "black box." Prisoners are forbidden congregate worship and other group activities. There have been two suicides. That any group impulse, any solidarity should arise in such a setting invites wonder. And yet my wife and I frequently receive letters from a prisoner concerned about the mistreatment of another prisoner. And many pris-oners sign their letters, "In the struggle," or, "Stay strong."

I don't wish to be understood as devaluing in any way the contribu-tion that the traditional culture of nonviolence can make to prison resis-tance. In 1997, there was an effort to organize a statewide prison strike in Ohio. The leading prisoner advocacy group in the state wrote a letter to all the wardens condemning the impending strike. The wardens posted the letter and, not surprisingly, the strike was less successful than it might have been. Thereafter, an affirmation of belief in nonviolent direct action was widely circulated in Ohio prisons and signed by many leaders of outside support groups. A new support group controlled by prisoners and former prisoners, the Prisoner Advocacy Network-Ohio, has explicitly declared its belief in nonviolent direct action. My concern is not to set up solidarity and nonviolence as opposite poles, between which a prisoner must choose, but rather, to point to the tangled, ideologically ambiguous path on which convicts may travel from the law of each one for himself to the practice of solidarity, and from there, to nonviolent direct action, and to ask respect for all stages in that journey.

### INSTEAD OF A CONCLUSION, CHIAPAS

In place of a conclusion, I want to tell you quickly about a recent trip Alice and I made to Chiapas, Mexico and to share my impression that there, too, the practice of solidarity is interwoven with the practice of nonviolence.

We talked with a woman who for years has worked with indigenous communities in the area. She will be publishing a book of interviews with women entitled "Voices from Mayan Communities in Rebellion in Chiapas." She told us:

In the 1960s, 1970s, and 1980s, three historical forces prepared the way for Zapatismo.

The first was Mayan tradition, in which "everything is done through assemblies."

The second was the Mexican Revolution of 1917. The Mexican Revolution declared a right to land. No one was supposed to own more than a certain amount. At least on paper, poor people were able to form associations called *"ejidos"* and to acquire land.

The third historical force was Vatican II and Catholic liberation theology. Base communities were formed: *Mayan* base communities in which there was a "marriage of traditions." We saw the marriage of traditions in a Catholic church we visited in a village called Chamula. There was no priest. Pine needles were strewn on the floor. Here and there, kneeling around a blanket, villagers chanted Mayan prayers before lighted candles.

The key demand that emerged from this confluence of traditions was for autonomy, that is, self-administration by the indigenous according to traditional law, *"uso de costumbre."* When Marxists showed up in Chiapas in the mid-1980s a movement formed by these forces was already in being. The movement influenced the Marxists, we were told, more than the Marxists influenced the movement.

The way it works in an individual village is as follows. The village may be wholly "autonomous" (the word the Zapatistas use to describe themselves) or it may have some autonomous families, and some families loyal to the governing political party, the PRI. The government tries to win people to the PRI by giving them things.

In the assembly of the autonomous, trusted individuals are asked to perform certain full-time functions: as storekeeper, or as a worker in a health clinic or a school. These persons "lead by obeying." Someone else cultivates their corn fields so that they can perform their new tasks. The store, the clinic, and the school serve all the families in the village, even those that are pro-PRI.

Outside groups can assist the villagers in their self-organization. The electrical workers' union has given workshops on how to tap into (steal from) the national electricity grid. The PRI says, "Vote for us and we'll bring electricity to your village." The Zapatistas respond, "We'll show you how to get electricity right now."

The Zapatista communities make joint decisions by a representative process. Each local assembly of the "autonomous"—whether it be all or some of the families in a particular village—is open to persons above a certain age. Each such assembly comes to a consensus and sends delegates to the next higher level. The delegates are bound to be spokespersons for the decisions of the local assemblies they represent.

It is an honor to be chosen as a representative, just as it is an honor to be chosen as a storekeeper or teacher. Consensus is sought at every level. A "straw vote" may be taken, only to give participants a sense of how widely particular outcomes are desired.

In the opinion of this woman, the Zapatista movement does not resemble other guerrilla movements. The movement it most resembles is the civil rights movement in the United States in the 1960s.

A second fascinating encounter was with a young man who works for an organization called Enlace ("links"). The group seeks to coordinate the desire of outside groups to be of assistance with the needs and desires of the autonomous communities. It does not tell the autonomous communities what they should study, or what development projects they should pursue. It takes direction from the communities themselves.

Sitting in the office of this organization in San Cristóbal de las Casas, I was indeed reminded of the COFO office in Jackson, Mississippi in 1964. Large bundles and boxes were stacked against the walls. People were constantly coming in and going out.

A third of the Mexican army—70,000 soldiers—is in Chiapas. Paramilitary forces are recruited from the villages to assault other indigenous people. There are 50,000 refugees. As was true in Nicaragua, teachers and workers in health clinics are particular targets.

We asked, Would it end as in Nicaragua? Would people become so weary of contra warfare that they would vote for whomever they thought might bring an end to hostilities?

The young man responded that a difference between Chiapas and Nicaragua was that the Zapatistas do not want power. Zapatista rifles were only a "symbol," he went on. (He made a motion with his hands to show a gun being loaded by tamping a charge down the barrel with a ramrod, as in an old single-shot musket.)

Likewise the ski masks worn by the Zapatistas recognize that for 500 years the indigenous have not had faces. "When we are perceived as individuals then we'll take off the masks," our friend finished.

A last conversation in Chiapas was with persons familiar with the current standoff at Amadór. That is the community on the western edge of the Lacondón jungle where the government is seeking to build a highway into the heart of the autonomous world. Construction has been stopped by a nonviolent "*cordón*" (picket line) of women. Since many of the soldiers are indigenous, the women appeal to them to recognize their true interests. The government seeks to prevent this dialogue by playing music through loud speakers. Every day the women, with babies on their backs, confront the soldiers in their riot gear.

I think the Farm Workers and the Pittston miners, George Skatzes, and the women of Amadór, Chiapas, are all telling us the same thing. The history of nonviolence is not over. It is just beginning.

Recently there has been a great deal of discussion about the racism of white workers. Unfortunately, little has been said or written about how white working-class racism can be overcome. In this essay, I examine a prison uprising in which black and white convicts struggled with racism and overcame it to a surprising degree.

### GEORGE SKATZES AND THE LUCASVILLE REBELLION
From April 11 to 21, 1993, what appears to have been the longest prison rebellion in United States history [during which lives were lost] took place at the maximum security prison in Lucasville, in southern Ohio.[1] More than 400 prisoners were involved. Nine prisoners and a guard were killed. After a negotiated surrender, five prisoners in the rebellion were sentenced to death.

The single most remarkable thing about the Lucasville rebellion is that white and black prisoners formed a common front against the authorities. When the State Highway Patrol came into the occupied cell block after the surrender they found slogans written on the walls of the corridor and in the gymnasium that read: "Convict unity," "Convict race," "Black and whites together," "Blacks and whites, whites and blacks, unity," "Whites and blacks together," "Black and white unity."

The five prisoners from the rebellion on death row—the Lucasville Five—are a microcosm of the rebellion's united front. Three are black, two are white. Two of the blacks are Sunni Muslims. Both of the whites were, at the time of the rebellion, members of the Aryan Brotherhood.

My wife and I know the Lucasville Five and are assisting with the appeal of one of the white men, who has since repented his affiliation with the Aryan Brotherhood. What we have learned should give pause to anyone inclined to dismiss all members of a group like the Aryan Brotherhood as incurably racist. Let me give you a synopsis of the childhood of George Skatzes (pronounced "skates"), his experiences during the 1993 rebellion, and the way that his actions ran out ahead of his organizational affiliation and political vocabulary.

In Marion, Ohio, where George grew up, whites lived on one side of the tracks and blacks on the other. George and his sister, Jackie, were the children of their mother's third marriage. Their parents were divorced when George was an infant and he grew up in his mother's home, where a succession of her boyfriends passed through. The house was in perpetual disorder; George and Jackie were embarrassed by the clothes they wore to school and never invited school friends to their house. George was often beaten by his mother or one of his two older stepbrothers. When he became an adult, he often tried to help his mother, once working overtime for five weeks and saving all his pay to buy her a freezer and refrigerator. But the gift was unappreciated.

George became aware that the neighbors considered his family to be "white trash." He felt more welcome on the black side of town than by the people next door. One of his best friends was the child of an interracial couple. "I might as well have been biracial myself," he recalls.

How could a person with these views have joined the Aryan Brotherhood at Lucasville? According to George, it was not because of an attitude of racial superiority. "You won't find anyone at Lucasville I judged because of the color of his skin," he insists, and the testimony of many black prisoners, both at trial and in private conversation with my wife and myself, supports this. "One race should not have to die for another to live," George Skatzes says. "We are all people."

Difficult as it may be for someone outside the walls to understand, George Skatzes states that he joined the Aryan Brotherhood because he perceived whites at Lucasville as a minority who needed to band together for self-protection. A majority of prisoners were black. The deputy warden, the warden, and the head of the statewide Department of Rehabilitation and Correction were black as well. On the one hand, all prisoners at Lucasville were oppressed. Conditions in the cell block used for administrative segregation were such that a petition was sent to Amnesty International and several prisoners cut off their pinky fingers and mailed them to the federal government. On the other hand, in Skatzes' experience, white prisoners like himself were punished for conduct that was condoned when committed by blacks.

Still insistent that these were the facts, Skatzes now says that joining the Aryan Brotherhood was "the biggest mistake of my life." In the course of responding to the day-by-day events of the rebellion, he found himself speaking not for white prisoners or for those white prisoners who belonged to the Aryan Brotherhood, but for the entire inmate body.

The disturbance at Lucasville was triggered by an attempt to force prisoners to submit to tuberculosis testing, by means of a substance containing alcohol injected under the skin. A number of Muslims said that receiving the injection was contrary to their religious beliefs, and suggested alternative means of testing. The warden responded that he was running the prison. He made plans to lock down the prison on the day after Easter and, if necessary, to force all prisoners to be injected. These plans became common knowledge. Accordingly, on the afternoon of Easter Sunday, prisoners returning from recreation on the yard overpowered a number of guards and took them hostage, occupying the L block of the prison.

During the next several hours, black prisoners killed five white prisoners believed to be snitches. A race war, like the one during the Santa Fe prison riot a few years earlier, seemed imminent.

At this point, two Muslims approached George Skatzes. George had not taken part in planning the rebellion. He celled in L block and had stayed there when the riot began, in order to protect his property and look after his friends. The black men who spoke to Skatzes were aware that, as a physically imposing older convict (in his late forties), "Big George" had often been asked to mediate disputes among prisoners. Siddique Abdullah Hasan and Cecil Allen told Skatzes that whites and blacks had gathered on different sides of the gymnasium and the atmosphere was very tense. They asked "Big George" to help them ensure that the protest would be directed against the prison administration, their common oppressor.

Skatzes agreed. He went to the gym and spoke to both the blacks and whites. He put his arm around the shoulders of a black man and said, "If they come in here, they're going to kill us no matter what color we are." He appealed to members of each group to mix with members of the other group.

The next day, April 12, George Skatzes (with a megaphone) and Cecil Allen (carrying a huge white flag of truce) went out on the yard to try to start negotiations. On Tuesday, Wednesday, and Thursday, April 13 through 15, Skatzes was the principal telephone negotiator for the prisoners. He took part in meetings of a leadership council representing the three main organized groups in L block: the Muslims, members of the Aryan Brotherhood (ABs), and the Black Gangster Disciples. On the afternoon and evening of Thursday, April 15, he negotiated the release of a hostage guard who was experiencing extreme emotional trauma, accompanied Officer Clark into the yard, and released him to the authorities. He made a radio address in which he said: "We are a unit here. They try to make this a racial issue [but] it is not a racial issue. Black and white have joined hands [at Lucasville] and have become one strong unit."

You see the point. The things that Skatzes *did*, in calming racial antagonisms, in working cooperatively with blacks, in characterizing the rebellion publicly as the work of "one strong unit," both black and white, hardly expressed the world view of the Aryan Brotherhood. In part, Skatzes' actions expressed his personal decency; they also responded to a practical situation that called for racial cooperation. Experience ran ahead of ideology. Actions spoke louder than organizational labels.

George Skatzes and the black prisoners among the Lucasville Five stand in solidarity publicly and struggle privately to understand each other. During a fast that they undertook together, their list of demands, drafted by one of the blacks in the group, began with a concern for proper medical treatment for Skatzes. At the super-maximum-security prison in Youngstown where the Five are now housed, a number of prisoners began another fast. After about a week, only Skatzes and Siddique Abdullah Hasan were still going without food. The prison approached each one with assurances that their complaints would be addressed. Each refused to break his fast until told directly by the other that he was ready to eat again. Hasan wrote to me: "I chose to stay on the fast to let them know that I was down with George's struggle, too, and I would not sit quiet and allow the system to mess over him. . . . [T]hey got the message and know that we are one."

## From Prison Resistance to Class Struggle

How, if at all, can this experience of prisoners overcoming racism be extrapolated? What is the relationship of prison resistance to the wider movement for social change?

A good deal of the recent writing about racism calls on white prisoners to give up "white-skin privilege" voluntarily in order to become legitimate participants in the class struggle. Such a voluntaristic approach to racism is unsatisfactory for exactly the same reason that Marx and Engels found Utopian Socialism to be inadequate. Workers do not become socialists because agitators have gone house to house preaching the virtues of common ownership. Workers become socialists in action, through experience. Thus, Eugene Debs first recognized the need for the broadest possible unity of the working class in economic struggle and founded the American Railway Union to take the place of the separate unions of the railway crafts. Then, after the Pullman strike, Debs came to understand that in a capitalist society, government will always intervene in the economic class struggle on behalf of the capitalist class, and helped to organize the Socialist Party.

Racism, too, will be transformed through experience and struggle. We should anticipate that the objective contradictions of capitalism will again and again call on workers somehow to set aside their antagonisms toward one another, so that they can effectively act together against the common oppressor. As workers' *actions* change in response to the need for a solidarity in which the survival of each depends on the survival of all, *attitudes* will change also.

There are at least two obvious differences between resistance in prisons and forms of struggle outside the walls. First, a prison is a total environment black and white workers in the larger society typically leave behind the integrated workplace setting when they punch out, returning to segregated living situations in the community. Inside a prison, blacks and whites must survive in one another's company twenty-four hours a day.

Second, anything good inside a prison must ordinarily be brought about by the prisoners themselves, from below, through self-organization. In this respect, prisons differ from the military. Like prisons, the military is a total institution, but in the military, desirable social change can come from above, and *did* come from above, when the Armed Forces were integrated after the Second World War.

I know another George—George Sullivan, a truck driver from Gary, Indiana—whose experience illustrates the effectiveness of the equal status contact imposed from above in the Armed Forces. George Sullivan grew up in southern Illinois, the same racist setting recalled by David Roediger in the opening pages of *The Wages of Whiteness*.[2] George Sullivan describes the racism he absorbed as a child:

> There never was any question in my mind that niggers weren't any good. I knew that, but it didn't necessarily mean they were bad people because everyone knew that a nigger's a coward and he won't cause you any trouble. There weren't any around where I lived.
>
> One did come to the house one time, scared me to death. I saw him at the door, there he was, and I didn't know what to do. Any time we would be doing something wrong, one of the comments my mother would make was, "I'll have some big nigger come and get you if you don't stop that." So I went to the door and there was this big nigger. I just knew that he had come after me. But that's the only association I had. I wasn't taught to hate them. It was like the feeling about animals. Their place is not in the house or it's not where you are. Animals live in the woods. Niggers live somewhere else.[3]

George Sullivan's relationship with blacks changed when he went into the military. The new policy of integration had just gone into effect. George reported to a barracks where he found that he was the only white.

After informing the sergeant that there had been a mistake, he was told, "No, we've been having some problems about not integrating enough. As new white guys come on the base they're going to be put in there. You just happen to be the first." Then this happened:

> I was a meat-cutter and I got a bit careless. I cut three or four of my fingers. I had them all bandaged up. I had just been promoted to sergeant but I still had my corporal stripes. I was sitting out in front of the barracks and the sergeant came by and he said, "Sullivan, get your stripes on." "I can't sew with one hand," I said, "and I don't have any money to take them over to the PX." He said, "You'll have stripes on your uniform by tomorrow or we'll take the stripes away from you."

> I was sitting there by myself just wondering what to do. One of the guys in the barracks who'd heard it, he came out and said, "Have you already got your stripes?" I said, "Yeah, I bought them already." He said, "Well, if you'll go get them I'll sew them on for you." So that was the first thing that really broke the ice. He sat and sewed those stripes on my uniform while we got to know each other.[4]

Neither George Skatzes nor George Sullivan were, or are, ideological radicals. But they are white workers who have substantially overcome the racism that surrounded them. Both learned through their experience to deal with people as individuals rather than to judge them by the color of their skin.

We need a synthesis of the pressure for social change illustrated by the military policy of integration, with working-class self-emancipation. Prison resistance begins to suggest such a synthesis. There, the common need to survive creates the pressure to cooperate. But prison administrators will not organize that cooperation from above. In fact, prison administrators do all that they can to forbid and break up self-organization by prisoners. Therefore, black and white prisoners must depend on themselves to build solidarity with each other.

In the 1960s and early 1970s, the self-organized protest movement of blacks created a model for students, women, workers, and eventually, soldiers. In the same way, the self-organized resistance of black and white prisoners can become a model for the rest of us in overcoming racism. Life will continue to ask of working people that they find their way to solidarity. Surely, there are sufficient instances of deep attitudinal change on the part of white workers to persuade us that a multi-ethnic class consciousness is not only necessary, but also possible.

### ENDNOTES

1    I have written about the Lucasville rebellion in "Black and White and Dead All Over: The Lucasville Insurrection," *Race Traitor*, no. 8 (Winter 1998); "Lessons from Lucasville," *The Catholic Worker*, vol. LXV, no. 7 (December 1998); "The Lucasville Trials," *Prison Legal News*, vol. 10, no. 6 (June 1999). I have also written a docudrama entitled "Big George," a play about the rebellion in two acts and twelve scenes, in which the dialogue is drawn entirely from words actually spoken.

2    David R. Roediger, *The Wages of Whiteness: Race and the Making of the American Working Class* (London: Verso, 1991), pp. 3-5.

3    George Sullivan, "Working for Survival," in *Rank and File: Personal Histories by Working-Class Organizers* (New York: Monthly Review Press, 1998), p. 202.

4    *Ibid.*, pp. 202-203.

A visitor from the imperialist heartland should be hesitant to pontificate about globalization and resistance.

In so many ways, Canada is a more civilized and a more developed society than the United States. In the 1960s, young men subject to the draft or already members of the Armed Forces of the United States fled to Canada. When my passport was taken away for traveling to Hanoi during wartime, I made a point of visiting Canada, for which a passport was not required. I hope that my words on those occasions may have added something to your resolve to provide sanctuary to war resisters from the States. In that same decade, both of my older children attended the Everdale Place, an experimental school not too distant from where we meet tonight. Later, your public health system gave heart not only to health care advocates in the States, but also to those of us who as Legal Services lawyers or Headstart teachers were trying to provide a public service administered in a decentralized and democratic manner. Less than two months ago, Canada's Finance Minister announced a moratorium on $700 million of the $1.1 billion debt owed to Canada by heavily indebted poor countries, so that those countries could spend that money "on urgent social priorities such as health care, education and poverty reduction." You have, I believe, a far more comprehensive and respectful approach to the self-determination of indigenous peoples than do we in the States. And you have abolished the death penalty.

My deepest sense of obligation is to individual comrades like Margaret Keith and Jim Brophy in their industrial health and safety work, or to Bruce Allen, who under his nom de web Praxis 1871 makes me sensitive to things I need to know about not only in Canada, but in the States as well, and indeed around the world.

For all of the foregoing, thank you, Canada.

At the same time, I believe you will join me in recognizing that Canada is still a capitalist economy, deeply enmeshed in the globalization that is our subject tonight. From this standpoint you in Canada and we in the United States are all in the same soup, or perhaps more precisely, all under the treads of the same neo-liberal juggernaut. Because of this common predicament that we share I venture to share some thoughts about globalization and resistance.

What should be the principles of our common resistance to globalization?

I am going to suggest certain principles, but I am concerned that the moment I do so, we will become lost in a discussion of labels. So let me begin in a different way by holding up as a model or mantra the activity of the resistance movement in the third society subject to NAFTA—and of course, more grievously subject to it than either the United States or Canada—namely, Mexico.

The Zapatista movement in Chiapas seems to me extraordinary in at least the following ways:

Without participating in electoral politics, the Zapatistas have ended seventy-one years of uninterrupted government by the Institutional Revolutionary Party, or PRI. How have they done this? One critical component is a vast effort at popular education. Mayan peasants, who had never before left their native villages, traveled all over Mexico meeting with popular organizations such as the rebelling students at the national university.

Of course the Zapatistas are not nonviolent in any traditional sense. But neither are they a traditional Latin American guerrilla movement. Without giving up either their arms or the principle of armed struggle, they have carried on for the last five years an essentially nonviolent resistance. For example, the Mexican government has sought to build roads into the Lacondón jungle that is the Zapatista stronghold. The government claimed that this was to help farmers get their produce to market. The real reason, obviously, was to be able to move soldiers and military gear into the area. At the western edge of the jungle is a village named Amadór. During the summer and fall of 1999, the soldiers seeking to build the road were met each day by a *cordón* (a picket line) of women from Amadór. Since many of the soldiers were indigenous, the women appealed to them to recognize their true interests and to put down their weapons. To prevent this dialogue the government played music through loud speakers. I lost track of this encounter for about a year. Then I noticed that after Vicente Fox became president, he announced the abandonment of a number of military bases in Chiapas. The first base to be abandoned was at Amadór.

I shall attempt to generalize from Zapatista reality by proposing the following principles:

1. *In resisting globalization, workers should rely on their own self-*

*activity expressed through organizations at the base that they themselves create and control.*

*2. We should seek to win over or neutralize the armed forces.*

*3. We need to build more than organizations, more even than a movement: we need to build a community of struggle.*

In offering these words as guiding principles, I once again emphasize that they are only words, and plead with you not to fetishize these words and not to engage in what the philosopher Alfred North Whitehead, following Marx, called the "misplaced concreteness" of mistaking words for things.

Finally by way of introduction, of course I understand that these principles will only take on life as the contradictions of capitalism provide opportunities for social transformation. Just since the first of the year, world over-capacity in the production of steel and automobiles has resulted in two steel company bankruptcies in Youngstown, and last Tuesday's announcement by Daimler Chrysler that it will halt promised renovation of its Windsor truck assembly plant and lay off an entire shift on July 1. The issue is not whether there will be economic instability. There will be. The issue is whether we, the movement for change, will be ready to do something with it.

## 1. SELF-ACTIVITY

First, then, *self-activity*. The closest equivalent in a language other than English I have thus far found is the Russian word *samodeyatelnost*, used by Trotsky in his youthful critique of Leninist centralism, and by Alexandra Kollontai, who used the term in the early years of the Bolshevik Revolution on behalf of the emerging women's movement and the Workers' Opposition. The closest synonym in English to "self-activity" is, perhaps, "participatory democracy." But there are others: government from below, self-organization. Again, it is not the words but the thing that matters.

I champion the idea of self-activity in contrast to the practice of national, bureaucratic, top-down trade unions. National trade unions, as they exist in the United States and Canada; as they existed in Great Britain, Germany, and elsewhere in Europe in the early twentieth century; as they have existed anywhere in the capitalist world and will exist anywhere in the globalized economy, are inherently opposed to the practice of self-activity by rank-and-file workers. This is true regardless of what persons may hold the top offices in those unions. The first principle of a resistance movement against globalization must be not to concentrate energy on campaigns for national union office, any more than we make campaigns for national political office our first priority. Of course it makes a difference who wins these campaigns. That doesn't mean we should spend our time working in them. Like the Zapatistas, we should influence national electoral campaigns by our non-electoral self-activity at the base.

Why is it that national trade unions will never be able to play a leading role in our movement to get rid of capitalism and substitute something better for it? Because national trade unions are irrevocably linked to capitalism. They will inevitably find ways to make their peace with profit-making corporations. They will always stop short of fundamental social transformation. They are and will remain Social Democratic, meaning, their historical project is reform not revolution, their nature is to try to make capitalism livable. This is a necessary project but, as Rosa Luxemburg said, it is a labor of Sisyphus: it could go on forever and never really change the system.

It may be helpful in this connection to explode certain historical myths about particular labor leaders. As a guest in your country, I shall avoid criticism of Canadian labor leaders, including all persons with the nickname "Buzz." Let me instead offer a desperately short vignette of two American labor leaders who for many symbolize the best in the early CIO and in the post World War-II labor movement in the States.

### John L. Lewis

It has long been recognized, even by historians who celebrate the major thrust of his work, that John L. Lewis was a dictatorial leader.

Lewis became international president of the United Mine Workers of America in 1919. Up to that time, the local unions, district organizations, and national conventions of the UMW had involved miners in the process of legislating wages, working conditions and production methods. Local unions began the collective bargaining process by proposing terms. Activists debated their merits in the pages of the UMW journal. Hundreds of elected local union delegates assembled in national convention to adopt a program of demands, usually consisting of a compromise among the local union resolutions. The wage scales eventually adopted left plenty of room for elected pit committees to exercise considerable control over the timing, methods and distribution of work.

Lewis changed all this. Even according to the UMW's official history, Lewis "transformed [the UMW journal from] what had once been an organ for miners to speak to each other into an organ for administration's use." By 1933, according to historian Walter Galenson, Lewis had removed the elected leaders of a majority of districts and replaced them with his own appointees. Would-be reform caucuses were branded as "dual," and their leaders subjected to expulsion and physical attack. In confronting the Save The Union Movement in 1926-1928, Lewis resorted to massive election fraud and ordered the home local of Save The Union leader John Brophy to expel him. International conventions were dominated by paid organizers and delegates from suspended districts. The union's tradition of bottom-up lawmaking was displaced by a regime of top-down command.

But, you may say, it's still the case that Lewis used section 7(a) of the National Industrial Recovery Act when it was passed in the spring of 1933 to rebuild the United Mine Workers, sending organizers through the coal fields with the slogan "The President Wants You To Join The Union"; and that this successful organizing drive, together with parallel efforts of the clothing workers under Sidney Hillman and David Dubinsky formed (in the words of Irving Bernstein) "an axle upon which trade unionism was to turn" for the next decade.

Professor James Pope of Rutgers University Law School has shown this received narrative to be a myth. It is true that between February 1933 and July 1934 the United Mine Workers grew from a demoralized remnant of less than 100,000 miners to a union with more than 500,000 paid-up members. It is untrue that these events were masterminded and controlled by John L. Lewis. Beginning well before Lewis initiated an organizing campaign, often proceeding in the face of opposition by UMW staff representatives and Lewis himself, 100,000 miners spread out over 1,000 square miles of mountainous terrain began and carried out an unauthorized strike movement that recreated the union from below.

I don't have time to tell the whole story; see James Gray Pope, "The Western Pennsylvania Coal Strike of 1933," Parts I and II, *Labor History*, v. 44, nos. 1 and 2 (2003). Let me quote a portion of Pope's conclusion:

> [T]he western Pennsylvania coal strikers of 1933 were attempting to establish a democratic form of unionism that diverged sharply from the predominant American pattern of hierarchical, business unionism. In the coalfields of eastern Pennsylvania, Illinois, Tennessee, New Mexico, Utah, Washington, and other states, insurgent movements pursued similar objectives. John L. Lewis used the UMW apparatus and his political influence to defeat these movements . . . . He . . . outlawed their organizations, broke up their meetings, blocked representation elections, and packed the UMW convention with his own appointees.

## WALTER REUTHER

Walter Reuther is a man in whose parents' home Eugene Debs is said to have visited, a man who did assembly line work in the Soviet Union in the 1930s. Here, if anywhere, should be the model of a so-called "social movement unionist." Many people in the labor movement say, If only we could go back to Walter! The New Directions caucus in the UAW, TDU, the Association for Union Democracy, and *Labor Notes* lend credence to this view by lionizing Victor Reuther, Walter's surviving brother.

Perhaps the single most devastating rebuttal to the Walter Reuther myth is the story of what he did to prevent the Mississippi Freedom Democratic Party (MFDP) from being seated at the 1964 Democratic Party convention in Atlantic City. This story is close to my heart. I was director of Freedom Schools in the 1964 Mississippi Summer Project. I saw the effect of what happened in Atlantic City on my associates in the Student Nonviolent Coordinating Committee (SNCC), on the fragile inter-racial character of the civil rights movement of the early 1960s, on the hopes we all shared for fundamental social change.

This story can be found in two recent books, neither of them anti-Reuther: Nelson Lichtenstein's biography of Reuther, *The Most Dangerous Man in Detroit*; and the second volume of Taylor Branch's work on the life and times of Dr. King, *Pillar of Fire*. [See also "Remembering SNCC," in this volume.] . . . . Lichtenstein sums up as follows: "[T]he legacy of this work would roll on and on. For SNCC and the generation for whom it spoke, there was an enormous sense of betrayal that extended from Johnson, Humphrey, and Reuther at the top to all those well-established civil rights advocates, like Rauh, Rustin, and Wilkins, who had advocated MFDP acquiescence."

In the bitter debate that consumed movement circles, Lichtenstein goes on, Reuther became the symbol of "realpolitik" and the devious use of power. Bayard Rustin argued for a broad Reutherite coalition, saying: "We must think of our friends in labor, Walter Reuther and the others, who have gone to bat for us. If we reject this compromise we would be saying to them that we didn't want their help." Moses, as Jim Forman recalled it, replied: "He didn't want anyone telling him down in Mississippi about Walter Reuther needing help, Reuther hadn't come to Mississippi." (Lichtenstein, p. 395.)

It is instructive to remember the experience of Joseph Rauh, a decent man who tried to serve two masters. The Atlantic City convention cost Rauh the trust of both Bob Moses (Branch, p. 472) and Walter Reuther (Lichtenstein, p. 395). Looking back Rauh said of Atlantic City: "Reuther always thinks he knows more than anybody else when he gets into a fight like this. . . . Walter Reuther made the greatest mistake of his life." (Lichtenstein, pp. 394, 395.)

Before trying to sum up this discussion of self-activity, let me make one quick further point. We have in mind the emergence of an international resistance to capitalist globalization. It is tempting to suppose that the evils of bureaucratic business unionism in North America have been avoided by more radical, socially-minded union movements in South Korea, or Brazil, or South Africa. May I voice a concern that we not suppose these pastures greener than our own? Professor Peter Rachleff of Macalester College in St. Paul has written an article, as I understand it soon to be published in *Labour/Le Travaille*, wherein he describes and analyzes a strike in winter 1999-2000 at a Volkswagen plant in Uitenhage, outside Port Elizabeth, South Africa. Sadly, his heavily-documented story is one all too familiar to activists on this side of the Atlantic. The company demanded the so-called flexibility required to remain competitive in a global economy: continuous run production, compulsory overtime without advance notice, 12-hour shifts, 70-hour workweeks, and so on. The National Union of Metal Workers of South Africa (NUMSA) agreed to all these changes without giving the workers an opportunity to vote them up or down. New shop stewards organized in protest. NUMSA suspended the stewards. Hundreds, eventually thousands of workers wildcatted on their behalf, and formed a crisis committee made up of representatives from nine local plants. The Confederation of South African Trade Unions (COSATU) supported NUMSA, as did President Mbeki. Rachleff details at length what he calls "a widening gap . . . between leaders and members in unions."

So what is the difference between the path of our labor movement Founding Fathers, like John L. Lewis and Walter Reuther, and the path that many of us are trying to walk today?

Those in the tradition of the Founding Fathers are preoccupied with taking power in *national* unions. Local union office is seen as a stepping stone. The rhetoric is of "taking back our union," when, in reality, no national union—not the Miners, not the Auto Workers, not the Steelworkers, not the Teamsters—has ever been controlled by its rank and file.

The other path takes its inspiration from the astonishing recreation from below throughout the past century of ad hoc central labor bodies: the local workers' councils known as "soviets" in Russia in 1905 and 1917; the Italian factory committees of the early 1920s; solidarity unions in Toledo, Minneapolis, San Francisco and elsewhere in the States in the early 1930s; and similar formations in Hungary in 1956, Poland in 1980-1981, and France in 1968 and 1995.

These were all *horizontal* gatherings of all kinds of workers in a given *locality*, who then form regional and national networks with counterpart bodies elsewhere. Unlike national trade unions, local unions can provide continuity between the moments when such ad hoc bodies come out of the ground like mushrooms, and indeed—to vary the metaphor—have the potential to be important building blocks and organizing centers for more spontaneous formations.

This is what workers do when they are truly emancipating themselves. It is the participatory democracy of the 1960s alive and well in the movement of the new century.

## 2. FRATERNIZING WITH THE TROOPS

Much more briefly, let me touch on the other two principles proposed.

Seeking to win over the armed forces responds to the question, "What do we do about the fact that the other side will always have more weapons?" and offers the simple answer: We seek to win over or neutralize the soldiers. This goes for police officers, including the Fraternal Order of Police in Philadelphia; for prison guards; for self-appointed deputies like members of the Ku Klux Klan in Mississippi; and for members of each nation's armed forces. We don't call them "pigs" or "fascists." We try to understand them as human beings.

This practice has three ideological variations. The first is pacifism, broadly-defined. At the Pentagon demonstration in October 1967, a man who had named himself "Superjoel" relates:

> I was between Abbie [Hoffman] and Dr. Spock. We're walking up on the grounds of the Pentagon. And on top of this pile of trash there's this bunch of flowers, daisies, right. I grabbed them. I saw these soldiers and they're all standing there, and they were my age. So I just took the flowers and one by one, boom, boom, boom, put 'em in the gun barrels.

> (*Steal This Dream: Abbie Hoffman and the Countercultural Revolution in America*, ed. Larry Sloman, p. 99.)

The crowd began to call out to the troops, "Join us!" More than three years later, on May 3, 1970, a student at Kent State University named Allison Krause—one of the four students killed the next day—put a flower in the gun barrel of a National Guardsman, saying: "Flowers are better than bullets." These events signified a change in the attitude of the antiwar movement toward the GIs, whose refusal to fight would ultimately bring the war to an end.

A second strain of ideology that calls for fraternization with the armed forces derives from Vatican II and liberation theology. Its most celebrated exemplar was Archbishop Oscar Romero. On March 23, 1980, Romero delivered a homily in which he addressed the Salvadoran armed forces and stated:

> Brothers, you are from the same people; you kill your brother peasants. . . . No soldier is obliged to obey an order that is contrary to the will of God. Now it is time for you to recover your consciences so that you first obey conscience rather than a sinful order. . . . In the name of God, then, in the name of this suffering people, whose cries rise to the heavens, every day more tumultuously, I ask you, I beg you, I order you in the name of God; stop the repression.

The next day Romero paid for these words with his life.

The third ideological tradition that calls for doing everything possible to win over the armed forces is Marxism. Leon Trotsky, after the triumph of the Red Army which he commanded, discussed this theme in his *History of the Russian Revolution* as it applied both to the revolution of February 1917, which overthrew the Tsar, and to the Bolshevik revolution the next fall.

Trotsky sketched the February events along lines that later scholarship has only confirmed. On February 23, International Women's Day, "the February revolution was begun from below, overcoming the resistance of its own revolutionary organizations, the initiative being undertaken on their own accord by the most oppressed and downtrodden part of the proletariat—the women textile workers, among them no doubt many soldiers' wives." (*History*, v. 1, p. 102.) Detachments of soldiers were called in to assist the police, but there were no encounters.

The next day, February 24, the number of demonstrators doubled. As the crowd moved toward the center of Petrograd, injured soldiers in some of the war hospitals waved whatever was at hand in support. At length the crowd stood face to face with mounted troops, the Cossacks. The Cossacks charged repeatedly. The crowd parted to let them through. "The Cossacks promise not to shoot," passed from mouth to mouth.

It was very much in the streets of Petrograd as it would be eighty-two years later in the road at Amadór.

> When women and soldiers faced each other on the turbulent streets, old women at the head of the demonstration stepped toward the mounted soldiers, pleading: "We have our

husbands, fathers, and brothers at the front. But here we have hunger, hard times, injustice, shame. The government mocks us instead of helping us. You also have your mothers, wives, sisters, and children. All we want is bread and to end the war." According to Trotsky, the women went "up to the cordons more boldly than men, [took] hold of the rifles, beseech[ed], almost command[ed]: 'Put down your bayonets—join us.'" Again and again the Cossacks refused to ride down the demonstrating women . . . .

(Trotsky, *History*, v. 1, p. 109; Tsuyoshi Takegawa, *The February Revolution: Petrograd, 1917*, chaps. 12-13.)

And what about Serbia? There one saw last fall what can fairly be called a nonviolent revolution. A political movement won an election. When the incumbent regime initially refused to recognize the election results, an outraged populace poured into the streets. On the evening of Friday September 29 the coal miners of the Kolubara region, who produce the coal required for half of Serbia's output of electricity, declared an indefinite general strike. The general in charge of the armed forces, and police from the Interior Ministry, showed up on Tuesday October 3 and Wednesday October 4. The miners adopted a dual strategy. On the one hand, they removed vital parts from the mine machinery and challenged the soldiers to mine coal with bayonets. On the other hand, they summoned 20,000 supporters from nearby communities. The police held their ground but made no arrests. The next day, Thursday October 5, hundreds of thousands of people in Belgrade—forty miles away—seized the parliament and the state TV station, and the police in Kolubara melted away. The Kolubara strike was coordinated not by a "trade union," but by a "workers' committee." All over Serbia following Kostunica's accession to power, local committees of workers displaced hated factory managers. I realize that a cynic might say that this was a transition from socialism to capitalism, not the other way around. But surely, Serbia also shows us that fundamental social transition, revolution, remain possible in the twenty-first century, and that neutralizing the armed forces by mass nonviolent direct action can be a critical component of the process.

### 3. BUILDING *A* COMMUNITY *OF* STRUGGLE

Finally, and still with desperate brevity, I invite you to look at the most difficult problem of all: building a community of struggle.

During the past fifty years, my wife and I have been associated with a commune in the hills of Georgia where we expected to spend the rest of our lives; with the Student Nonviolent Coordinating Committee and Students for a Democratic Society; with the work community of a Legal Services office where I was employed for eighteen years; and with three large local unions led by persons who were, if not radicals, at least militant reformers. Every one of these entities went out of existence or continued, after internal struggle, as a two-dimensional caricature of its former self. And in every case the reason for the disintegration or decay of the community of struggle was that the human beings who made it up could not resolve their problems with each other, could not remain, as we used to say in the South, a band of brothers and sisters standing in a circle of love. It wasn't COINTELPRO, the FBI, or Ronald Reagan that did us in. We did it to ourselves.

In the case of the commune, the issue was whether we had all to believe in the same religious creed in order to resolve deep personal problems. SNCC and SDS fractured, I believe, under the combined pressure of: 1) the emergence of black power, 2) the frustrations of trying to end the war in Vietnam, 3) the advent of Marxist grouplets confident that they had all the answers and we did not. With all three local unions, it was a matter of personalities in each reform slate splitting over issues connected with the next election.

I wish I could believe that these were problems confined to the United States. I fear they are not. Look at the Russian Revolution. Look at the Cultural Revolution in China. Look at Polish Solidarity. Even in Canada, it may be that you have occasionally experienced what I am trying to describe: the apparently limitless capacity of the Left for self-destruction and fratricide. A resistance movement against globalization, it would seem, must have some response to these intractable evils.

My own response is still very much in process, but let me share it, such as it is. I think there is a difficulty with the concept of "organizing." No doubt most of us would piously reject the idea of a Leninist vanguard party. But the concept of "organizing" that most of us might applaud also tends to be vanguardist. The organizer says—does he or she not?— "I know what you ought to think, or at a minimum, what organization you should join and pay dues to." There is an inequality from the outset between organizer and organizee. Moreover, given that inequality, as well as the inequality between the organizer and the supervisor to whom he or she reports, there is less listening and consensual problem-solving than there should be, resentments are not expressed and fester, and individual careerism comes to the fore at the first opportunity.

In Latin America—for example, once again, in the work of Archbishop Romero—there is the different concept of "accompaniment." I do not organize you. I accompany you, or more precisely, we accompany each other. Implicit in this notion of *"accompañando"* is the assumption that neither of us has a complete map of where our path will lead. In the words of Antonio Machado: *"Caminante, no hay camino. Se hace camino al andar."* "Seeker, there is no road. We make the road by walking."

Accompaniment has been, in the experience of myself and my wife, a discovery and a guide to practice. Alice first formulated it as a draft counselor in the 1960s. When draft counselor meets counselee, she came to say, there are two experts in the room. One may be an expert on the law and administrative regulations. The other is an expert on what he wants to do with his life. Similarly as lawyers, in our activity with workers and prisoners, we have come to prize above all else the experience of jointly solving problems with our clients. They know the facts, the custom of the workplace or the penal facility, the experience of past success and failure. We too bring something to the table. I do not wish to be indecently immodest, but I will share that I treasure beyond any honorary degree actual or imagined the nicknames that Ohio prisoners have given the two of us: "Mama Bear" and "Scrapper."

I have begun to wonder whether the concept of "accompaniment," in addition to clarifying the desirable relationship of individuals in the movement for social change to one another, also has application to the desirable relationship of groups. A great deal of energy has gone into defining the proper relationship in the movement for social change of workers and students; blacks and whites; men and women; straights and gays; gringos, ladinos and *indígenas*; and no doubt, English-speakers and French-speakers. An older wave of radicalism struggled with the supposed leading role of the proletariat. More recently other kinds of division have preoccupied us. My question is, what would it do to this discussion were we to say that we are all accompanying one another on the road to a better society?

I came to this notion in an interesting way. Marty Glaberman, an honored friend and colleague, kept telling me that the fullest expression of spontaneous workers' councils was the Hungarian Revolution of 1956 and that the best book describing them was *Hungary '56* by Andy Anderson. Finally he sent me the book. I read it. And what to my wondering eyes did appear but the following:

At the 20th Congress of the Russian Communist Party in February 1956, Khrushchev denounced the misdeeds of Stalin. In April 1956, Hungarian students formed the Petofi Circle, named for a patriotic poet of the nineteenth century. "Soon, the meetings of the Petofi Circle were attracting thousands of people." The issue was freedom to speak and write the truth. As of September 1956, protest was still in the hands of intellectuals. The demonstrations that became a revolution in October were organized by the Petofi Circle and other student groups. Workers joined in, magnificently, with far-reaching demands. But students came first.

This information set something free inside myself. For twenty-five years I have been conscientiously pursuing the project of accompanying the working class. But in my former incarnation, in the 1960s, it was students who sat in at a Woolworth lunch counter to kick off the civil rights movement of the following decade, and it was students who first went out into the streets against the war. Workers opposed the war just as strongly as did middle-class constituencies. Working-class soldiers, black and white, ultimately refused to fight and ended it. But as in Hungary in 1956, so in the 1960s—not only in the United States, but also for example in France in 1968—students came first.

Having begun to see examples of this sequencing, I started to find it everywhere. In Russia throughout the year 1904 protest was voiced at a doctors' congress, at a conference of teachers, at a series of banquets organized by liberals. At Father Gapon's meetings with workers the demand was voiced: "Workers must join the campaign against the autocracy." The decision to present a petition to the Tsar, which led to "Bloody Sunday" in January 1905 and thus to the beginning of the 1905 revolution, was made in Gapon's apartment on November 28, 1904, "the evening after a bloody assault by soldiers on student demonstrators." ("Russia: 1905," in *A Force More Powerful: A Century of Nonviolent Conflict*, ed. Peter Ackerman and Jack DuVall, pp. 21-24.) Only in the fall of 1905, almost a year after rolling general strikes began to spread across Russia, was the so-called soviet formed in St. Petersburg. And where did it meet? According to its chairman, Trotsky, in the universities. "The doors of the universities," he writes, had "remained wide open. . . . 'The people' filled the corridors, lecture rooms and halls. Workers went directly from the factory to the university." The first meeting of the soviet was held on the evening of October 13, 1905, at the Technological Institute. The second meeting the next night had to be moved to the physics auditorium of the same institution. Trotsky says that on that evening "the higher educational establishments were overflowing with people." (*1905*, pp. 83-84, 105, 108.)

Why do students so often come first? One can speculate. To whatever extent Gramsci is right about the hegemony of bourgeois ideas, students and other intellectuals break through it: they give workers the space to think and experience for themselves. Similarly the defiance of students may help workers to overcome whatever deference they may be feeling toward supposed social superiors.

I want to conclude by affirming my hope for the rebirth of the movement for social change in the United States. George W. Bush may do for us what we have been unable to do for ourselves since the collapse of SDS and SNCC at the end of the 1960s. He may organize a new movement. Protest against the death penalty, against George W. Bush as executioner extraordinaire, and against the institutionalized racism of the United States penal system, will be a leading edge of the new movement. Old issues, such as the right to vote and gender equality, will reintroduce themselves in the context of resistance to the doctrinaire neo-liberalism and lack of compassion of the Bush administration. Students, workers, women, and prisoners will all be involved.

It will be a vast, ragged coalition full of cross currents and internal contradictions. Unions like the Steelworkers and the Teamsters may be in the streets on occasion, as in Seattle [in 1999], because they wish to protect the livelihoods of their members from imported steel and Mexican truck drivers. Appearances notwithstanding, this is not international class solidarity and does not express concern for what happens to workers in other countries. Yet for countless individuals who were in the streets with one another, the jubilant shared experience of "turtles and Teamsters together at last" was real, and expressed the spirit of accompaniment I have been trying to describe.

Hopefully, then, as social transformation once again comes onto the agenda in the United States, new networks of solidarity will spring into being between our movement and [for example] the struggles of Local 3903 at York University and Local 598 in Falcolnbridge; between our movement and your resistance to a private prison at Penetanguishene; between our movement and the work of Marion Traub-Warner and others to protect Nike workers at the Kuk-Dong garment factory in Mexico; between our movement and current efforts to reinvest in your health care system; between our movement and the Fathers Day Coalition at the Hamilton Air Show; between our movement and the folks from all over the world who will gather on the Plains of Abraham in April and, for Desert Scorn, in November in Qatar.

Daniel Singer's first book was *Prelude to Revolution: France in May 1968*, published in 1970. There he posed the question: "Could it be that a socialist revolution is beginning, that Marxism is returning to its home ground, the advanced countries for which it was designed?" And he answered his own question, Yes. The main message of the May crisis was that a "revolutionary situation can occur in an advanced capitalist country."[1]

Singer saw in France in 1968 a revolution from below, a spontaneous upheaval. It began in the universities of Paris. Then it spread to factories all over France, as ten million workers occupied the places where they worked. Singer expressed passionate disdain for the Communist-dominated trade union movement which, he argued, functioned as a brake on the revolution from below. This was workers' direct action expressed in sit-downs and factory takeovers. It was the creation of a "dual power" parallel to that of the government, in the form, *not* of trade unions, but of revolutionary action committees. Singer asserted that in France in 1968 students and workers sought "a new form of democracy, including industrial democracy, that does not just rest on an occasional ballot." Whether articulated by students or by workers, the ideology of May 1968 was a "revulsion against anything coming from above, against centralism, authority, the hierarchical order."[2]

For Daniel Singer, what happened in France in 1968 became for the remainder of his life the paradigm for an interrelationship of social forces that held out hope for a transition from capitalism to socialism, after all. We may term it the "Singer model." The outstanding characteristics of the Singer model are that 1) students act before (or at any rate, independently of) workers, but 2) when workers intervene in support of students or against the same enemies, "rebellion [turns] into potential revolution." Singer stressed that in France "the students clearly did not think that their struggle was a separate one. They wanted to break out of their ghetto and turn to the workers."[3]

This suggested model of revolution was something new under the sun. Singer recognized that "workers cannot conquer economic power under capitalism as the bourgeoisie did under feudalism." Building a new society within the shell of the old would be less possible for the working class than it had been for the bourgeoisie.[4] Nevertheless Singer saw in the French events the possibility of a series of steps whereby the working class, acting "in parallel" to the revolt of the young, could approach the transition to socialism.

This new theory of the transition from capitalism to socialism drew on French and Italian ideas about "structural reform" or "revolutionary reform" (popularized in English by André Gorz). May 1968, as befits a prelude, exhibited only scattered illustrations of these ideas. In a few cases workers not only occupied their factories but attempted to restart production. Perhaps the most significant prefigurative institution was the workers' practice of gathering at the workplace "in general assemblies meeting every day" to decide what to do next,[5] a practice that reappeared during the French general strikes of 1995. The term that held most promise for the future, in Latin America as well as in Europe, was "*autogestión*" or "self-management." Here, Singer wrote, "would lie the opportunity to move quickly from workers' control to a share of the management and then to full management by collective producers."[6]

What should we think about the Singer model? Thirty-some years after he put it forward, does it still make sense? How do Singer's ideas compare with those of Lenin, Rosa Luxemburg, and C. L. R. James? How does what happened in France in 1968 resemble or differ from what happened in Russia in 1905, in Poland in 1980-81, or in the Vietnam antiwar movement?

### Rosa Luxemburg, and the *1905* Revolution

Lenin's *What Is To Be Done?*, published in 1902, remains the inevitable starting point for discussion.

Therein, it will be recalled, Lenin insisted that the experience of trade unionism in all countries demonstrated "that the working class, exclusively by its own effort, is able to develop only trade-union consciousness." The spontaneous labor movement, Lenin wrote elsewhere in the same pamphlet, "is pure and simple trade unionism." Political, socialist consciousness could only be brought to workers from without, by Marxist intellectuals whose task was to "divert" the labor movement from its spontaneous, trade-unionist striving.

The analysis set forth by Lenin in *What Is To Be Done?* is often thought to have been refuted by the Russian Revolution of 1905. In

Russia that year, the working class embarked on "perhaps the most extensive general strike in history"[7] and created autonomous institutions from below: first local strike committees, and then the improvised citywide labor bodies known as "soviets" (in Russian, "councils"). Rosa Luxemburg, who had harshly criticized Lenin's pamphlet for its "pitiless centralism" and condemned its author for having the "sterile spirit of the overseer," found in the 1905 revolution a dramatic confirmation of her faith in the capacity of the working class for spontaneous, self-directed activity.

In 1905 Luxemburg returned from Germany to her native Poland, threw herself into revolutionary work, and was arrested. After her release from prison, she wrote her pamphlet, *The General Strike, the Political Party and the Trade Unions.*

Luxemburg's central thesis is that the rolling general strike that gripped working-class Russia in 1905 was not artificially "made," not "decided," not "propagated," by a revolutionary central committee. If anyone had undertaken to win the working class to the idea of a general strike by house-to-house canvassing, she wrote, it would have been "idle and profitless and absurd." Not only in 1905, but during the previous decade, the role of the Russian Social Democratic Party had been "insignificant," as over and over again, in one locality after another, seemingly minor incidents of workplace life had triggered explosions of whole working-class communities, led by workers themselves.[8]

It now appears that the Russian revolution of 1905 was far more spontaneous than Lenin had thought possible but less self-directed from below than Rosa Luxemburg supposed at the time. Indeed, the Russian revolution of 1905 appears to exemplify "the Singer model." Students (as well as a variety of middle-class professionals) acted first, and then, transforming protest into revolution, the working class weighed in.

The Russian Revolution of 1905 is generally thought to have begun on "Bloody Sunday" in January 1905, when Father Gapon led several thousand factory workers to the Tsar's Winter Palace in St. Petersburg. The workers carried a petition requesting a minimum wage and an eight-hour work day, freedom of speech, press and association, the release of all political prisoners, the right to organize unions, and election of a constituent assembly. Soldiers opened fire, killing dozens.

But there was a pre-history to Bloody Sunday. Against the background of military defeat by the Japanese and the assassination of the minister of the interior, conventions of teachers and doctors were broken up by the police. A congress of delegates from institutions of local administration (*zemstvos*) passed a resolution favoring a national assembly with real powers. Beginning in late November 1904, liberals organized a series of banquets in twenty-six cities ostensibly to celebrate the fortieth anniversary of judicial reform. Maxim Gorky wrote to his wife about one such banquet: "There were more than 600 diners . . . in general, the intelligentsia. Outspoken speeches were made, and people chanted in unison, 'Down with the autocracy!' 'Long live the constituent assembly!' and 'Give us a constitution!'"[9] Students in both Moscow and St. Petersburg launched demonstrations in late November and early December, sometimes ending in violent conflict with the police. Few workers were involved. One historian of the 1905 revolution declares flatly: "The movement for social change that sparked the crisis of 1905 began, not in the working class, but among the educated, privileged social strata."[10] It appeared, writes another, "that almost the entire middle and upper classes—that is, the educated classes—were speaking out against the government."[11]

On November 28, 1904, there was a bloody assault by soldiers on student demonstrators. That evening thirty-five workers crowded into Father Gapon's apartment in St. Petersburg. The group decided, in the words of one participant, that the workers should "add their voice" to that of the students. Father Gapon was asked to draw up a petition to present to the Tsar.[12]

Yearlong turmoil among both workers and students followed Bloody Sunday. Finally, when in the fall of 1905 workers gathered to form a new kind of institution called a "soviet," they assembled at the universities!

The universities came to serve as meeting places in the fall of 1905 because of a late-summer government decree granting the universities administrative autonomy. The result was the opposite of that intended. In Moscow,

> [t]housands of students from all over the city gathered daily in the university lecture halls during the first weeks of September to attend marathon meetings . . . . On September 11, the majority of students present supported a resolution pledging to fight hand in hand with the laboring masses for the overthrow of the tsarist regime . . . . When classes resumed on September 15, some 3,000 students showed up at the university, but fewer than half sat in the classrooms. The rest marched through the halls, interrupting classes and singing revolutionary songs.

On the evening of September 21, the working class joined the students. Amid tremendous excitement a crowd of over 3,000 persons—almost a third of them striking workers—forced its way into the Law Auditorium. Allegedly, a police officer stationed at the university entrance told arrivals: "If you are looking for the Socialist Revolutionaries, turn to the right; the Social Democrats are this way, to the left."[13]

In St. Petersburg, on October 11, 1905, "some ten thousand factory workers, students and others assembled in various professional and local groupings on the campus of St. Petersburg University. A meeting of railroad employees voted unanimously to strike."[14] One of the first groups to elect delegates to the St. Petersburg soviet were three thousand union printers, meeting on the evening of October 13 by candle light in the university cafeteria.[15]

Similar scenes took place in other cities with universities. In Kharkov, in October 1905 "[t]he strike leaders and their followers established their headquarters at the University of Kharkov and used its property freely."[16]

Thus in Russia in 1904-05, as in France May 1968, events when closely scrutinized conform closely to the "Singer model." Students and intellectuals acted first, in the *zemstvo* congresses, banquets, and other middle-class gatherings of November-December 1904. Even at the height of working-class self-activity, during the general strikes of fall 1905, universities continued to be the meeting places of the movement.

## POLAND IN *1980-81*

Poland soon provided what had been hinted at in France. In *The Road to Gdansk*, Daniel Singer chronicled successive revolts by Polish workers in 1970, 1976, and 1980-81. These upheavals established as institutions central to Polish society the workers' council, and later, the inter-factory workers' council. More than a structural reform, these institutions represented to Singer what in Russia in 1917 had been called "dual power."

In 1956, Singer wrote, following the death of Stalin (1953) and Khrushchev's speech about Stalin's misconduct (February 1956), workers' councils were "revived all over Poland." Then in 1970, at the Wartski shipyards in Szczecin, each of thirty-six departments "elected three delegates, who could be recalled at any time and had to get their shop's approval for any major decisions. The delegates in turn elected a five-member strike committee . . . ." Similar formations appeared in December 1970 in Gdansk and Gydnia.[17]

In January 1971 the 10,000 workers at the Szczecin shipyard struck for a second time.

> This time the organization was somewhat different. Each section had five delegates but also elected directly one member of the strike committee. The latter was no longer dominated by party cardholders but led by workers most radicalized during

the previous weeks, such as the ex-sailor Edmund Baluka. The commission on resolutions was busiest of all, having to deal with scores of proposals, ranging from details concerning one shop to proposed solutions for national problems. Surrounded by troops, threatened, the Warski shipyard paralyzed by the strike was a school for democracy.[18]

In the summer of 1980 workers' councils appeared again in the Baltic shipyards, and this time the workers' leading demand was to institutionalize their councils as "free trade unions independent of party and employers."[19]

The experience of Polish Solidarity makes it clear that the Singer model should not be understood to apply only to situations where students and intellectuals act first. It can also apply, in modified form, to a situation in which after several cycles of protest it becomes almost irrelevant to ask, Who acted first?, but in which students and intellectuals maintain throughout a separate identity.

Historian Roman Laba argues that in 1970-1972 Polish workers took the initiative in creating, first, factory committees, and then, regional interfactory committees, without significant input from intellectuals. Historian Lawrence Goodwyn adds that in 1980, when Solidarity erupted at the Gdansk shipyards, intellectuals who came from Warsaw to help "did not know how to read the scenes in the Lenin shipyard" and inappropriately sought to soften the demands of the workers.

Assume all this to be so. One might compare the scene at the shipyard in August 1980, to the Democratic Party convention in Atlantic City, New Jersey, in August 1964, when African Americans from Mississippi rejected the compromise supported by Walter Reuther, Bayard Rustin, Roy Wilkins, Joseph Rauh, and other leaders, adamant that "we didn't come all this way for no two seats."

The essential message of the Singer model remains. Students and intellectuals need to be understood as a social force in their own right. They are not and should not be encouraged to become merely "organizers" (Lenin) nor should it be supposed that their contribution is "insignificant" (Luxemburg). Whichever group takes the initiative in a particular historical situation, students and intellectuals need to relate to workers horizontally, as one of two equal hands seeking to create a better world.

## THE MOVEMENT AGAINST THE VIETNAM WAR

Lest I seem to be generalizing on too slender a basis of fact, I want to look quickly at another experience of the second half of the twentieth century.

The Singer model resonates for me because it corresponds to my own experience in the 1960s. I was part of the civil rights movement in the American South, led by the youthful organizers of the Student Nonviolent Coordinating Committee. And I was myself a leader of the movement against the war in Vietnam that students began at a time when the AFL-CIO and almost all trade unions in the United States supported the war (just as the AFL-CIO presently supports the "war against terrorism").

Initially there may have been some hostility on the part of antiwar protesters toward working-class young men who were drafted to fight in Vietnam. But at least as early as the fall of 1967, in the great demonstration at the Pentagon, the antiwar movement began to address soldiers with the words, "Join us!" From then until the war ground to a close in 1975, we recognized that the antiwar movement could succeed only when working-class young men in uniform refused to fight.

Eventually they did refuse to fight, as chronicled in countless movies and memoirs, and in a brilliant historical study by Christian Appy, *Working-Class War.*[20] Infantrymen became convinced that they were being used as bait, to attract enemy attack and thus to locate targets for air strikes and artillery fire.[21] The burning of whole villages and massacre of their inhabitants—as at My Lai—became a commonplace way to vent anxiety and frustration.[22] Soldiers came to feel "a desperate need to find some moral language, however strained, to justify their actions."[23] At least a third of the "enemy" casualties in Vietnam were civilians.[24]

In the end, soldiers came to feel that they were fighting a war for nothing.[25] By 1969-70, officers were fully aware of the risk that their own men might try to kill them.[26] In the last analysis, the sense of returning veterans that the antiwar protesters had been right struggled with the feeling that no one who had not been there had any right to speak.

In however awkward and disjointed a manner, the Vietnam years in the end show workers joining with students to protest a war that oppressed them both.

## CONCLUSION

In his last book, *Whose Millennium?*, Daniel Singer summed up the themes of his earlier French and Polish case studies.

Rosa Luxemburg is front and center. Singer rightly argues that her criticisms of Lenin's vision of a revolutionary party and of the young Russian Revolution never caused her to cross to the side of the counter-revolution. Nevertheless, he insists, "she pleaded with Lenin and Trotsky that, if there was a way out, it led through more, not less, democracy." She

left us the imperishable words that "freedom is always and exclusively freedom for the one who thinks differently"; and, "without general elections,
without unrestricted freedom of press and assembly, without a free struggle
of opinion . . . only the bureaucracy remains as the active element"; and,
"the errors committed by a truly revolutionary movement are infinitely
more fruitful than the infallibility of the cleverest Central Committee."[27]

Paris in 1968 left us the slogan: "Be realistic, demand the impossible!" A few years ago, [the international demonstrations at] Seattle,
Quebec and Genoa would have seemed impossible. Now the realm of
the possible has been expanded. Students act first, not to direct or organize workers, but to express their own needs, consciences, and dreams.
Workers then join in: at the Nantes aircraft factory in France, after work
in downtown Budapest, in resisting the Vietnam War, all along the band
of shipyards on Poland's Baltic coast. And as Daniel Singer seems to have
correctly proposed, because of workers' participation, revolution in the
industrial societies of the global North once again appears possible.

## ENDNOTES

1   Daniel Singer, *Prelude to Revolution: France in 1968* (New York: Hill
and Wang, 1970), pp. xii, 4.

2   *Id.*, pp. 7-10, 21.

3   *Id.*, pp. 23, 66-67.

4   *Id.*, p. 100.

5   *Id.*, p. 238.

6   *Id.*, p. 378.

7   Henry Reichman, *Railwaymen and Revolution: Russia, 1905* (Berkeley:
University of California Press, 1987), p. 206.

8   See "The Mass Strike, the Political Party and the Trade Unions," in *Rosa
Luxemburg Speaks*, ed. Mary-Alice Waters (New York: Pathfinder Press, 1970).

9   Quoted in Orlando Figes, *A People's Tragedy: The Russian Revolution,
1891-1924* (London: Jonathan Cape, 1996), p. 172.

10  Laura Engelstein, *Moscow, 1905: Working-Class Organization and
Political Conflict* (Stanford: Stanford University Press, 1982), pp. 55, 64.

11  Sidney Harcave, *First Blood: The Russian Revolution of 1905* (New
York: The Macmillan Company, 1964), p. 58.

12  N. M. Varnashev, "Ot Nachala de Kontsa Gapanovskoi Organizatsiei
(Vospominania) [From Beginning to End of Gapon's Organization:
Recollections]," in *Istoriko-revoliutsionnyi Sbornik*, ed. V. I. Nevski (Leningrad:
Government Publishers, 1924), pp. 201-202, quoted in Walter Sablinsky, *The
Road to Bloody Sunday: Father Gapon and the St. Petersburg Massacre of 1905*
(Princeton, NJ: Princeton University Press, 1976), p. 135.

13  Engelstein, *Moscow, 1905*, pp. 71-72, 130-131.

14 Reichman, *Railwaymen and Revolution*, p. 208.

15 Victoria E. Bonnell, *Roots of Rebellion: Workers' Politics and Organizations in St. Petersburg and Moscow, 1900-1914* (Berkeley: University of California Press, 1983), p. 173.

16 Harcave, *First Blood*, p. 182.

17 Daniel Singer, *The Road to Gdansk: Poland and the USSR* (New York: Monthly Review Press, 1981), pp. 161, 170.

18 *Id.*, p. 173.

19 *Id.*, pp. 220, 223.

20 Christian G. Appy, *Working-Class War: American Combat Soldiers and Vietnam* (Chapel Hill: University of North Carolina Press, 1993).

21 *Id.*, pp. 182-190.

22 *Id.*, pp. 190-205.

23 *Id.*, p. 200.

24 *Id.*, p. 203.

25 *Id.*, Chapter 7.

26 *Id.*, p. 246.

27 Daniel Singer, *Whose Millennium? Theirs or Ours?* (New York: Monthly Review Press, 1999), pp. 240-241.

The problem of the transition from capitalism to socialism has nagged at and puzzled me all my adult life.

As a high school student I pursued my political education during the half hour trip to school on the New York City subway. I devoured Edmund Wilson's *To the Finland Station*. I read Ignazio Silone's *Bread and Wine*, still my favorite novel. And I also read a book by an ex-Trotskyist named James Burnham, *The Managerial Revolution*.[1]

Burnham argued that the bourgeois revolution occurred only after a long period during which bourgeois institutions had been built within feudal society. The position of the proletariat within capitalist society, he contended, was altogether different. The proletariat has no way to begin to create socialist economic institutions within capitalism. Hence, he concluded, there would be no socialist revolution.

I have no distinct memory, but I assume that when I got off the subway and back to my parents' home I reached for Emile Burns' *Handbook of Marxism* or some such source to find out why Burnham was wrong. The problem was I couldn't find an answer. Nor have I have been able to find one during the more than half century since. In 1987 I rephrased Burnham's argument in *The Journal of American History*:[2]

> The transition from capitalism to socialism presents problems that did not exist in the transition from feudalism to capitalism. In late medieval Europe, a discontented serf, a Protestant artisan, an experimental scientist, or an enterprising moneylender could do small-scale, piecemeal things to begin to build a new society within the old. He could run away to a free city, print the Bible in the vernacular, drop stones from a leaning tower, or organize a corporation, all actions requiring few persons and modest amounts of capital, actions possible within the interstices of a decentralized feudal society. The twentieth-century variant of this process, in Third World countries, also permits revolutionary protagonists in guerrilla enclaves, like

Yenan in China or the Sierra Maestra in Cuba, to build small-scale alternative societies, initiating land reform, health clinics, and literacy. But how can people take such meaningful small steps, begin such revolutionary reforms, in an interdependent society like that of the United States? A localized strategy runs into the problem of what might be called "socialism in one steel mill": the effort to do something qualitatively new, requiring tens of millions of dollars, in a hostile environment. . . .

In the year 2002 one might rephrase the problem this way: If, as anti-globalization protesters affirm, another world is possible, how do we begin to build it, here and now?

# *I*

Edward Thompson, too, was intensely concerned with the transition from capitalism to socialism, especially during the decade 1955-1965 in which he wrote and published *William Morris* and *The Making of the English Working Class.*

One of Thompson's first attempts to discuss the transition to socialism was an essay called "Socialist Humanism: An Epistle to the Philistines," published in 1957 in *The New Reasoner*.[3]

There Thompson asserted that "mankind is caught up in the throes of a revolutionary transition to an entirely new form of society—a transition which must certainly reach its climax during this century." Several other comments about "the period of transition," "the phase of the transition," and "the transitional stage" are scattered throughout the essay. What is of greatest interest is Thompson's response to the thesis that the working class has not developed and cannot develop under capitalism a new society within the shell of the old. Here is what he wrote:

> The best, most fruitful ideas of Trotskyism—emphasis upon economic democracy and direct forms of political democracy—are expressed in fetishistic form: "workers' councils" and "Soviets" must be imposed as the only orthodoxy. But Britain teems with Soviets. We have a General Soviet of the T.U.C. [Trade Union Congress] and trades soviets in every town: peace soviets and national soviets of women, elected parish, urban district and borough soviets.[4]

In these remarks, Thompson implicitly asks us to choose between two views of the transition from capitalism to socialism. One is expressed in the song by Wobbly Ralph Chaplin, "Solidarity Forever," when the song affirms: "We can bring to birth a new world from the ashes of the old." In this perspective the new world will arise, phoenix-like, after a great catastrophe or conflagration. The emergence of feudalism from pockets of local self-help after the collapse of the Roman Empire is presumably the exemplar of that kind of transition.

A second view of the transition from capitalism to socialism compares it to the transition from feudalism to capitalism. The Preamble to the IWW Constitution gives us a mantra for this perspective, declaring that "we are forming the structure of the new society within the shell of the old."

Thompson opted for the second paradigm. Confronting the question, "Where is the proletarian new society within the shell of the old?" Thompson answered as follows in another essay from the late 1950s, "Homage to Tom Maguire." There he discussed the genesis in the late nineteenth century of the Independent Labor Party, a party which—Thompson declared—"grew from the bottom up." According to Thompson:

> the ILP gave political expression to the various forms of independent or semi-independent working-class organization which had been built and consolidated in the West Riding [of Yorkshire] in the previous thirty years [that is, from the 1860s to the 1890s]—co-operatives, trade unions, friendly societies, various forms of chapel or educational or economic "self-help."[5]

This was a more concrete description of the "British soviets" invoked by Thompson in his essay on socialist humanism. Sheila Rowbotham remembers how, about this time, "Edward Thompson started to tell me about the northern [that is, north of Britain] socialism, how for a time changing all forms of human relationships had been central in a working-class movement."[6]

Edward Thompson's fullest engagement with the building of a working-class new society inside the shell of capitalism came in a book called *Out of Apathy*, published in 1960. Thompson wrote three essays for this volume. One is justly remembered and often reprinted: entitled "Outside the Whale," it is a tour de force in which Thompson details the retreat of Auden and Orwell from the enthusiasms of the 1930s. The other two essays, unjustly forgotten, are the introduction and conclusion to the volume.[7]

In these essays Thompson introduces a metaphor central to his view of the transition from capitalism to socialism: the rabbit warren. For a society to be criss-crossed by underground dens and passageways created by an oppositional class is, in Thompson's 1960s vocabulary, to be "warrened." British society, he wrote, "is warrened with democratic processes—committees, voluntary organizations, councils, electoral procedures." Because of the existence of such counter-institutions, in Thompson's view a transition to socialism could develop from what was already in being, and from below. "Socialism, even at the point of revolutionary transition—perhaps at this point most of all—must grow from existing strengths. No one . . . can impose a socialist humanity from above."[8]

Thompson condemned the neglect of the issue of transition by persons calling themselves radicals. "[W]hat we mean to direct attention to is the extraordinary hiatus in contemporary labour thinking on this most crucial point of all—how, and by what means, is a transition to socialist society to take place." Further, in his view: "The absence of any theory of the transition to socialism is the consequence of capitulation to the conventions of capitalist politics."[9]

Here Thompson reaches a critical point in his argument. The difficulty in thinking about the transition from capitalism to socialism, he contends, derives in part from a mistaken notion about the difference between bourgeois and socialist revolutions to be found in the writings of . . . Joseph Stalin! Thompson finds the distinction most fully and dangerously expressed in Stalin's *On the Problems of Leninism* (1926). Here is what Thompson says in *Out of Apathy*:

> The conceptual barrier [to thinking about the transition from capitalism to socialism] derives . . . from a false distinction in Leninist doctrine between the bourgeois and the proletarian revolution. The bourgeois revolution (according to this legend) begins when "more or less finished forms of the capitalist order" already exist "within the womb of feudal society." Capitalism was able to grow up with feudalism, and to coexist with it—on uneasy terms—until prepared for the seizure of political power. But the proletarian revolution "begins when finished forms of the socialist order are either absent, or almost completely absent." Because it was supposed that forms of social ownership or democratic control over the means of production were incompatible with capitalist state power: "The bourgeois revolution is usually consummated with the seizure of power, whereas in the proletarian revolution the seizure of power is only the beginning."[10]

Thompson's footnote to this passage reads: "The quotations here are taken from Stalin's *On the Problems of Leninism* (1926); but the influence of this concept is to found far outside the Communist tradition."

I can confirm that the passages quoted by Thompson will be found on page 22 of volume 8 of the *Works* of Stalin (Moscow: Foreign Languages Publishing House, 1954).[11]

How does Thompson propose that we rebut the distinction between the bourgeois and proletarian revolutions? Thompson writes:

> [I]f we discard this dogma (the fundamentalist might meditate on the "interpenetration of opposites") we can read the evidence another way. It is not a case of *either* this *or* that. We must, at every point, see *both*—the surge forward *and* the containment, the public sector *and* its subordination to the private, the strength of trade unions *and* their parasitism upon capitalist growth, the welfare services *and* their poor-relation status. The countervailing powers are there, and the equilibrium (which is an equilibrium *within* capitalism) is precarious. It could be tipped back towards authoritarianism. But it could also be heaved *forward*, by popular pressures of great intensity, to the point where the powers of democracy cease to be countervailing and become the active dynamic of society in their own right. This is revolution.[12]

Thompson is thinking dialectically. X need not be A or non-A. X can be both A and B, depending on the context, because both the context and X itself are constantly changing.

I cannot resist further quotation from these most politically important of all the words Edward Thompson ever wrote.

> Certainly, the transition can be defined, in the widest historical sense, as a transfer of class power: the dislodgment of the power of capital from the "commanding heights" and the assertion of the power of socialist democracy. This is the historical watershed between "last stage" capitalism and dynamic socialism—the point at which the socialist potential is liberated, the public sector assumes the dominant role, subordinating the private to its command, and over a very great area of life the priorities of need override those of profit. But this point cannot be defined in narrow political (least of all parliamentary) terms; nor can we be certain, in advance, in what context the breakthrough will be made. What is more important to insist upon is that it is necessary to *find out* the breaking point, not by theoretical speculation alone, but *in practice* by unrelenting reforming pressure in many fields, which are designed to reach a revolutionary culmination. And this will entail a confrontation, throughout society, between two systems, two ways of life.

Throughout the emphasis is on the positive, building on existing strengths, as opposed to a scenario of catastrophe and apocalypse. In Thompson's words:

> [S]uch a revolution demands the maximum enlargement of *positive* demands, the deployment of constructive skills within a conscious revolutionary strategy—or, in William Morris' words, the "making of Socialists." . . . Alongside the industrial workers, we should see the teachers who want better schools, scientists who wish to advance research, welfare workers who want hospitals, actors who want a National Theatre, technicians impatient to improve industrial organization. Such people do not want these things only and always, any more than all industrial workers are always "class conscious" and loyal to their great community values. But these affirmatives coexist, fitfully and incompletely, with the ethos of the Opportunity State. It is the business of socialists to draw the line, not between a staunch but diminishing minority and an unredeemable majority, but between the monopolists and the people—to foster the "societal instincts" and inhibit the acquisitive. Upon these positives, and not upon the débris of a smashed society, the socialist community must be built.[13]

Edward Thompson touched upon these same themes five years later, in the course of his polemic with Perry Anderson and Tom Nairn entitled "The Peculiarities of the English." The occasion was the comment of Anderson and Nairn that after Chartism, which crested about 1850, the English working class ceased to be a revolutionary force. Note once again the dialectical caste of Thompson's response as well as the recurrent comparison of working-class institutions to a "warren."

> [T]he workers, having failed to overthrow capitalist society, proceeded to warren it from end to end. This "caesura" [after 1850] is exactly the period in which the characteristic class institutions of the Labour movement were built up—trade unions, trade councils, T.U.C., co-ops, and the rest—which have endured to this day. It was part of the logic of this new direction that each advance within the framework of capitalism simultaneously involved the working class more deeply in the *status quo*. As they improved their position by organization within the workshop, so they became more reluctant to engage in quixotic outbreaks which might jeopardize gains accumulated at such cost. Each assertion of working-class influence

within the bourgeois-democratic state machinery, simultaneously involved them as partners (even if antagonistic partners) in the running of the machine. . . .

We need not necessarily agree with Wright Mills that this indicates that the working class can be a revolutionary class only in its formative years; but we must, I think, recognize that once a certain climactic moment is passed, the opportunity for a certain *kind* of revolutionary movement passes irrevocably. . . .

[I]t is possible to envisage three kinds of socialist transition, none of which have in fact ever been successfully carried through. First, the syndicalist revolution in which the class institutions displace the existing State machine; I suspect that the moment for such a revolution, if it was ever practicable, has passed in the West. Second, through a more or less constitutional political party, based on the political institutions, with a very clearly articulated socialist strategy, whose cumulative reforms bring the country to a critical point of class equilibrium, from which a rapid revolutionary transition is pressed through. [Attentive Thompson watchers will recognize this second scenario as that set forth five years before in *Out of Apathy*.] Third, through further far-reaching changes in the sociological composition of the groups which entail the break-up of the old class institutions and value system, and the creation of new ones.[14]

Writing in 1965, Edward thought that some combination of the second and third strategies might hold most promise. The bottom line for all discussion, in his view, was: "It is abundantly evident that working people have, within capitalist society, thrown up positions of 'countervailing power.'" The New Left—already in 1965 he calls it "the former New Left"—had sought to pursue "reformist tactics within a revolutionary strategy." But whatever the verbal trappings, he concluded:

. . . we have stated a problem, but are no nearer its solution. The real work of analysis remains: the sociological analysis of changing groups within the wage-earning and salaried strata; the points of potential antagonism and alliance; the economic analysis, the cultural analysis, the political analysis, not only of forms of State power, but also of the bureaucracies of the Labour Movement.[15]

Edward Thompson did not himself pursue the analysis for which he called. In 1965, the same year in which "The Peculiarities of the English" was published, he took a full-time position at Warwick University and disappeared in the general direction of the eighteenth century. Much that was marvelous ensued, and in the early 1980s Thompson emerged from academia to spend half a dozen years in ceaseless agitation against the nuclear arms race, an agitation that may have hastened his premature death. My point is only that, to the best of my knowledge, he did not pursue further what he had termed the unresolved problem of the transition from capitalism to socialism. We shall have to attempt that task ourselves.

## II

If another world is possible, and we want to begin to build it within the womb or shell of capitalist society, how should we proceed? What institutions can serve the working class in "warrening" (Edward Thompson's phrase) the old society with the emerging institutions of the new?

The most obvious answer is trade unions. In "Value, Price and Profit," Karl Marx wrote in 1865: "Trades Unions work well as centres of resistance against the encroachments of capital." The next year, in instructions drafted for the British delegation to the 1866 congress of the First International, Marx expressly compared the work of trade unions as "centres of organization of the working class" to what "the medieval municipalities and communes did for the middle class."[16]

However, the limitations of trade unions soon became apparent. Capitalism was furthest advanced in Great Britain. In their *History of Trade Unionism*, published in 1894, and *Industrial Democracy*, published in 1898, Sidney and Beatrice Webb summed up the evolution of trade unions in that country. The Webbs found that the "revolutionary period" in the history of the British labor movement was at the beginning, in 1829-1842, and that the business unionism of the British labor movement at the close of the nineteenth century was good, or at any rate inevitable.[17]

The Webbs' conclusions powerfully influenced Lenin, who together with his wife Krupskaya translated the Webbs' *Industrial Democracy* while in Siberian exile.[18] In *What Is To Be Done?*, published in 1902, Lenin proposed a revolutionary strategy that accepted the findings of the Webbs with regard to the development of trade unions. "The history of all countries," he wrote, "shows that the working class, exclusively by its own effort, is able to develop only trade-union consciousness." Socialist consciousness could only be brought to workers "from without." The spontaneous labor movement, Lenin wrote elsewhere in the same pamphlet, "is pure and simple trade unionism." Hence the task of socialists was "to *divert* the labour movement, with its spontaneous trade-unionist striving," and bring it under the wing of revolutionary Social Democracy.[19]

Only three years later—dialectically, as it were—the Russian revolution of 1905 imposed a powerful corrective to Lenin's analysis in *What Is To Be Done?* Without significant assistance from middle-class revolutionaries or from the various revolutionary parties, the Russian working class embarked on a yearlong general strike and created autonomous institutions from below: the improvised central labor bodies known as "soviets." Throughout this course of self-activity workers sacrificed and died for political objectives as well as economic ones. Rosa Luxemburg found in the revolution of 1905 a dramatic refutation of what she termed Lenin's "pitiless centralism," which, in her view, imposed a "blind subordination" of all party organs to the party center and expressed "the sterile spirit of the overseer."[20]

There the debate has rested ever since.

### ENDNOTES

1 James Burnham, *The Managerial Revolution: What is Happening in the World* (Westport, CT: Greenwood Press, 1941).

2 Staughton Lynd, "The Genesis of the Idea of a Community Right to Industrial Property in Youngstown and Pittsburgh, 1977-1987," *Journal of American History*, v. 74, no. 3 (Dec. 1987), pp. 926-958, reprinted in Staughton Lynd, *Living Inside Our Hope: A Steadfast Radical's Thoughts on Rebuilding the Movement* (Ithaca, NY: Cornell University Press, 1997).

3 E. P. Thompson, "Socialist Humanism: An Epistle to the Philistines," *The New Reasoner* (Summer 1957), pp. 105-143. I should like to thank Peter Linebaugh for locating this hard-to-find essay and sending me a copy.

4 Thompson, "Socialist Humanism," pp. 105, 106, 107, 110, 139 (references to "transition"), 140 (reference to Trotskyism).

5 E. P. Thompson, "Homage to Tom Maguire," in E. P. Thompson, *Making History: Writings on History and Culture* (New York: W. W. Norton, 1994), pp. 24, 26.

6 Sheila Rowbotham as quoted in Bryan D. Palmer, *E. P. Thompson: Objections and Oppositions* (New York: W. W. Norton, 1994), p. 41.

7 The other essays are "At the Point of Decay" and "Revolution," in E. P. Thompson, ed., *Out of Apathy* (London: Stevens, 1960), pp. 3-15, 287-308.

8 Thompson, "At the Point of Decay," p. 6, and "Outside the Whale," p. 194, in E. P. Thompson, ed., *Out of Apathy*.

9 Thompson, "Revolution," pp. 294, 296.

10 *Id.*, pp. 300-301.

11 The late Marty Glaberman called my attention to a similar passage in Trotsky's *History of the Russian Revolution* (New York: Simon and Schuster, 1937), v. 3, pp. 168-169, wherein Trotsky argued that the vanguard party must

provide for the proletariat the "social advantages" that a network of pre-revolutionary institutions gave the bourgeoisie.

12 Thompson, "Revolution," pp. 301-302.

13 *Id.*, pp. 303-305 (emphasis in original).

14 E. P. Thompson, "The Peculiarities of the English," in E. P. Thompson, *The Poverty of Theory and Other Essays* (New York: Monthly Review Press, 1978), pp. 281-282.

15 *Id.*, p. 282.

16 Karl Marx and Friedrich Engels, *Collected Works*, v. 20 (New York: International Publishers, 1975), pp. 149, 191-192, quoted and discussed in Kenneth Lapides, ed., *Marx and Engels on the Trade Unions* (New York: Praeger, 1987) and Hal Draper, *Karl Marx's Theory of Revolution* (New York: Monthly Review Press, 1978), v. 2, pp. 99-101.

17 See for a fuller discussion "The Webbs, Lenin, Rosa Luxemburg," in Lynd, *Living Inside Our Hope*, pp. 207-220.

18 As noted in *id.*, p. 261, n.15: "Solomon M. Schwarz, a Russian Social Democratic labor organizer in the early years of this century, agrees that Lenin 'must have been influenced by the views he formed while translating Sidney and Beatrice Webbs' *Industrial Democracy*.' Schwarz observes: 'The immense bibliography of the second and third editions of Lenin's *Sochinenia* contain not one major work on the subject [of trade unionism] that came out after the Webbs'.' Solomon M. Schwarz, *The Russian Revolution of 1905: The Workers' Movement and the Formation of Bolshevism and Menshevism* (Chicago: University of Chicago Press, 1967), p. 326 n."

19 V. I. Lenin, "What is to be Done?" in *Collected Works of V. I. Lenin*, v. 4 (New York: International Publishers, 1929), pp. 136-138.

20 Rosa Luxemburg, *The Russian Revolution and Leninism or Marxism?* ed. Bertram D. Wolfe (Ann Arbor: University of Michigan Press, 1970), pp. 84-86, 94.

*T*o *Begin With*
 The greatest honor I have ever received is to be asked to speak to you on the occasion of the IWW's 100th birthday. But I am not standing here alone. Beside me are departed friends.

 John Sargent was the first president of Local 1010, United Steelworkers of America, the 18,000-member local union at Inland Steel just east of Chicago. John said that he and his fellow workers achieved far more through direct action before they had a collective bargaining agreement than they did after they had a contract. You can read his words in the book *Rank and File*.

 Ed Mann and John Barbero, after years as rank and filers, became president and vice president of Local 1462, United Steelworkers of America, at Youngstown Sheet & Tube in Youngstown, and toward the end of his life Ed joined the IWW. Ed and John were ex-Marines who opposed both the Korean and Vietnam wars; they fought racism both in the mill and in the city of Youngstown, where in the 1950s swimming pools were still segregated; they believed, as do I, that there will be no answer to the problem of plant shutdowns until working people take the means of production into their own hands; and in January 1980, in response to U. S. Steel's decision to close all its Youngstown facilities, Ed led us down the hill from the local union hall to the U. S. Steel administration building, where the forces of good broke down the door and for one glorious afternoon occupied the company headquarters. Ed's daughter changed her baby's diapers on the pool table in the executive game room.

 Stan Weir and Marty Glaberman, very much alone, moved our thinking forward about informal work groups as the heart of working-class self-organization, about unions with leaders who stay on the shop floor, about alternatives to the hierarchical vanguard party, about overcoming racism and about international solidarity.

These men were in their own generation successors to the Haymarket martyrs and Joe Hill. They represented the inheritance that you and I seek to carry on.

## *How I First Learned About the IWW*

It all began for me when I was about fourteen years old.

Some of you may know the name of Seymour Martin Lipset. He became a rather conservative political sociologist. In the early 1940s, however, he was a graduate student of my father's and a socialist, who wrote his dissertation on the Canadian Commonwealth Federation.

Marty Lipset decided that my political education would not be complete until I had visited the New York City headquarters of the Socialist Party. The office was on the East Side and so we caught the shuttle at Times Square. I have no memory of the Socialist Party headquarters but a story Marty told me on the shuttle changed my life.

It seems that one day during the Spanish Civil War there was a long line of persons waiting for lunch. Far back in the line was a well-known anarchist. A colleague importuned him: "Comrade, come to the front of the line and get your lunch. Your time is too valuable to be wasted this way. Your work is too important for you to stand at the back of the line. Think of the Revolution!" Moving not one inch, the anarchist leader replied: "This is the Revolution."

I think I asked myself, Is there anyone in the United States who thinks that way? A few years later, in my parents' living room, I picked up C. Wright Mills' book about the leaders of the new Congress of Industrial Organizations, *The New Men of Power*. Mills argued that these men were bureaucrats at the head of hierarchical organizations. And at the very beginning of the book, in contrast to all that was to follow, Mills quoted a description of the Wobblies who went to Everett, Washington on a vessel named the *Verona* in November 1916 to take part in a free speech fight. As the boat approached the dock in Everett, "Sheriff McRae called out to them: Who is your leader? Immediate and unmistakable was the answer from every I.W.W.: 'We are all leaders.'"

So, I thought to myself, perhaps the Wobblies were the equivalent in the United States of the Spanish anarchists. But here a difficulty held me up for twenty years. If, as the Wobblies seemed to say, the answer to the problems of the old AF of L was industrial unionism, why was it that the new industrial unions of the CIO acted so much like the craft unions of the old AF of L?

## Industrial Unionism and the Right to Strike

The Preamble to the IWW Constitution, as of course you know, stated and still states:

"The trade unions foster a state of affairs which allows one set of workers to be pitted against another set of workers in the same industry . . . ."

Clearly these words, when they were written, referred to a workplace at the beginning of the last century where each group of craftspersons belonged to a different union. Each such union had its own collective bargaining agreement, complete with a termination date different from that of every other union at the worksite. The Wobblies called this typical arrangement "the American Separation of Labor." The Preamble suggested a solution:

> These conditions can be changed and the condition of the working class upheld only by an organization formed in such a way that all its members in any one industry, or all industries if necessary, cease work whenever a strike or lockout is on in any department thereof, thus making an injury to one an injury to all.

The answer, in short, appeared to be the reorganization of labor in industrial rather than craft unions.

It seemed to Wobblies and to like-minded rank-and-file workers that if only labor were to organize industrially, the "separation of labor"— as the IWW characterized the old AF of L—could be overcome. All kinds of workers in a given workplace would belong to the same union and could take direct action together, as they chose. Hence in the early 1930s Wobblies and former Wobblies threw themselves into the organization of local industrial unions.

A cruel disappointment awaited them. When John L. Lewis, Philip Murray, and other men of power in the new CIO negotiated the first contracts for auto workers and steelworkers, these contracts, even if only a few pages long, typically contained a no-strike clause. All workers in a given workplace were now prohibited from striking as particular crafts had been before. This remains the situation today.

Nothing in labor law required a no-strike clause. The leaders of the emergent CIO gave the right away. To be sure, the courts helped, holding before World War II that workers who strike over economic issues can be permanently replaced, and holding after World War II that a contract which provides for arbitration of grievances implicitly forbids strikes. But the courts are not responsible for the no-strike clause in the typical CIO contract. Trade union leaders are responsible.

Charles Morris' new book, *The Blue Eagle at Work*, argues that the original intent of Federal labor law was that employers should be legally required to bargain, not only with unions that win National Labor Relations Board elections, but also with so-called "minority" or "members-only" unions: unions that do not yet have majority support in a particular bargaining unit. We can all agree with Professor Morris that the best way to build a union is not by circulating authorization cards, but by winning small victories on the shop floor and engaging the company "in interim negotiations regarding workplace problems as they arise." But Morris' ultimate objective, like that of most labor historians and almost all union organizers, is still a union that negotiates a legally-enforceable collective bargaining agreement, including a management prerogatives clause that lets the boss close the plant and a no-strike clause that prevents the workers from doing anything about it. In my view, and I believe in yours, nothing essential will change—not if Sweeney is replaced by Stern or Wilhelm, not if the SEIU breaks away from the AFL-CIO, not if the percentage of dues money devoted to organizing is multiplied many times—so long as working people are contractually prohibited from taking direct action whenever and however they choose.

## GLABERMAN, MANN, SARGENT, AND WEIR

All this began to become clear to me only in the late 1960s, when a friend put in my hands a little booklet by Marty Glaberman entitled "Punching Out." Therein Marty argues that in a workplace where there is a union and a collective bargaining contract, and the contract (as it almost always does) contains a no-strike clause, the shop steward becomes a cop for the boss. The worker is forbidden to help his buddy in time of need. An injury to one is no longer an injury to all.

As I say these words of Marty Glaberman's, almost forty years later, in my imagination he and the other departed comrades form up around me. We cannot see them but we can hear their words.

Ed Mann: "I think we've got too much contract. You hate to be the guy who talks about the good old days, but I think the IWW had a darn good idea when they said: 'Well, we'll settle these things as they arise.'"

John Sargent: "Without a contract we secured for ourselves agreements on working conditions and wages that we do not have today. . . . [A]s a result of the enthusiasm of the people in the mill you had a series of strikes, wildcats, shut-downs, slow-downs, anything working people could think of to secure for themselves what they decided they had to have."

Stan Weir: "[T]he new CIO leaders fought all attempts to build new industrial unions on a horizontal rather than the old vertical model.

. . . There can be unions run by regular working people on the job. There have to be."

## RUMBLES IN OLYMPUS

Here we should pause to take note of recent rumbles—in both senses of the word—on Mount Olympus. What is happening in the mainstream labor movement, and what do we think about it?

This is a challenging question. Our energies are consumed by very small, very local organizing projects. It is natural to look sidewise at the organized trade union movement, with its membership in the hundreds of thousands, its impressive national headquarters buildings, its apparently endless income from the dues check-off, its perpetual projects for turning the corner in organizing this year or next year, and to wonder, Are we wasting our time?

Moreover, there is not and should not be an impenetrable wall between what we try to do and traditional trade unionism at the local level. My rule of thumb is that national unions and national union reform movements almost always do more harm than good, but that local unions are a different story. Workers need local unions. They will go on creating them whatever you and I may think, and for good reason. The critical decision for workers elected to local union office is whether they will use that position merely as a stepping stone to regional and national election campaigns, striving to rise vertically within the hierarchy of a particular union, or whether they will reach out horizontally to other workers and local union officers in other workplaces and other unions, so as to form classwide entities—parallel central labor bodies, or sometimes, even official central labor bodies—within particular localities.

Such bodies have special historical importance. The "soviets" in the Russian revolutions of 1905 and 1917 were improvised central labor bodies. Both the Knights of Labor and the IWW created such entities, especially during the first period of organizing in a given community when no single union was yet self-sufficient. My wife and I encountered a body of exactly this kind in Hebron in the occupied West Bank, and the Workers' Solidarity Club of Youngstown was an effort in the same direction. The "workers' centers" that seem to spring up naturally in communities of immigrant workers are another variant. What all these efforts have in common is that workers from different places of work sit in the same circle, and in the most natural way imaginable tend to transcend the parochialism of any particular union and to form a class point of view.

Because many Wobblies will in this way become "dual carders" [belonging both to the IWW and to a more traditional trade union], and often vigorously take part in the affairs of local unions, the line between our work and the activity of traditional, centralized, national trade unions needs to be drawn all the more clearly. From my point of view the choice is between, on the one hand, endless rearranging of the deck chairs on a sinking *Titanic*, and on the other hand, turning our faces toward the beginnings of a new world.

As you know I am a historian. And what drives me almost to tears is the spectacle of generation after generation of radicals seeking to change the world by cozying up to popular union leaders. Communists did it in the 1930s, as Len DeCaux became the CIO's public relations man and Lee Pressman its general counsel; and Earl Browder, in an incident related by historian Nelson Lichtenstein, ordered Party members helping to lead the occupation of a General Motors plant near Detroit to give up their agitation lest they offend the CIO leadership. Trotskyists and ex-Trotskyists in the second half of the twentieth century repeated this mistaken strategy with less excuse, providing intellectual services for the campaigns of Walter Reuther, Arnold Miller, Ed Sadlowski, and Ron Carey. And Left intellectuals almost without exception hailed the elevation of John Sweeney to the presidency of the AFL-CIO in 1995. Professors formed an organization of sycophantic academics, and encouraged their students to become organizers under the direction of national union staffers. In a parody of Mississippi's "Freedom Summer," so-called "union summers" used the energy of young people but denied them any voice in decisions.

In all these variations on a theme, students and intellectuals sought to make themselves useful to the labor movement by way of a relationship to national unions, rather than by seeking a helpful relationship with rank-and-file workers and members of local unions. In contrast, students at Harvard and elsewhere organized their own sit-ins to assist low-wage workers at the schools where they studied, and then it was John Sweeney who showed up to offer support to efforts that, to the best of my knowledge, young people themselves controlled.

Yes, national union leaders wish to increase union "density." But what characterizes national union leaders of the past and of the present is an absolute unwillingness to let rank-and-file workers decide for themselves when to undertake the sacrifice that direct action requires.

Consider John Sweeney. Close observers should have known in the fall of 1995 that Sweeney was hardly the democrat some supposed him to be. Andrea Carney (who is with us today) was at the time a hospital worker and member of Local 399, SEIU in Los Angeles. She tells in *The New Rank and File* how the Central American custodians whom the SEIU celebrated in its "Justice for Janitors" campaign joined Local 399 and then decided that they would like to have a voice in running it. They connected with Anglo workers like Ms. Carney to form a Multiracial Alliance that contested all offices [save that of local union president] on the local union executive board. In June 1995 they voted every officer out of office except the president. In September 1995, as one of his last acts before moving on to the AFL-CIO, Brother Sweeney removed all the newly-elected officers and put the local in trusteeship.

Closely following Sweeney's accession to the AFL-CIO presidency were his betrayal of strikes by Staley workers in Decatur, Illinois, and newspaper workers in Detroit. In Decatur, workers organized a spectacular "in plant" campaign of working to rule. After Staley locked them out, there were the makings of a parallel central body and a local general strike including automobile and rubber workers. Striker and hunger striker Dan Lane spoke to the AFL-CIO convention that elected Sweeney, and Sweeney personally promised Lane to further the campaign to cause major consumers of Staley product to boycott the company if Lane would give up his hunger strike. But Sweeney did nothing. Meantime the Staley local had been persuaded to affiliate with the national Paperworkers' union, which proceeded to organize acceptance of a concessionary contract.

In Detroit (as Larry who is here could describe in more detail), strikers begged the new AFL-CIO leadership to convene a national solidarity rally in their support. Sweeney said No. On the occasion of Clinton's second inauguration in 1997, leaders of the striking unions— including Ron Carey—decided to call off the strike without consulting the men and women who had been walking the picket lines for a year and a half. Only then did the Sweeney leadership summon workers from all over the country to join in a, now meaningless, gathering in Detroit.

SEIU president Andrew Stern apparently believes that the lesson is that the union movement should be more centralized. What kind of labor movement would there be if he had his way? Local 399 had a membership of 25,000 spread all over metropolitan Los Angeles. The SEIU "local union" where I live includes the states of Ohio, Kentucky, and West Virginia. This is topdown unionism run amok. The lesson for us is that, however humbly, in first steps however small, we need to be building a movement that is qualitatively different.

## SOLIDARITY FOREVER

And so of course we come in the end to the question, Yes, but how do we do that? Another world may be possible, but how do we get there? The Preamble says: "By organizing industrially we are forming the structure of the new society within the shell of the old." But if capitalist factories and mainstream trade unions are not prototypes of the new society, where is it being built? What can we do so that others and we ourselves do not just think and say that "another world is possible," but actually begin to experience it, to live it, to taste it, here and now, within the shell of the old?

In recent years I have glimpsed for the first time a possible answer, what Quakers call "way opening." It begins with the Zapatistas. Suppose the traditional conception of the creation of a new society is expressed in the equation, Rising Class plus New Institutions Within The Shell Of The Old equals State Power. What the Zapatistas have suggested, echoing an old Wobbly theme, is that the equation does not need to include the term "State Power." Perhaps we can change capitalism without taking state power. Perhaps we can change capitalism from below.

There remains the most difficult problem of all. "An injury to one is an injury to all" means that we must act in solidarity with working people everywhere, so that, in the words of the Preamble, "the workers of the world organize as a class."

This means that we cannot join with steel industry executives in seeking to keep foreign steel out of the country: we need a solution to worldwide over-capacity that protects steelworkers everywhere. We cannot, like the so-called reform candidate for president of the International Brotherhood of Teamsters a few years ago, advocate even more effort to keep Mexican truck drivers from crossing the Rio Grande. We should emulate the Teamsters local in Chicago where a resolution against the Iraq war passed overwhelmingly after Vietnam vets took the mike to share their experience, and the local went on to host the founding national meeting of Labor Against The War.

I believe the IWW has a special contribution to make. Wobblies were alone or almost alone among labor organizations a hundred years ago to welcome as members African Americans, unskilled foreign-born workers, and women. Joe Hill not only was born in Sweden and apparently took part in the Mexican Revolution, but, according to Franklin Rosemont, may have had a special fondness for Chinese cooking. This culture of internationalism can sustain and inspire us as we seek concrete ways to express it in the twenty-first century.

I have concluded that no imaginable labor movement or people's movement in this country will ever be sufficiently strong that it, alone, can confront and transform United States capitalism and imperialism.

I am not the only person who has reached this conclusion, but most who do so then say to themselves, I believe, "OK, then I need to cease pretending to be a revolutionary and support reform instead."

I suggest that what we need is an alternative revolutionary strategy. That strategy, it seems to me, can only be an alliance between whatever movement can be brought into being in the United States and the vast, tumultuous resistance of the developing world.

Note that I say "alliance," as between students and workers, or any other equal partners. I am not talking about kneejerk, uncritical support for the most recent Third World autocrat to capture our imaginations.

We in Youngstown have taken some very small first steps in this direction that I would like to share.

In the late 1980s skilled workers from Youngstown, Aliquippa, and Pittsburgh made a trip to Nicaragua. Ned Mann, Ed Mann's son, is a sheet metal worker. He helped steelworkers at Nicaragua's only steel mill, at Tipitapa north of Managua, to build a vent in the roof over a particularly smoky furnace. Meantime the late Bob Schindler, a lineman for Ohio Edison, worked with a crew of Nicaraguans doing similar work. He spoke no Spanish, they spoke no English. They got on fine. Bob was horrified at the tools available to his colleagues and, when he got back to the States, collected a good deal of Ohio Edison's inventory and sent it South. The next year he went back to Nicaragua, and traveled to the northern villages where Benjamin Linder was killed while trying to develop a small hydro-electric project. Bob did what he could to complete Linder's dream.

About a dozen of us from Youngstown have also gone to a labor school south of Mexico City related to the Frente Auténtico del Trabajo, the network of unions independent of the Mexican government.

These are tiny first steps, I know. But they are in the right direction. Why not take learning Spanish more seriously and, whenever we can, encourage fellow workers to join us in spending time with our Latin American counterparts?

And on down the same road, why not, some day, joint strike action from workers for General Motors in Puebla, Mexico, in Detroit, and in St. Catherine's, Ontario?

Instead of the TDU candidate for president of the Teamsters criticizing Jimmy Hoffa for doing too little to keep Mexican truck drivers out of the United States, why not a conference of truck drivers north and south of the Rio Grande to draw up a single set of demands?

Why not, instead of the United Steelworkers joining with United States steel companies to lobby for increased quotas on steel imports, a task force of steelworkers from all countries to draw up a common program about how to deal with capitalist over-production, how to make sure that each major developing country controls its own steelmaking capacity, and how to protect the livelihoods of all steelworkers, wherever they may live?

Perhaps I can end, as I began, with a story.

About a dozen years ago my wife and I were in the Golan Heights, a part of Syria occupied by Israel in 1967. There are a few Arab villages left in the Golan Heights, and at one of them our group was invited to a barbecue in an apple orchard. There was a very formidable white lightning, called *arak*. It developed that each group was called on to sing for the other. I was nominated for our group. I decided to sing "Joe Hill" but I felt that, before doing so, I needed to make it clear that Joe Hill was not a typical parochial American. As I laboriously began to do so, our host, who had had more to drink than I, held up his hand. "You don't have to explain," he said. "Joe Hill was a Spartacist. Joe Hill was in Chile and in Mexico. But today," he finished, "Joe Hill is a Palestinian."

Joe Hill is a Palestinian. He is also an Israeli refusenik.

He is imprisoned in Abu Ghraib and Guantanamo, where his Koran is subject to constant shakedowns and disrespect.

He works for Walmart and also in South African diamond mines.

He took part in the worldwide dock strike a few years ago and sees in that kind of international solidarity the hope of the future.

Recently he has spent a lot of time in occupied factories in Argentina, where he shuttles back and forth between the workers in the plants and the neighborhoods that support them.

In New York City, Joe Hill has taken note of the fact that a business like a grocery store (in working-class neighborhoods) or restaurant (in midtown Manhattan) is vulnerable to consumer boycotts, and if the pickets present themselves as community groups there is no violation of labor law.

In Pennsylvania, he has the cell next to Mumia Abu Jamal at S.C.I. Greene in Waynesburg. In Ohio, he hangs out with the "Lucasville Five": the five men framed and condemned to death because they were leaders in a 1993 prison uprising.

He was in Seattle, Quebec City, Genoa, and Cancun, and will be at the next demonstration against globalization wherever it takes place.

In Bolivia he wears a black hat and is in the streets, protesting the privatization of water and natural gas, calling for the nationalization of these resources, and for government from below by a people's assembly.

As the song says, "Where workingmen are out on strike, it's there you'll find Joe Hill."

Let's do our best to be there beside him.

# CONCLUSIONS

Here are my conclusions as of autumn 2009, when I delivered the three talks that make up this section.

Essay 23 was an appreciation of the historian William Appleman Williams. The occasion was a gathering at the University of Wisconsin on the fiftieth anniversary of the publication of his *Tragedy of American Diplomacy*. I call your attention especially to the brief ending of my talk. One of Williams' last books was called *Empire as a Way of Life*. It is dedicated to his grandmother and his summation describes an incident between his grandmother and himself when Williams was a little boy. I intuit that he means to suggest something fundamental about America's relation to the rest of the world. See what you think.

As for "Someday They'll Have A War And Nobody Will Come," these remarks were first delivered as the initial David Dellinger memorial lecture to the War Resisters League in New York City, and later presented to the 2009 conference of the Peace History Society. Therein I seek to critique the law of conscientious objection in the United States. The law provides that only persons sincerely opposed to participation in "war in any form" on the basis of "religious training and belief" should be recognized as Conscientious Objectors and excused from military service.

This statute is an example of what Herbert Marcuse called "repressive tolerance." In the first place, only a small number of persons who were brought up as members of the Amish, the Mennonites, the Hutterites, the Quakers, the Jehovah's Witnesses, and similar small religious groups, can qualify. In the second place, since the United States now has a voluntary military, hardly anyone presently serving in the Army, Navy, Marines or Air Force is likely to be recognized as a lifelong objector to war in any form.

An entirely different perspective opens up if we go back to the judgments of the Nuremburg Tribunal and ask what relevance these have to an Ehren Watada who encounters what he perceives to be war crimes after voluntarily enlisting in the Armed Forces. I argue that such "particular war objectors" must be legitimized, and that if they were, war would become much more difficult for nation states to wage.

The last of these three talks was delivered on the ninety-first anniversary of the Armistice that ended World War I, at the time proclaimed to be "the war to end war" and "the war to make the world safe for democracy." It was presented at the Fernand Braudel Center of the State University of New York in Binghamton. My comments address what seem to me the two "sixty-four dollar" or ultimate questions: What is the nature of capitalist crisis at a time when capitalism has more than ever become a globalized system? And, What sources of solidarity exist that we can support and nurture with the hope of replacing capitalism with another and a better world?

The first ten pages of *The Tragedy of American Diplomacy* set forth the following propositions:

First, in a prefatory quotation from the German philosopher Karl Jaspers, we find the idea that "genuine tragedy . . . grows out of success itself." Tragedy is not just something sad and painful. Genuine tragedy is the product of an incomplete and transitory victory; as Williams wrote elsewhere, of "the confrontation and clash of opposing truths"; of an accomplishment that, when wedged into the total structure of history, gives rise to its own rebuttal and leads to an undoing. So it was with Oedipus, who killed his own father, and with Hamlet, who could not kill his stepfather Claudius. Thus tragedy, for Williams, is a close cousin to what Karl Marx called a dialectical process of development. The question Williams presents to historians, and to the American people, is whether it is possible to extricate oneself from an unfolding foreign policy tragedy lacking only a fatal Fifth Act.

Also in these first few pages we find Williams insisting that "American leaders were not evil men," only an elite who sincerely believed that the rest of the world should be made over in America's image. The economic interests of the ruling elite are, for the most part, not personal, "pocketbook" interests, Williams stressed. Men like Alexander Hamilton, John Jay, and James Madison, or John Hay and Theodore Roosevelt, or more recently, John Foster Dulles, Dean Acheson, Robert McNamara, and Richard Cheney—all men who shuttled back and forth between the commanding heights of economic and political power—were concerned to preserve an economic system. These men assumed that representative government required a foundation of securely-protected private property. Hence, in aggressively promoting the spread of American capitalism, they assumed that they were simultaneously making the world safe for democracy.

Indeed throughout his writings Williams seems to have cherished the hope that influential members of the Establishment—such as, in days of yore, the Earl of Shaftesbury and John Quincy Adams, in his own time perhaps a William Fulbright—might perceive the folly of the strategy in pursuit of which men of their class were leading a compliant government.

Early on in *The Tragedy*, also, Williams demanded of radical readers that we face the fact that by the 1890s most Americans supported a foreign policy of capitalist economic expansion. Overseas economic expansion was widely perceived to be the functional equivalent of the continental frontier that was no longer available as the United States entered the twentieth century. An outlet for American farm products and manufactures that could not be consumed at home was felt to be necessary to forestall economic collapse. "Once a pioneer began to produce surpluses," Williams wrote, "he became a farm businessman looking for markets." Support for a foreign policy that would promote American exports was expressed, according to Williams, not only by Democratic Party spokesmen like William Jennings Bryan and Woodrow Wilson, but also by Populist agitators such as "Sockless" Jerry Simpson.

## *THE OPEN DOOR POLICY*

The bulk of *The Tragedy* sets forth Williams' core concept that the strategy guiding American foreign policy at least since the 1890s has been what Williams called "the Open Door policy."

The Open Door policy seeks all the advantages of economic imperialism without the burdens of outright colonialism. In the language of foreign policy discourse after World War II, it is a policy that has been "neo-colonial" from the beginning. One way to understand the idea is to consider the law of contracts. Contracts, as portrayed in the first year of law school, are entered into between parties of equal bargaining power. But that is not the real world. In the real world, if one contracting party has sufficient power it can simply demand acceptance of its terms by the weaker party. What is ostensibly an agreement between equals may conceal a relationship in which a tenant, or a consumer, or a worker desperate for a job, is taken advantage of egregiously.

Williams asked us to see the relationship between the United States and smaller, developing economies in a similar way. "[I]n expanding its own economic system throughout much of the world," he wrote, "America has made it very difficult for other nations to retain their economic independence." Consistent with United States rhetoric about self-determination and humanitarian concern for others, the government of a former colony in Latin America, or Africa, or Southeast Asia, may be allowed to become and remain nominally independent. But "American corporations exercise extensive authority, and even commanding power, in the political economy of such nations."

The New Deal, Williams argued in *The Tragedy*, continued and deepened the pattern of "free trade imperialism or informal empire." In Williams' view, "[t]hinking of the New Deal . . . as a reform movement tends to blind both its critics and its defenders . . . ." New Deal reforms, according to Williams, "rationalized the system as it existed, and did not lead to significant modifications of its character."

Ninety pages of *The Tragedy of American Diplomacy* sought to show that the development of Cold War hostility between the United States and the Soviet Union after World War II offered another illustration of Open Door imperialism. It was "the decision of the United States to employ its new and awesome power in keeping with the traditional Open Door policy which crystallized the cold war," Williams wrote (*Tragedy*, p. 295).

In these pages Williams restated an analysis presented in his first book, *American-Russian Relations, 1781-1917*, published in 1952. There Williams set forth the belief that the United States must recognize, and adapt to, socialist revolution as represented by the Soviet Union. He attacked, as the clearest expression of the view that he opposed, George Kennan's thesis in Kennan's famous "Mr. X" article that "[t]he United States has it in its power . . . to promote tendencies which must eventually find their outlet in either the breakup or the gradual mellowing of Soviet power" (*American-Russian Relations*, pp. 258, 279-283).

The problem, however, is that Kennan appears to have been right. Both a mellowing or "perestroika" and a breakup of Soviet power did indeed take place. To be sure, history in hindsight is easier than history as prediction and prophecy, but Williams, having chosen to write prophetic history, cannot complain if his history must be corrected by what actually happened.

A more convincing example of the Open Door policy in action is Williams' account of the origin of hostilities between the United States and Cuba after the accession to power by Castro, presented in *The United States, Cuba and Castro*, published in 1962.

Here again, Williams encountered the problem of History As Prediction. He wrote that as of September 1962, the Russians "had not establish[ed] Soviet bases in Cuba as the United States has done in such nations as Turkey along the frontiers of the Soviet Union," nor had the Soviet Union, Williams said, "constructed . . . launching pads for Soviet missiles" (*Cuba and Castro*, p. 143). Before the book was published several weeks later Williams was obliged to add a postscript in which he argued that the discovery in Cuba of launching sites for Soviet missiles, precipitating the Cuba Missile Crisis, did not invalidate his underlying thesis.

Nonetheless, I find Williams' account of how the Open Door policy was applied in Cuba more persuasive than his parallel narrative concerning the Soviet Union. Williams asked us to look at three things: the Cuban Constitution of 1940, which Castro had vowed to put into effect; the International Monetary Fund's refusal to loan money to the new Cuban government on terms that would have made repayment possible; and the Agrarian Reform Law announced in 1959.

Williams began by asking us to credit the desire of Cuba's new revolutionary government to provide tangible benefits to the Cuban people.

> More than a quarter million dollars was promptly invested in housing projects, schools, recreational facilities, and various other public works. Many of them were opened to the public within a month after Batista was defeated. Many salaries were raised. Electric power rates were cut. More telephones became available at lower cost. Rents were decreased as much as 50 percent . . . . Mortgage rates were reduced. And the price of meat was lowered.

However, standing between such aspirations and a long-term program of improvement were the fact that more than half a million workers were out of work and the need for substantial capital investment. Cuba was at the time an economy dependent on the export of sugar. Castro wanted to diversify, to encourage food production for the home market, and to develop light industry producing textiles and other consumer goods, all of which required capital investment. Whence was that capital to come?

The new Cuban government approached the International Monetary Fund for the long-term loan that it needed. Williams told the story of this effort based on published materials and on what he described as his own "persistent efforts to discover still further information." It seems clear that the IMF was prepared to loan money only if the Cubans accepted a so-called "stabilization program." That program, as applied in Argentina a few months earlier, would have required "credit restraint" and a "balanced- or nearly-balanced budget." So-called stabilization would therefore have prevented massive investment based on deficit financing. In Williams' words, it would have meant "telling Castro that he could have a loan if he gave up the social revolution to which he was committed."

In a May 1959 address in Buenos Aires to an economic conference sponsored by the Organization of American States, Castro noted that the foreigners who had the necessary capital wanted what they termed a "favorable climate" for their operations in poorer countries. Cuba refused this

ultimatum. The loan it had requested did not materialize, and Cuba turned
to the Soviet Union as a market for its sugar and for military support.

The effort by the United States to impose its vision of a desirable world by means of the World Bank and International Monetary
Fund, exemplified by Cuban events in 1959, has continued. American
administrators of the two bodies have insisted that developing economies
seeking their help must commit to smoothing the way for foreign capital investment by privatizing nationalized industries and public services.
Fittingly, it was Fidel Castro who many years ago sought to counterpose
the demand that the debts of such governments, by means of which the
United States sought to impose its own cookie-cutter notions of what
constitutes a "free" society, should simply be canceled.

Consider the impact of the North American Free Trade Agreement
on the economy of Mexico. Not long after NAFTA went into effect
(and the Zapatista rebellion began) in January 1994, my wife and I attended a seminar organized by the Frente Auténtico del Trabajo, or FAT,
a network of independent Mexican trade unions. Another participant
was a man who cultivated a farm near the city of Puebla. His father and
grandfather had grown corn for the local and regional market. He could
no longer do so, our friend told us, because NAFTA prohibited import
duties and so he could be undersold by corn from Iowa. Instead he was
raising sheep. "We see," I responded, "you are selling mutton." "No, no."
Julio responded, "if I sold meat I would also be undersold by Iowa. I am
selling wool!" Listening with a heavy heart, I could only wonder how long
it would be before fibers from the United States would undersell Julio in
that market also.

And we should not forget that the *quid pro quo* for removal of
Mexican tariffs was to be free access to the United States for Mexican
goods and services. But it is more than fifteen years since the adoption
of NAFTA and Mexican truck drivers are still not permitted to cross the
Rio Grande and to drive freely in the United States.

These consequences of NAFTA further illustrate a remark of
President William McKinley in 1896, quoted by Williams. The purpose
of the Open Door policy, McKinley stated,

> was "to afford new markets for our surplus agricultural and
> manufactured products without loss to the American laborer
> of a single day's work that he might otherwise procure."

A third foreign policy crisis that self-evidently presented itself to
Williams, at the full tide of his powers, was Vietnam. Williams edited
a volume entitled *The Vietnam War* made up of documents presented

and introduced by himself, Thomas McCormick, Lloyd Gardner, and Walter LaFeber.

The Open Door policy does not seem to be a very good explanation of what happened in Vietnam. There was concern in the United States about Southeast Asia in the years immediately following World War II, but Professor McCormick said that this "did not flow from direct American interest in the region." American policymakers were anxious to expand exports to Vietnam not from the United States, but from Japan, lest that country drift toward Communism. Even within that framework, they perceived French Indochina to possess less market potential than any other country in the region.

Once the United States committed itself to nation-building in South Vietnam, incentives quite different from those hypothesized by the Open Door thesis appeared to drive policy. President Lyndon Johnson believed that he could not marshal support for the War on Poverty at home if he lost Vietnam to Communism. Professor LaFeber comments: "Americans virtually took over the responsibility for running South Vietnam. This policy . . . less resembled the traditional U.S. open-door approach than British rule in India."

Finally, far from assisting the United States economically, intervention in Vietnam produced inflation that tore apart the U.S. economy, destroyed much of the dollar's value by 1971, and "helped bring on the quadrupling of gasoline prices in 1973-1974." Throughout the years of intense United States involvement there was very little private investment in Vietnam by American companies.

Thus, in the three major foreign policy crises of Williams' lifetime—the confrontations with the Soviet Union, with Cuba, and with the Vietnam insurgency—the Open Door hypothesis fits the facts best when applied to Cuba and less well when applied to the Cold War with the Soviet Union and to Vietnam. Nevertheless, overall Williams' presentation of economic expansion as the heartbeat of United States foreign policy for at least the past century is compelling. The number of significant spokespersons Williams shows to have been explicit advocates for expanding United States exports abroad, by whatever means necessary, is staggering.

The third and last edition of *The Tragedy of American Diplomacy* ends in a way that is itself truly tragic. Chile, Williams wrote in August 1971, "has demonstrated the possibility of choosing [a revolutionary path] in a democratic election." Two years later, on September 11, 1973, the democratically-elected Allende government was overthrown by the United States just as the United States had previously engineered the overthrow of democratically-elected governments in Iran (1953) and Guatemala (1954).

Today the democratically-elected Hamas government in Palestine awaits a similar fate. Thus far it has been stripped of most of the area it was elected to govern and left to administer impoverished, and now devastated, Gaza.


## *ANTI-ABOLITIONISM*

It seems unfair to criticize a man who is no longer with us and is not in a position to defend himself. But I cannot try to supplement Williams' insights with my own *Weltanschauung*—to use one of his favorite words—unless I first emphasize a sharp and fundamental difference between Williams' world view and my own.

I met Bill Williams for the first and only time during the winter of 1961-1962. He greeted me at the Madison airport and we spent an evening of discussion at his home with William Taylor. Professor Taylor was full of excitement about the work on women's history he was undertaking with Christopher Lasch.

What astounded me in the discourse of both men was their hostility toward the nineteenth century antislavery movement. They regarded the abolitionist movement as a propaganda arm of Northern capitalism. I was in my first year of teaching at a college for African American women in Atlanta. I had been recruited by Howard Zinn, whose subsequent book on the Student Nonviolent Coordinating Committee was sub-titled "The New Abolitionists." Many of our students, such as the future author of *The Color Purple*, were picketing segregated department stores in downtown Atlanta. In confronting these young women in the American history survey course, I was coming to recognize the centrality of slavery in United States history. The contrary perspective of Williams and Taylor caused me consternation.

What Williams had to say about the coming of the Civil War and Abraham Lincoln in subsequently-published books only increased my distress. Williams asserted in *The Contours of American History* (p. 286) that

> the basic cause of the Civil War was the *Weltanschauung* of laissez faire. Unwilling to compete within the framework and under the terms of the Constitution, northern antislavery advocates of laissez faire finally undertook to change the rules in the middle of the game . . . by denying the South further access to the expanding market place.

In another book, *America Confronts a Revolutionary World*, Williams argued that "the cause of the Civil War was the refusal of Lincoln and other northerners to honor the revolutionary right of self-determination by the Confederate South" (p. 113).

One wonders, what about that other value affirmed by the Declaration of Independence, the idea that all men are created equal? According to Williams, Southerners who insisted on their right to independence recognized "the possibility that it would prove necessary to end slavery to secure independence and self-determination." Williams thought that Southerners walked through the door into independence knowing that it might mean the end of slavery (*America Confronts*, pp. 117-118). As Williams saw it, Lincoln's course of conduct in declining to let the Southern states depart in peace was "counterrevolutionary," expressing "the possessive individualism of marketplace capitalism" (*America Confronts*, p. 121).

To put it in the light most favorable to Williams, he was concerned that this country must acquire the ability to let other societies exercise their right to self-determination by finding their own ways into the future. Williams wanted America to learn how to "live and let live" in a revolutionary world. But I cannot follow Williams in including the slave South among the developing societies entitled to self-determination, or in wishing that the Southern states had been given the opportunity to prolong the life of their peculiar institution, or in believing that the Confederacy, left to its own devices, might have abolished slavery.

## MY COUNTRY IS THE WORLD

Accordingly, as fellow believers with Professor Williams in the concept of tragedy and in the dialectical process, I think we must conclude that his own worldview was in some respects two-dimensional and incomplete.

Williams' history sometimes seems Hegelian. Concepts like "the Open Door policy," "self-determination," "mercantilism," and "laissez faire" figure in Williams' pages as if they, not human beings, were the essential historical protagonists, and as if history itself were a war of the *Weltanschauungen*.

How might we try to put into words what is missing? How may we provide what Hegel called an *Aufhebung*, that is, an overcoming of apparent contradiction such that a new synthesis emerges?

To begin with, what William Appleman Williams called empire as a way of life is something more than a desire for markets in which surplus goods can be sold. Deep currents of racism, of male insecurity, and of a propensity to violence, enter in. Early in 2007 I was part of a citizens' panel in Tacoma, Washington. Lt. Ehren Watada was being court martialed for his refusal to deploy to Iraq. The idea of our proceeding was to listen to the evidence that the officer in charge of the court martial would not permit to be heard.

By far the most gripping testimony came from veterans of the Iraq war, and the particular evidence I cannot get out of my head came from Geoffrey Millard. He described how his unit had set up a particular Traffic Control Point. As vehicles approached the checkpoint, servicemen had to make split-second decisions as to whether an approaching vehicle contained friends or foes. An eighteen-year-old Private First Class pressed the butterfly trigger on his 50-caliber machine gun and put more than 200 rounds into an approaching car. He watched as the results of his decision were extracted from the vehicle: a mother, a father, a boy aged four, and a girl aged three.

That evening the unit discussed what had happened in the presence of a "full bird colonel." Millard said there is a mistaken belief that racism among the troops comes from the bottom up and that higher-ranking officers are more enlightened. According to Millard, that evening's discussion ended when the colonel stopped the briefing, exclaiming loudly: "If these fucking hajis [would] learn to drive, this shit wouldn't happen." (*Peace Not Terror: Leaders of the Antiwar Movement Speak Out Against U.S. Foreign Policy Post 9/11*, ed. Mary Susannah Robbins, pp. 198-199.)

The colonel said "hajis." He might have said "towel heads" or "sand Niggers." Had the unit been in Vietnam he would have said "gooks" or "slants."

Additional light on the subject is shed by William Calley, the former Army lieutenant convicted of twenty-two counts of murder at My Lai, Vietnam. Mr. Calley spoke to the Kiwanis Club of Greater Columbus, Georgia, in August 2009. The Columbus *Ledger-Enquirer*, reporting the event, recalled the words Calley spoke at his court martial when he was allowed to address the court before sentencing. Calley stated on that occasion: "If I have committed a crime, the only crime I have committed is in judgment of my values [*sic*]. Apparently I valued my troops' lives more than I did those of the enemy."

These words bring us to the heart of the matter. United States imperialism, like slavery in the United States, has economic origins. But the stereotypes and projections by means of which imperialism is justified are also real. If we are to overcome what William Appleman Williams termed "empire as a way of life" we shall have to struggle on more than one terrain. At the same time that we resist factory shutdowns and the export of capital to low-wage societies outside the United States, we shall have to learn how to critique the self-satisfied vision of our country as a light to other nations, as the leader of the free world. We must find ways to affirm, in opposition to William Calley, that the nation into which one is born is of secondary importance because all human beings are of equal value.

For reasons I do not fully understand, Williams set himself apart from the tradition of American radicalism beginning with Thomas Paine and running through antislavery agitators like Garrison, Thoreau, and Frederick Douglass to the Haymarket anarchists and the IWW. Williams mentioned Paine but preferred Samuel Adams. Williams conceded that Adams demanded the death sentence for Daniel Shays and the indebted farmers who supported Shays. But Adams, according to Williams, was a "Calvinist revolutionary crusading for a Christian corporate commonwealth" and thus eligible for admission to Williams' pantheon whereas Paine was not.

Paine, after close encounters with the governing classes of three nations (including the American gentlemen who snubbed him after they had used him), was accused of atheism and died a lonely death. But his words grew wings. Paine had written in *The Rights of Man*, "my country is the world." William Lloyd Garrison placed on the masthead of *The Liberator* when it appeared in 1831, "Our country is the world, our countrymen are mankind." In the 1840s, when Frederick Douglass was en route to England on his first trip outside the United States, he was taunted by slaveholders. His friends the Hutchinson singers responded with a toast, "Our country is the world, our countrymen all mankind." When he returned to the United States, Douglass said, "I have no love for America as such; I have no patriotism, I have no country." A generation later the Haymarket anarchist Albert Parsons addressed a packed Chicago courtroom before he was sentenced to death. "Opening his arms wide" Parsons declared: "The world is my country, all mankind my countrymen." And Eugene Debs, at the time of World War I, expressed in *The Appeal to Reason* the sentiment that would cause him to be sent to the Atlanta Penitentiary: "I have no country to fight for; my country is the earth; I am a citizen of the world."

The most riveting articulations of this tradition come from Henry David Thoreau. In his essay on "Civil Disobedience," he famously observed that the "fugitive slave, and the Mexican prisoner on parole, and the Indian come to plead the wrongs of his race" should find good citizens in "the only house in a slave State in which a free man can abide with honor," namely, in prison behind bars. Less well-known is another fragment of the same essay:

> If I have unjustly wrested a plank from a drowning man, I must restore it to him though I drown myself. This, according to Paley [a writer on moral questions], would be inconvenient. But he that would save his life, in such a case, shall lose it. This people must cease to hold slaves, and to make war on Mexico, though it cost them their existence as a people.

In "Slavery in Massachusetts," written after fugitive slave Anthony Burns was abducted in broad daylight on the streets of Boston, Thoreau summoned his countrymen to be "men first, and Americans only at a late and convenient hour."

The idea that "my country is the world" has been reborn, and as it were mainstreamed, in the rhetoric of international human rights that burst into being at the end of World War II, above all at the Nuremburg Tribunal. And in the last few years the United States Supreme Court, in a magnificent series of decisions about indefinite detention without criminal charges, has turned historian and liberally cited authorities from the period of the American Revolution in support of the concept of international human rights. Probing what it termed the "ambient law" of the Revolutionary era, the Court has concluded that in that era courts were open to claims based on "a norm of international character accepted by the civilized world." (*Sosa v. Alvarez-Machain*, 542 U.S. 692, 714, 725.) Even more dramatically the Court has twice cited Lord Mansfield's 1772 decision in *Somersett v. Stewart*, releasing "an African slave purchased in Virginia and detained on a ship docked in England and bound for Jamaica." James Somerset's "status as an alien," like that of the so-called enemy combatants at Guantanamo, was not a bar to habeas corpus relief. (*Rasul v. Bush*, 542 U.S. 466, 481 n. 11; *Boumediene v. Bush*, 128 S.Ct. 2229, 2248.)

The idea of international human rights has its own kind of power. Anthropologist Shannon Speed offers a revealing anecdote from her many years in Chiapas, Mexico. In July 1995 she traveled nearly ten hours "in the crowded back of an old truck on a very rough dirt road." Finally

> the truck came to a halt in the road in front of a small plaza with a basketball court, a church, and a meeting-house. I jumped down and stood blinking like a stunned animal in the unrelenting sun. Children peered at me . . . . I continued to stand there in the road, unsure how to proceed. The tension in the air was palpable. Finally . . . a man approached me. He peered severely into my face and asked, *"Vienes de derechos humanos?"* "Are you from human rights?" *"Sí, sí,"* I told him . . . . His face broke into a relieved smile. I was from human rights. I was on their side. I was one of them.
>
> (*Rights in Rebellion: Indigenous Struggle and Human Rights in Chiapas*, pp. 60-61.)

### GIVE BACK THE KNIFE

Having fulfilled my scholarly duty to be properly critical of Professor Williams, I should like to conclude by celebrating him.

After Williams, it should no longer be possible for historians to present any specific intervention or act of aggression as an inexplicable departure from our country's normal practice of beneficent peacemaking. Williams has shown us that for the United States empire has been a way of life from the time of the first English settlements in North America. The Open Door policy is a particular imperial strategy, more helpful in explaining some situations than in explaining others. But the underlying reality of economic expansion, justified by self-righteous chatter about a City on the Hill, has always been there.

Perhaps the best evidence for this proposition are the four appendices to Williams' book engagingly entitled *Empire As a Way of Life: An Essay on the Causes and Character of America's Present Predicament Along With a Few Thoughts About an Alternative*, published by Oxford University Press in 1980. Therein Williams lists 153 incidents of American Interventionist Activity (excluding declared wars) from 1798 to 1941.

A second great legacy to American historians is Williams' insistence—awkwardly expressed, never fully explained, and sometimes illustrated by rather bizarre examples—that the United States must choose between empire and community. "Our true goal should be an American community," Williams wrote in *Contours of American History* (p. 6).

Humankind can seek relationships based on "power and passivity" or relationships arising from "involved, participating, and reciprocal love." Either set of relationships may be called a community, but in the case of a community based on power and passivity it is a benevolent despotism. Benevolent despotisms exist but they "break down because they fail to satisfy the demands for love and participation."

The second kind of community is democratic and equitable, straightforward and loving. Love comes before power, and participation before passivity. Equity and equality come before efficiency and ease.

> Man . . . creates best in conjunction with, not under direction by. And he most nearly approaches love in evolving relationships with other human beings, rather than in organized and structured association with other role players.

(*Contours*, p. 9.)

The most moving passages in *Empire as a Way of Life* occur at the very beginning and the very end. In closing his Preface, Williams says:

I was born and reared in our American womb of empire, but my experience and my study of history have enabled me to understand that we must leave that imperial incubator if we are to become citizens of the real world. Our future is . . . a community to be created ourselves so that we can be citizens—not imperial overlords—of the world.

(*Empire*, p. xii.)

In these words Paine's critic endorses Paine's most fundamental affirmation.

The very end of *Empire as a Way of Life* tells a story involving Williams' maternal grandmother, Maude Hammond Appleman, to whom the book is dedicated.

It seems that young Williams, growing up in a small Midwestern community, became impatient to own a fine and expensive knife on display at the best hardware store in town. His family was not dirt poor. But, as Williams puts it, "the imperial ethos does not teach one to wait." He stole the knife.

Maude Hammond Appleman told her grandson that he **had** to return the knife. And so he "walked back along those long and lonely blocks to the store." I came face to face, he tells us,

with the member of the small community who owned the store. And I said: I stole this knife and I am sorry and I am bringing it back.

And he said: Thank you. The knife is not very important, but you coming down here and saying that to me is very important.

Remembering all that [Williams concludes], I know why I do not want the empire. There are better ways to live and there are better ways to die.

(*Empire*, p. 226.)

I must begin with a scholarly correction. The title of this talk, "Someday They'll Have A War And Nobody Will Come," is one of those quotations that has been in your head forever and that you are sure is right. However, it's wrong. The correct quotation—which I consider less felicitous—turns out to be, "Sometime they'll give a war and nobody will come." Moreover, I was quite certain that the quotation came from a play by Irwin Shaw called "Bury The Dead." That's wrong also. The quotation is from Carl Sandburg's "The People, Yes."

Both "Bury The Dead" and "The People, Yes" were published in 1936. Thus neither was a product of the period between September 1939, when Germany invaded Poland, and June 1941, when Germany invaded the Soviet Union, the period that Communist Parties termed the period of "phony war" and during which persons in and close to the Party strenuously opposed war preparations. Indeed, in 1936 the Communist Party was encouraging young men to go to Spain to fight in the International Brigades. Accordingly, I presume that the passionate antiwar sentiments of these two literary works expressed what we might call the "World War I syndrome." In some liberal and radical circles there was still in 1936 a wide and deep opposition to war caused by the horrors of 1914-1918.

David Dellinger, in whose memory I delivered the original version of this talk, was one of a very small number of persons whose pacifism continued into and throughout World War II. David was one of the Union Theological Seminary Eight who not only refused to fight in the second world war but refused to register for the draft. David served two terms in federal prison and helped to lead long hunger strikes protesting racial segregation, censorship of mail, and other objectionable prison practices.

While David was doing his second prison term for war resistance, his wife Betty was pregnant. David tells in *From Yale to Jail* how when he was on hunger strike at Lewisburg the warden came to his cell and said,

"She's dying. She has sent a message telling you to go off the strike so she can die in peace." David said, "Take me to her." The warden refused and David concluded, correctly, that the warden was lying. The prisoners won one of the major goals of their hunger strike, concerning the censorship of mail. David was given a pile of letters from Betty telling him that she was well and supported the strike. The Dellingers' oldest child, Patchen, was born soon after.

When the Union Eight were released from prison, Union offered them readmission on condition that they would avoid any course of action that would publicize their draft resistance. Five of the eight refused and went instead to Chicago Theological Seminary.

Another opponent of the military Goliath, David Mitchell, pioneered in the 1960s the position that I wish to explicate tonight. David Mitchell said that he was not a pacifist. He refused to participate in the Selective Service process because he believed that the actions of the United States in Vietnam were war crimes, as war crimes had been defined at Nuremburg after World War II. He spent two years in prison.

With these forerunners in mind we turn to the message of another hero, Ehren Watada. In the military, justice is administered by courts martial. In the court martial process, there is a proceeding similar to the convening of a grand jury. It is called an Article 32 hearing. The hearing officer decides whether there is sufficient evidence to justify a court martial. On August 17, 2006, at Fort Lewis, Washington, there was an Article 32 hearing for Lt. Watada. Early in the hearing the prosecution played video clips from his recent speeches. In one of these speeches, at the national convention of Veterans for Peace, Lt. Watada said: "Today, I speak with you about a radical idea. . . . The idea is this; that to stop an illegal and unjust war, the soldiers . . . can choose to stop fighting it."

Of course in itself this was not a new idea. It was another way of saying, Someday they'll have a war and nobody will come.

But what is unusual is Lt. Watada's basis for saying No. Like David Mitchell in the 1960s, Ehren Watada is not a pacifist. He offered to go to Afghanistan but refused to go to Iraq. He refused to go to Iraq for the same reason David Mitchell refused to go to Vietnam, not because of objection to all wars, but because of a conviction that war crimes were being committed in this particular war, giving rise to an obligation, under the principles declared at Nuremburg, to refuse military service.

Carl Mirra has edited a collection of oral histories of the second Iraq War entitled *Soldiers and Citizens: An Oral History of Operation Iraqi Freedom from the Battlefield to the Pentagon.* Therein two interviewees— one a veteran, the other a veteran's wife who now does military counseling—express the view that the current legal definition of conscientious objection is too confining, too "tight." It is confining and tight because it requires a soldier who is troubled by actions he has been ordered to commit to object to participation in all wars in order to refuse conscientiously. Self-evidently conscience cannot be thus circumscribed, and Nuremburg did not intend that it should be. A soldier can and must be able to say No to orders in a particular war that he perceives to be war crimes and that deeply offend conscience.

Take a minute to recognize how radical a change this would be. The concept of Conscientious Objection, as set forth in Selective Service law during and after World War II and in the existing regulations of all the military services, is based on the Christian teaching of forgiveness of enemies, of doing good for evil, of turning the other cheek, of putting up the sword. To become a conscientious objector the applicant must object to participation in "war in any form," which is to say, to *all* wars.

This is a noble idea. I happen to adhere to it, personally. But it is unlikely ever to be the conviction of more than a very few persons of military age. It is a legal system written to accommodate the tender consciences of members of certain small Christian sects that came into being during the Radical Reformation: Hutterites, Quakers, Amish, Mennonites, Brethren, and the like. And let's be honest, **Conscientious Objection thus defined exists because the powers that be know that it will never be the world view of more than a handful of persons.**

Moreover, it should be obvious that in a volunteer military an even tinier minority of service men and women can be expected to object to war in any form. Had this been their belief, why would they have volunteered in the first place? True, it is possible to become a Conscientious Objector while serving in the military. Certain remarkable individuals like Camillo Mejia and Kevin Benderman have deployed to Iraq, been horrified by what they experienced, and on reflection concluded that they will never again fight in any war. But common sense tells us that such Conscientious-Objectors-From-Experience-In-A-Particular-War will be few. This is, especially so because, as was the case with both Mejia and Benderman, the military will court martial and imprison such objectors without giving them the legally-required opportunity to appeal an initial rejection of conscientious objector status.

The system can tolerate traditional Conscientious Objectors. For those who remember Herbert Marcuse's concept of "repressive tolerance," this is an example: precisely by making room for such atypical refuseniks, the system as a whole can continue undisturbed.

But it might be otherwise if the David Mitchell-Ehren Watada approach became law. Then you might have hundreds, even thousands of soldiers saying, in effect: "I can't tell you how I might feel in another war.

But I can tell you where I stand about this one. This particular war is a war that requires the commission of war crimes. It may even be a war that as defined at Nuremburg *is* a war crime in its totality, because it is an aggressive war, a crime against the peace. I ain't gonna study this war no more."

If that idea were once let loose in the land, one might indeed have a war to which very few would come.

So let's try to form a more precise idea of refusal to fight based on the belief that a particular war involves war crimes.

## I. THE NUREMBURG PRINCIPLES

At the end of World War II humanity imagined a new design of international relations. In that new web of relationships, all nations would recognize certain human rights, all persons and governments would be required to avoid certain war crimes and crimes against humanity, all conquering states would commit themselves to prescribed behavior with respect to prisoners and occupied territories.

The initial conceptualization of these new rights and obligations took place at Nuremburg. For more than a half century, the verdicts at Nuremberg in trials of German leaders after World War II have provided the fundamental standards by which alleged war crimes are to be assessed.

The Charter of the International Military Tribunal (IMT) identified three kinds of war crimes:

(a) War crimes: namely, violations of the laws or customs of war. Such violations shall include, but not be limited to, murder, ill-treatment or deportation to slave labor or for any other purpose of civilian population of or in occupied territory, murder or ill-treatment of prisoners of war or persons on the seas, killing of hostages, plunder of public or private property, wanton destruction of cities, towns or villages, or devastation not justified by military necessity;

(b) Crimes against humanity: namely, murder, extermination, enslavement, deportation, and other inhumane acts committed against any civilian population, before or during the war; or persecutions on political, racial or religious grounds, in execution of or in connection with any crime within the jurisdiction of the Tribunal, whether or not in violation of domestic law of the country where perpetrated;

(c) Crimes against peace: namely, planning, preparation, initiation or waging of a war of aggression, or a war in violation of international treaties, agreements or assurances, or participation in a common plan or conspiracy for the accomplishment of any of the foregoing.[1]

Apart from the definition of war crimes, three principles set forth in the Charter are of particular importance here.

The first is that the defense of "superior orders"[2] is expressly rejected. Article 8 of the Charter specified: "The fact that the defendant acted pursuant to order of his Government or of a superior shall not free him from responsibility, but may be considered in mitigation of punishment if the Tribunal determines that justice so requires."[3]

The second Nuremburg principle is that international law must take precedence over the law of any particular nation. Expansion and clarification of the Nuremburg Principles was carried forward by the U.N. International Law Commission in 1950, when it adopted and codified them in broad application to international law, drawing in some cases on the judgments of the Tribunal.

Here the Commission highlighted at the outset the principle "that international law may impose duties on individuals directly without any interposition of internal law," and, as a corollary, that individuals are not relieved of responsibility under international law "by the fact that their acts are not held to be crimes under the law of any particular country." The Commission went on to point out that this implies "what is commonly called the 'supremacy' of international law over national law," and to cite the declaration of the IMT that "the very essence of the Charter is that individuals have international duties which transcend the national obligations of obedience imposed by the individual State."[4]

The third, and for my purposes most important, Nuremburg principle is that aggressive war is a crime no matter what nation may commit it. The nations which framed the Charter, the judges of the Tribunal, and in particular, the representatives of the United States, considered that henceforth the crimes defined at Nuremberg should apply to all nations, including those that conducted the trials. Among these crimes was the "crime against peace" of aggressive war.

Robert Jackson, Associate Justice of the United States Supreme Court and Chief Counsel for the United States during the Nuremberg proceedings, reported that the definition of aggressive war occasioned "the most serious disagreement" at the conference which drafted the Charter. Jackson stated that the United States "declined to recede from its position even if it meant the failure of the Conference." He described the conflict as follows:

> The Soviet Delegation proposed and until the last meeting pressed a definition which, in our view, had the effect of declaring certain acts crimes only when committed by the Nazis. The United States contended that the criminal character of such acts could not depend on who committed them and that international crimes could only be defined in broad terms applicable to statesmen of any nation guilty of the proscribed conduct.[5]

Telford Taylor corroborates Jackson's account. According to Taylor, "the definition of the crimes to be charged . . . was an important question of principle which at first appeared to be intractable." The Soviets, Taylor says, wanted to charge the Nazi leaders with "[a]ggression against or domination over other nations *carried out by the European Axis* . . . ." The Soviets were willing to define "war crimes" and "crimes against humanity" as violations of international law no matter by whom committed. But the Russians—and the French—resisted creating a new crime of aggressive war.[6]

At the final meeting of the London conference, the Soviet qualifications were dropped and agreement was reached on a generic definition acceptable to all. In his Opening Statement to the Tribunal, Justice Jackson articulated the consensus reached by the United States, France, Great Britain and the Soviet Union. He made it clear that while this law was being first applied "against German aggressors, the law includes, and if it is to serve a useful purpose it must condemn aggression by any other nations, including those which sit here now in judgment."[7] Telford Taylor quoted this solemn affirmation by Justice Jackson on the first page of Taylor's subsequent book on Nuremberg and Vietnam.[8]

In trials conducted by the victorious occupying nations in other courts in occupied territory, phraseology limiting the jurisdiction of the tribunals to persons "acting in the interests of the European Axis countries" was dropped, making way for expansion of the Nuremburg Principles beyond the immediate prosecution of agents of the defeated European powers. As Taylor wrote, "Nuremburg is a historical and moral fact with which, from now on, every government must reckon in its internal and external policies alike." Recalling the declaration of the Tribunal regarding the impartial application of its principles to all, Taylor wrote: "We may not, in justice, apply to these defendants because they are Germans, standards of duty and responsibility which are not equally applicable to the officials of the Allied Powers and to those of all nations."[9]

And on the last page of his book on Nuremberg, published shortly before his death, Taylor once again affirmed what he obviously considered to be the heart of the Nuremberg proceedings. Reflecting on the growing demand in the 1990s for the establishment of a permanent tribunal for the trial of international crimes, Taylor recalled

> that the Nuremberg Tribunal had jurisdiction only over "the major war criminals of the European Axis countries." Considering the times and circumstances of its creation, it is hardly surprising that the Tribunal was given jurisdiction over the vanquished but not the victors. Many times I have heard Germans (and others) complain that "only the losers get tried."

Taylor continued:

> Early in the Korean War, when General Douglas MacArthur's forces landed at Inchon, the American and South Korean armies drove the Koreans all the way north to the border between North Korea and China, at the Yalu River. About a week later the Chinese attacked in force and their opponents were driven deep into South Korea.
>
> During the brief period when our final victory appeared in hand, I received several telephone calls from members of the press asking whether the United States would try suspect North Koreans as war criminals. I was quite unable to predict whether or not such trials would be undertaken, but I replied that if they were to take place, the tribunal should be established on a neutral base, preferably by the United Nations, and given jurisdiction to hear charges not only against North Koreans but South Koreans and Americans (or any other participants) as well.

And Taylor concluded: "I am still of that opinion. The laws of war do not apply only to the suspected criminals of vanquished nations. There is no more or legal basis for immunizing victorious nations from scrutiny. The laws of war are not a one-way street."[10]

It is crystal clear, then, that after the Nuremberg trials, the United States was committed to having its own conduct judged according to the principles of international law applied in those proceedings.

## II. THE NUREMBURG PRECEDENT IN UNITED STATES COURTS AND MILITARY TRIBUNALS

During and after the Vietnam War, United States courts and military tribunals were asked to apply the Nuremberg Principles to the conduct of individual soldiers. The civilian judicial system washed its hands of the issue and (to use another Biblical metaphor) passed by on the other side. Military tribunals were far more forthright than their civilian counterparts in facing the problem but did not succeed in resolving the dilemma.

### A. David Mitchell And The Fort Hood Three

When David Mitchell was found guilty by the trial court and the federal court of appeals, his attorneys sought a writ of certiorari from the United States Supreme Court. The Supreme Court of the United States decided not to consider the case. Justice William Douglas dissented from the denial of certiorari. He stated in part that petitioner's

> defense was that the "war" in Vietnam was being conducted
> in violation of various treaties to which we were a signatory,
> especially the Treaty of London of August 8, 1945, 59 Stat.
> 1544, which in Article 6(a) declares that "waging of a war of
> aggression" is a "crime against peace," imposing "individual re-
> sponsibility." Article 8 provides: "The fact that the Defendant
> acted pursuant to order of his Government or of a superior
> shall not free him from responsibility, but may be considered in
> mitigation of punishment . . . ."
>
> . . . Mr. Justice Jackson, the United States prosecutor at
> Nuremberg, stated: "If certain acts in violation of treaties are
> crimes, they are crimes whether the United States does them
> or Germany does them, and we are not prepared to lay down a
> rule of criminal conduct against others which we would not be
> willing to have invoked against us." (International Conference
> on Military Trials, Dept. State Pub. No. 3880, p. 330.)
>
> Article VI, cl. 2, of the Constitution states that "treaties"
> are a part of "the supreme law of the land; and the Judges in
> every State shall be bound thereby."
>
> There is a considerable body of opinion that our actions in
> Vietnam constitute the waging of an aggressive "war."
>
> This case presents the questions:
>
> (1) whether the Treaty of London is a treaty within the mean-
> ing of Article VI, cl. 2;
> (2) whether the question of the waging of an aggressive "war"
> is in the context of this criminal prosecution a justiciable
> question;
> (3) whether the Vietnam episode is a "war" in the sense of the
> Treaty;
> (4) whether petitioner has standing to raise the question;
> (5) whether, if he has, it may be tendered as a defense in this
> criminal case or in amelioration of the punishment.
>
> These are extremely sensitive and delicate questions. But they
> should, I think, be answered. . . .[11]

In *Mora et al. v. McNamara et al.*, three young men already drafted
into military service—Dennis Mora, James Johnson, and David Samas—
refused to deploy to Vietnam. They offered essentially the same defense
as had David Mitchell, adding the provisions of the US Army Field
Manual, *The Law of Land Warfare* (FM 27-10, 1956). This time two
justices of the United States Supreme Court, Justices Douglas and Potter
Stewart, dissented from denial of certiorari.[12]

### B. Howard Levy

Captain Howard B. Levy, M.D., also a draftee, refused to teach medicine to Green Beret soldiers at Fort Jackson, South Carolina.

The hearing officer at Capt. Levy's court martial, Colonel Earl Brown, the law officer, suddenly injected the possibility of a defense based on Nuremberg.

> Now the defense has intimated that special forces aidmen are being used in Vietnam in a way contrary to medical ethics. My research on the subject discloses that perhaps the Nuremberg Trials and the various post war treaties of the United States have evolved a rule that a soldier must disobey an order demanding that he commit war crimes, or genocide, or something to that nature. However, I have heard no evidence that even remotely suggests that the special forces of the United States Army have been trained to commit war crimes, and until I do, I must reject this defense.[13]

In colloquy with the prosecutor that followed, Colonel Brown stated that if the aidmen were being "trained to commit war crimes, then I think a doctor would be morally bound to refuse" to train them.[14]

Counsel for Dr. Levy were given one extra day to assemble witnesses to put on a Nuremberg defense. The defense found three witnesses. Donald Duncan was a former Special Forces Sergeant, who became disaffected while serving in Vietnam and resigned from the Army. Robin Moore was the author of a best-selling book, *The Green Berets*. Captain Peter Bourne was an Army psychiatrist who had served in Vietnam. The defense also proffered as exhibits 4,000 articles describing war crimes in Vietnam, including war crimes by the Special Forces, and a brief by Professor Richard Falk, an international law expert at Princeton, assisted by Richard Barnet of the Institute for Policy Studies. Finally, the defense submitted a list of thirty-eight witnesses to be called should Col. Brown determine that a prima facie case of Nuremberg violations had been made out.[15]

An out-of-court hearing followed. *The Law of Land Warfare* prohibits assassination of enemy soldiers or civilians. Duncan and Moore described assassination by United States forces and by the Vietnamese personnel that they trained. *The Law of Land Warfare* prohibits "putting a price on an enemy's head," but Duncan and Moore testified that in Vietnam it was a common practice. Most riveting, it seems, was defense testimony about torture and murder of unarmed prisoners, although *The Law of Land Warfare* prohibits killing prisoners "even in the case of . . . commando operations."[16]

Assessing the Nuremberg defense presented by Dr. Levy's counsel, Col. Brown simply ruled that Levy had failed to make a prima facie showing.[17]

Levy, like Mitchell and Mora before him, sought review by the Supreme Court of the United States. In *Parker v. Levy*, 417 U.S. 733 (1974), the Supreme Court upheld the validity of Levy's court martial conviction. Military tribunals quote and rely on the high court's pronouncement in *Parker v. Levy* that "the military is, by necessity, a specialized society," and hence "the fundamental necessity for obedience, and the consequent necessity for imposition of discipline, may render permissible within the military that which would be constitutionally impermissible outside it."[18] Justice Stewart angrily read his dissenting opinion from the bench.

### C. After Vietnam

The evasion of Nuremberg by the United States Supreme Court in the Mitchell, Mora, and Levy cases continues to cast a long shadow.

Further departing from the Nuremburg principles, the United States has now explicitly endorsed the doctrine of preemptive war. In a speech at the 2002 graduation exercises at West Point, President George W. Bush remarked that for much of the last century, America's defenses had relied on the Cold War doctrines of deterrence and containment. But, the president argued, containment means nothing against "terrorist networks with no nation or citizens to defend," "the war with terror will not be won on the defensive," and the United States must be prepared for "preemptive action when necessary."[19] In September 2002, the Bush Administration promulgated a new National Security Doctrine which stated, in part, that "we will not hesitate to act alone, if necessary, to exercise our right of self-defense by acting preemptively against such terrorists, to prevent them from doing harm against our people and our country."[20]

This new doctrine would appear expressly to violate the condemnation of aggressive war on which the United States insisted at Nuremberg. A conviction that his country is an aggressor in violation of international law is the essence of Lt. Watada's conclusion that what he is being ordered to do is unlawful. **He considers that he is not engaging in "civil disobedience" but rather obeying settled international law that Nuremburg decreed he would disregard at his peril**. In his case, then, and in future cases like his, a potential or actual soldier may be entitled to refuse orders not only because they require "war crimes" or "crimes against humanity," but also because they demand obedience to a "crime against peace": aggressive war.

## III. CONCLUSION

To conclude: The little girl quoted in *The People, Yes* deserves the last word.

The little girl saw her first troop parade and asked, "What are those?"
"Soldiers."
"What are soldiers?"
"They are for war. They fight and each tries to kill as many of the other side as he can."
The girl held still and studied.
"Do you know . . . I know something?"
"Yes, what is it you know?"
"Sometime they'll give a war and nobody will come."[21]

### ENDNOTES

1   The Charter was part of the Treaty of London, Aug. 8, 1945 (59 Stat. 1544), which established an International Military Tribunal. *The Nuernberg Case as Presented by Robert H. Jackson, Chief Of Counsel for the United States* (New York: Cooper Square Publishers, 1971), pp. 22-23. The first session of the general assembly of the United Nations unanimously affirmed the principles of international law in the Charter, and directed the International Law Commission to formulate them into an International Criminal Code. Res. 95 (1), Dec. 11, 1946. The text of the Charter may be found in Michael R. Marrus, *The Nuremburg War Crimes Trial, 1945-46: A Documentary History* (Boston: Bedford Books, 1997), pp. 51-55.

2   This was later often called the "Eichmann defense," in reference to the spectacular trial of Adolf Eichmann in Jerusalem in 1961. Eichmann had been head of the Jewish Affairs Section of the Reich Security Head Office and was viewed as one of those chiefly responsible for the attempted "final solution of the Jewish question." Eichmann's defense rested in part on the claim that he had acted on superior orders and, moreover, under duress that left him no moral choice. The Israeli court rejected this argument, holding that "the accused closed his ears to the voice of conscience." The court quoted the judgment of a District Military Court following the IMT that if an order was "manifestly unlawful, it cannot be used as an excuse." Cited in Robert K. Woetzel, *The Nuremberg Trials in International Law, with a Postlude on the Eichmann Case* (New York: Praeger, 1962), p. 269. The Court of Appeals in Eichmann's case further concluded in 1962 that "the appellant had received no 'superior orders' at all. He was his own superior, and he gave all orders in matters that concerned Jewish affairs. . . ." Cited in Hannah Arendt, *Eichmann in Jerusalem* (New York: Viking Press, 1963), p. 227.

3   Marrus, *The Nuremburg War Crimes Trial*, p. 53. Nevertheless, several of the defendants in the Trial of the Major War Criminals and many defendants in subsequent trials used the argument of superior orders to defend themselves. The Judgments of the International Military Tribunal (IMT) rejected this defense in all cases, generally on the ground that the Charter prohibited it. In some cases, the defense was rejected even for the purpose of mitigating a sentence. For example, in the case of Wilhelm Keitel (Chief of the High Command of the Armed Forces, directly under Hitler) the Tribunal concluded: "There is nothing in mitigation. Superior orders, even to a soldier, cannot be considered in mitigation where crimes as shocking and extensive have been committed consciously, ruthlessly, and without military excuse or justification."

4   "Principles of International Law Recognized in the Charter of the Nuremburg Tribunal and in the Judgment of the Tribunal," adopted by the U.N. International Law Commission, 2 August 1950, U.N. Doc. A/1316, 2 Y.B.I.L.C. 374 (1950), Principle I, par. 99; Principle II, par. 100, 102.

Article 8 was revised by the International Law Commission to read: "The fact that a person acted pursuant to order of his Government or of a superior does not relieve him from responsibility under international law, provided a moral choice was in fact possible to him." In this formulation, the provision of Article 8 allowing mitigation of punishment was dropped on the ground that "the question of mitigating punishment is a matter for the competent court to decide," rather than a matter of general principle. At the same time, the provision concerning moral choice was added, based upon the following declaration of the judgment:

The provisions of this article . . . are in conformity with the law of all nations. That a soldier was ordered to kill or torture in violation of the international law of war has never been recognized as a defense to such acts of brutality. . . . The true test, which is found in varying degrees in the criminal law of most nations, is not the existence of the order but whether moral choice was in fact possible.

*Id.*, par. 105.

5   *Report of Robert H. Jackson, United States Representative to the International Conference on Military Trials* (New York: AMS Press, 1949), pp. vii-viii.

6   Telford Taylor, *The Anatomy of the Nuremberg Trials* (New York: Alfred A. Knopf, 1992), pp. 65-66 (emphasis added). Scholarship during the past half century has confirmed the account by Jackson and Taylor. An authoritative article appearing in 2002 states:

the difficulties centered on whether the substantive definition of aggression would specify Nazi or Axis aggression (the Soviet position), or would define the crime [against peace] in a clean, universal way that might, in another era, even include American acts (the Jackson position). . . . In the end, the Charter for the new tribunal embodied Jackson's view . . . .

Jonathan A. Bush, "'The Supreme ... Crime' and its Origins: The Lost Legislative History of the Crime of Aggressive War," *Columbia Law Review*, v. 102, No. 8 (Dec. 2002), p. 2369.

7 Opening Statement for the United States, Nov. 21, 1945, *The Nuernberg Case as Presented by Robert H. Jackson Chief of Counsel for the United States* (New York: Cooper Square Publishers, 1971), p. 93.

8 Telford Taylor, *Nuremberg and Vietnam: An American Tragedy* (New York: Bantam Books, 1971), pp. 11-12. Taylor went on to say:

However history may ultimately assess the wisdom or unwisdom of the war crimes trials, one thing is indisputable: At their conclusion, the United States government stood legally, politically and morally committed to the principles enunciated in the charters and judgments of the tribunals. [Taylor shows that the president of the United States, thirty or more American judges who took part in the tribunals, General Douglas MacArthur, and the United States delegation to the United Nations general assembly, all squarely endorsed the Nuremberg principles in one way or another.]

Thus the integrity of the nation is staked on those principles, and today the question is how they apply to the conduct of our war in Vietnam, and whether the United States Government is prepared to face the consequences of their application.

... [T]he Son My [My Lai] courts-martial are shaping the question for us, and they can not be fairly determined without full inquiry into the higher responsibilities. Little as the leaders of the Army seem to realize it, this is the only road to the Army's salvation, for its moral health will not be recovered until its leaders are willing to scrutinize their behavior by the same standard that their revered predecessors applied to Tomayuki Yamashita 25 years ago.

*Id.*, pp. 94, 182.

9 Taylor, *Final Report*, pp. 234, 235.

10 Taylor, *Anatomy of the Nuremberg Trials*, p. 641. The speaker, although a vigorous opponent of the Vietnam War, took a similar position in declining to take part in the War Crimes Tribunal created by Lord Bertrand Russell. See Bush, "'The Supreme ... Crime,'" p. 2393 n.224, citing Staughton Lynd, "The War Crimes Tribunal: A Dissent," *Liberation*, v. 12 (Dec. 1967-Jan. 1968), p. 76.

11 Douglas, J., dissenting, in *Mitchell v. United States*, 386 U.S. 972 (1967), quoted in *We Won't Go: Personal Accounts of War Objectors* (Boston: Beacon Press, 1968), ed. Alice Lynd, pp. 102-04.

12 *Id.*, pp. 182-84.

13 Tr. at 875, quoted in Robert N. Strassfeld, "The Vietnam War on Trial: The Court-Martial of Dr. Howard B. Levy," 1994 *Wisconsin Law Review* 839, 902.

14 Tr. at 878, quoted in *id.*, p. 903. According to Professor Strassfeld, Colonel Brown had often discussed the implications of the Nuremberg and Tokyo war crimes trials as a law instructor at West Point in the late 1940s, and

had been deeply impressed by the movie *Judgment at Nuremberg*.

15 *Id.*, pp. 905-08.

16 *Id.*, pp. 908-15.

17 *Id.*, pp. 922-23.

18 *United States v. Moore*, 58 M.J. 466, 2003 CAAF LEXIS 694 (2003), quoting *Parker v. Levy*, 417 U.S. 733, 743, 758 (1974).

19 http://www.whitehouse.gov/news/releases/2002/06/20020601-3.html (emphasis added).

20 *The National Security Strategy of the United States of America* (Washington, D.C.: Sept. 2002), p. 5 (emphasis added).

21 Carl Sandburg, *The People, Yes* (New York: Harcourt, Brace and Company, 1936), p. 43.

G reetings on the ninety-first anniversary of Armistice Day, 1918. That was the day there came to an end the war that the United States government called "The war to end war" and "The war to make the world safe for democracy."

I recognize that for you World War I must seem ancient history, something like the siege of Troy. Let me take a moment to indicate some of the many ways in which this war and its aftermath gave rise both to the world in which we live, and also to that other world which insurgents in Chiapas, Mexico, as well as protesters in Seattle, Quebec, Genoa, and Cancun, assure us may be possible.

My mother described to me her experience on Armistice Day at Wellesley, where she was student body president. When the end of fighting in Europe was confirmed, students spontaneously marched into the college chapel singing a popular song of the day, "Good morning, Mr. Zip, Zip, Zip." My mother and her friends felt that this was not the way they wished to welcome the end of a war in which hundreds of thousands of young men had spent years trying to slaughter each other. A memorial service was organized. There was a reading from Rudyard Kipling's poem "Recessional," which asks that after "The captains and the kings depart" we who sit vigil with the memory of the dead must not "forget."

During World War I a new song was created by Ralph Chaplin, an imprisoned member of the Industrial Workers of the World. The melody had been reworded twice before during an earlier conflict. In the opening days of the Civil War, Julia Ward Howe was trying to make her way through Washington, D.C. in a carriage. Her carriage was brought to a standstill by columns of marching Union soldiers. They were singing "John Brown's body lies a-mouldering in the grave, but his soul goes marching on." Immobilized, listening, Ms. Howe jotted down words for a Battle Hymn of the Republic. Its opening verse remembered the terrible swift sword of the Book of Revelation. The vintage where the grapes of wrath are stored is not wine, but blood. But in later verses there are also other words, such as: "He hath sounded forth the trumpet that shall never call retreat, He is sifting out the souls of men before his judgment seat, Be swift my soul to answer Him, be jubilant my feet, Our God is marching on." Chaplin, immobilized in a different way behind bars, kept the tune but changed Howe's message. His song, "Solidarity Forever," declared: "In our hands is placed a power greater than their hoarded gold, Greater than the might of armies magnified a thousandfold, We can bring to birth a new world from the ashes of the old, For our Union makes us strong."

What did this terrible war mean to those who fought in it? My favorite movie was as I was growing up (and remains) *Grand Illusion*, in which the class experiences that bind together working people in France and Germany are represented to be stronger than the bonds connecting all persons born in France or their German counterparts. A French mechanic who has escaped from a German prison camp is sheltered by a German peasant woman. She shows him around her house, pointing to photographs of groups of soldiers that hang on her walls. The pictures, she explains, were taken at the sites of battles where her husband and brothers were killed. She describes these battles bitterly as "Our greatest victories."

My son sings a song about a Christmas truce between the opposing armies. I do not know whether it is apocryphal or true. According to the song, as midnight approaches on Christmas eve a tenor voice from the German trenches strikes up "Silent Night," and then, little by little, soldiers from both armies emerge from the trenches bearing gifts of food and drink to share with their enemies.

Armistice eve is described in a novel by Eric Maria Remarque. The guns have largely fallen silent in anticipation of peace. There came a day so quiet that the army communiques merely reported, "*Im Westen nichts neues*," or "All quiet on the Western Front." The hand of the protagonist, a German soldier, reaches out for a butterfly. The hand falls limp as a bullet kills him.

Following the Armistice German revolutionary Rosa Luxemburg was released from prison, where she had been confined for opposing the war. Her first public remarks after she was set free called for an end to the death penalty. Two months later she herself was assassinated.

In the United States, similarly, during the war Eugene Debs made a speech in Canton, Ohio. He said: "When I say I am opposed to war I mean ruling class war, for the ruling class is the only class that makes war . . . . I would be shot for treason before I would enter such a war . . . . I have no country to fight for; my country is the earth; I am a citizen of the world." Solely for uttering these words he was sentenced to long years in federal prison. The impression that he made on both his fellow prisoners and his jailors is suggested by the fact that when he was released the warden of the Atlanta Penitentiary let all the prisoners out of their cells so that they might wave good-bye.

In addition, of course, wartime discontent was the immediate cause of the Bolshevik Revolution, and defeat in World War I was—less directly—a cause of German Fascism.

This, then, is my tradition, the context into which I was born and out of which I speak. Prominent among the multi-colored strands of this tradition are opposition to war and opposition to capitalism. And no less than New Leftists of the 1960s or today's young anarchists, a Ralph Chaplin, a Rosa Luxemburg, a Eugene Debs demanded that we put our bodies where our mouths are and walk our talk.

## I

I believe that an adequate orientation to the creation of another world requires two components. The first is structural analysis. Without it, we cannot know where we are so as to imagine a travel plan to a new place. The second is prefigurative experimentation, the construction and nurturing of new institutions. Without them, we cannot begin to experience what a new society would be like. We need to try to create a horizontal network of self-governing local entities comprising a "dual power" that begins to manage our common affairs in a new way.

Let's start with structural analysis. I believe that the most compelling candidate for an adequate structural analysis is Marxist political economy. It offers us the concepts of: class conflict as the moving part or steam engine of history; of the nation state as an executive committee of the ruling class; of the unemployed as an industrial reserve army dragging down wage rates; of the changing organic composition of capital as the cause of a falling rate of profit; of the export of capital as a means of countering the falling rate of profit by seeking out low-wage workers in other economies; of uneven capitalist development, as capitalist nations that are "behind" in the race for world economic dominance leapfrog over nations that industrialized earlier; of war as the product of such imperialist competition.

This bundle of ideas provides a remarkable tool chest. However, for the sixty-five years of my adulthood Marxist economists have been making predictions that didn't come true and have failed to explain the big things that mattered. They said at the end of World War II that the United States economy would revert to depression as military spending fell away. Later, they said that the Soviet Union was good and China was bad, or the reverse, without recognizing the creeping capitalism common to both societies. They completely failed to predict either the worldwide student insurgency of the 1960s or the accelerated capitalist globalization beginning in the 1970s. Presently they appear to have lapsed into senile incoherence, muttering words like "multitude" or post-something-or-other, that are inaccessible to the rational mind and unrelated to any happenings in the real world.

Accordingly, I wish to share some ground-level, seat-of-the-pants observations of capitalist laws of development as they have played out in Youngstown, Ohio during the thirty-three years Alice and I have lived in the area. These observations are profoundly influenced by Marxism. But hopefully they are not limited to sterile discussion about which of several one-sided theoretical constructs will rule the academic roost for the time being.

When the Lynds moved to Youngstown in 1976 what had previously been the second or third steel-producing region of the United States was still in relatively good shape. There was an ongoing erosion of jobs in steel. A city population that had once been over 150,000 had shrunk to about 100,000. But supermarkets were still open around the clock to accommodate all three shifts in the mill. There were well over 10,000 union jobs in basic steel at which workers could earn a good living with access not only to a pension and Medicare after normal retirement but also to ample collectively-bargained benefits in the event of an early shutdown.

Comparable employment was available at two other major enterprises in the area, the General Motors automobile assembly plant in Lordstown and the Packard Electric (now Delphi Packard) complex that made electric harnesses and other parts for General Motors vehicles. Each of these facilities also employed more than 10,000 workers.

By the summer of 1980 not a single ton of steel was being made in Youngstown. Today, employment at steel mills in other parts of the Mahoning Valley, at the car plant in Lordstown, and at Delphi Packard, amounts to a couple of thousand workers or less at each location. Meantime Delphi has become the largest multinational employer in Mexico, with a work force there of over 40,000.

What happened? The answer appears to be somewhat different for each of the employment centers mentioned above, that is, for the manufacture of steel, vehicles, and vehicle parts.

Each year for three successive years a major Youngstown steel mill shut down, and each year the Valley arrived at a more sophisticated analysis. In 1977, 100,000 persons signed a petition blaming the shutdown of the Campbell Works on burdensome EPA regulations and took it to Washington by chartered buses. When the Brier Hill mill closed in 1978 some commentators pointed out that Brier Hill had been acquired by a shipping conglomerate, the Lykes Corporation, and used by Lykes as a cash cow for other corporate acquisitions. By the time U.S. Steel delivered the coup de grace to Youngstown steelmaking at Thanksgiving 1979, Youngstown was ready to place blame where it belonged. This time the chartered buses went to U.S. Steel headquarters in Pittsburgh and protestors came in from the cold to occupy the lower floors of the giant building. In January 1980, rebellious steelworkers broke down the door of U.S. Steel's Youngstown administration building and occupied the entire structure for an afternoon. The daughter of Ed Mann, spokesperson for the rebellion, changed her baby's diapers on the pool table in the executive game room. However, the mills closed.

Clearly the steel industry in Youngstown was done in by imports from abroad. But we need to ask, What made it possible for foreign steel companies to ship enormously heavy rolls of steel across thousands of miles of ocean and yet undersell United States companies in their domestic market? It was a classic case of the uneven development of capitalism. The reason German and Japanese steel mills could compete in the United States market, on its face an unlikely development, was that overseas facilities destroyed by American bombing during World War II were rebuilt with technology more up-to-date than that used in this country.

Thus at a time when foreign mills had begun to make steel in Basic Oxygen or electric furnaces, and to shape it in continuous casters, American steelmakers continued to use open hearth and blast furnaces. U.S. Steel built its new Fairless Works in Pennsylvania after World War II with open hearth furnaces. Every ton of steel poured in Youngstown during the years when the mills closed was made in an open hearth furnace. We calculated that it might cost $20 million to purchase and reopen any of the area's mills but that any such mill could not survive for long unless more than $200 million could be obtained to modernize it. We couldn't find the money.

In the case of automobile assembly plants as well, foreign imports have obviously been one cause of the loss of market share in the United States by American carmakers. But an even more important factor may have been the so-called "legacy costs," that is, the collectively-bargained pension and health care benefits promised to their workers by American companies. In the United States these benefits are paid by private employers, rather than by the national government as in other capitalist economies. This is so because of a conjuncture of events during World War II.

The new CIO unions had agreed to a wage freeze while the war lasted to demonstrate their patriotism. But prices rose dramatically, and as the war dragged on it was agreed that unions might collectively bargain for pension and health benefits to compensate workers for their loss of purchasing power. After the tide of war turned at Stalingrad in 1943, and in the flush of victory after 1945, it apparently did not occur to anyone that industry in the United States might one day encounter competition that would make it difficult to pay these promised benefits.

When active employees outnumbered retirees, as in American car plants then or in Honda and Toyota plants in the United States today, legacy costs could be paid from a reasonable portion of profits. But in the older plants of the Big Three, as there came to be one, two, three or more retirees for every worker still producing on the shop floor, it did not require the theory of surplus value to see that GM, Chrysler and Ford would not be able to compete. According to one account (Sam Gindin, "Lessons from the Humbling of General Motors," June 28, 2009, pp. 6-7), at the end of the 1970s General Motors had 470,000 hourly workers and 133,000 retirees and surviving spouses, but thirty years later when GM declared bankruptcy had 64,000 workers and 500,000 retirees: 7.7 retirees for every active worker.

Finally we come to the third major employer in the Mahoning Valley, Delphi Packard. To the best of my knowledge Delphi does not have significant competition from imported vehicle parts. Delphi does have legacy costs as do other major industries in the United States. But in the case of Delphi plants in the Youngstown area there may have been a third factor. These plants were originally organized by the United Electrical Workers, a Communist-led union more democratic and more militant than most other CIO unions.

When the UE was thrown out of the CIO, and the IUE displaced the Electrical Workers as bargaining representative, some of the old militancy and democracy remained. Throughout the 1950s and 1960s there were a number of wildcat strikes. One worker remembered: "We fought for everything: personal days, breaks, hospitalization." In 1968 a foreman came into the plant drunk and physically threatened several workers. "All of Packard was shut down."

Another popular mode of struggle was the so-called—this will amuse you—"tea party." If grievances were not resolved in a timely manner, union representatives would call together, ostensibly for a tea break, enough workers to shut down the operation. A foreman who thought female workers used the rest room too often took it upon himself to conduct a poll of women's menstrual cycles. The line was shut down until the idea was abandoned. In general, when problems arose union representatives might turn off the power and personally block access to the switch.

The company reacted by transferring work, first to more compliant plants in the southern United States that were non-union and low-wage, and then to Mexico. Management adopted the slogan "no more bricks and mortar" in the Youngstown area. Delphi joined other area companies on the yellow brick road of downsizing and concession bargaining.

These snapshots from the deindustrialization of one community suggest no single explanation for what happened. The conclusion that stands out is that capitalism can apparently be counted on to cause continued disruption and crisis. From time to time the illusion is projected that capitalism has attained a plateau of stability and that workers can make plans for the future of themselves and their children with confidence. In the early 1900s Social Democratic theorists Edward Bernstein and Karl Kautsky proposed that international capitalism had reached such a steady state. Then came the first World War. In boom periods like the 1920s economists have imagined that the good times would last forever. When the Berlin Wall came down, the Cold War was declared to have been won and conservative commentators envisioned "the end of history." Today it is hard to remember that after the elections of 2000 and 2004 many pundits expected a permanent Republican majority and unchanging United States dominance of the world economy.

But an economy premised on the cutthroat competition of each against all cannot make good on such projections. All the Harvard and Yale men in the world, trained to try to keep the system together despite the selfishness of its component parts, cannot repair the unending damage done by the desire for profit maximization.

I am reminded of an incident when the U.S. Steel mills in Youngstown closed in 1979. A particular worker had heard the U.S. Steel Chairman of the Board solemnly state on local TV that the company had no plans to close its Mahoning Valley mills. The area superintendent for the company repeated this assurance. Relying on those representations, this worker decided to buy a new house. On his way home after signing the purchase papers he was delayed at one of the community's many railroad crossings. He turned on the radio as he awaited the reopening of the crossing. The radio informed him that the company had just announced that it would close its Youngstown mills immediately.

So my structural analysis comes to a simple conclusion. The one thing on which we can rely is that crises of capitalism will continue. As Immanuel Wallerstein has written: The present period is one of transition, impossible to predetermine, "intrinsically uncertain and, therefore, precisely open to human intervention and creativity" ("Globalization or the Age of Transition?," *International Sociology*, v. 15, no. 2, June 2000, pp. 249, 265). Opportunities will endlessly present themselves to try to change things for the better by creating another world. To that topic I now turn.

## II

Here is an analogy, a metaphor. Some of you, like myself, may have done a good deal of wilderness canoeing and backpacking. What has been established up to this point is that capitalist crises will predictably recur in the future. But while we know there will be dramatic changes in objective conditions, we do not have nor are we likely to obtain a precise analysis of where we need to go and how to get there. It is as if we were in the remote back country without a map.

This brings to mind an experience. I was canoeing in the Algonquin Wilderness in Ontario with my son and the young woman who would become his wife. We had a miserable day transitioning from one chain of lakes to another by wading with our canoe, in the rain, down a shallow stream overgrown with brambles. At length, just at dusk, we came out into the northernmost body of water in the second chain of lakes. There was a small island just ahead of us. The rain had more or less stopped. Like Phidippides after the battle of Marathon, we were prepared to exclaim: "Victory is ours."

We beached our canoe and my son began to chop wood for a supper fire. I warned him to be careful with the hatchet. A moment later he put it into the back of his left hand.

It had taken us two days to reach this remote island. If you can imagine the strain put on the top of each hand by canoeing, it was clear that Betsy and I would have to transport Lee to safety. We had to travel two days' distance in one and get Lee to a doctor. The route back was through an unfamiliar series of lakes. All that night I lay on my side in a very small tent that I shared with a second traveler, periodically reaching into the back pocket where I kept our map, carefully dragging it to the front of the tent and unfolding it, and yet again trying to read it with a flashlight. At each inspection the map became a little more creased and illegible.

We made it out of the wild by 10 o'clock the next evening. But here's the point: We didn't get there just by following a map. Sitting in the stern of the canoe I would study the line of low hills ahead of us. Where I saw a dip or notch in the hills I would hypothesize either a brook leading from one lake to the next or a low-lying portage. We oriented ourselves to our surroundings and found our way to where we needed to arrive.

So it is with our movement, I suggest. We do not have a map sufficiently precise and comprehensive to tell us exactly how to reach the Other World which we believe is possible. **But we are not lost.** We can orient ourselves to our surroundings and move ahead with cautious confidence.

Imagine yourselves for a moment on land rather than water, in the middle of nowhere. It is difficult to be completely lost. The sun rises in the East, or Orient, as the very word "orientation" suggests. At night the two furthermost stars in the Big Dipper point to the North Star. I have never had much luck with moss, which always seems to be on every side of the trees that I inspect, not just on the North side. A more reliable indicator in the woods is the sound of running water. That sound is a message that nearby there is a stream which can only run downhill and if followed long enough is almost sure to empty into a lake or river.

The most important thing is to keep your cool, your poise. Then, more likely than not, you will be able to orient yourself to the general direction in which you need to go.

So here are three kinds of orientation that I believe will help us find our way forward. To name them in the order in which they became clear to my wife and myself, they are: 1. Archbishop Romero's idea of "accompaniment"; 2. Solidarity unionism; and 3. Rather than aspiring to take state power, to govern from below by insisting on what Subcomandante Marcos and Bolivian President Evo Morales call *"mandar obediciendo,"* that is, to govern in obedience.

### A. Accompaniment

"Accompaniment" is a term coined by Archbishop Oscar Romero of El Salvador that the Lynds encountered during several trips to Sandinista Nicaragua in the 1980s.

Romero confronted a situation in which the FMLN, supported by many Salvadoran *campesinos*, had initiated guerrilla warfare. What should be the response of Catholics influenced by liberation theology but resistant to picking up the gun? In the annual pastoral letters that he wrote during the years before his assassination, Romero projected a course of action with two essential elements. First, be yourself. If you are a believing Christian don't be afraid of professing it. If you are an intellectual don't pretend that you make your living by manual labor. Second, place yourself at the side of the poor and oppressed. Accompany them on their journey.

It seemed to Alice and myself that "accompaniment" described a course of conduct that we had been developing for twenty years. In August 1965 the Lynds took part in a gathering in Washington, D.C. known as the Assembly of Unrepresented People. The idea was that on the 20th anniversary of the bombing of Nagasaki those so inclined would gather on the steps of Congress and declare peace with the people of Vietnam. In effect we would say, "Somebody else may be at war with you but we are not." At the time I considered it a great idea. I still do.

Prior to the march down the mall toward the Capitol, there had been a weekend of workshops. Alice attended one of these on the subject of Conscientious Objection. When the workshop ended she asked the facilitator whether she might be able to be a draft counselor. He replied,

"I guess you could if you could get anyone to come to you. I know of one woman draft counselor."

Over the next five years Alice became a counselor for students at Yale out of our home in New Haven; then, after we moved to Chicago, an employee of the Midwest Committee for Draft Counseling; and finally, coordinator for the American Friends Service Committee of draft counseling throughout the Chicago area. She formulated what she called the idea of two experts.

The idea was that in encountering one another, a draft counselor and a young person subject to conscription should regard themselves as equals, each bringing a different kind of expertise to the table. The counselor presumably knew about the law and regulations governing the Selective Service system, as well as the customary procedure of local draft boards. The counselee was an expert in his own life experience, his religious experience growing up, the likely responses of his parents or girl friend to alternative courses of action that he might choose, and how that choice would affect future job prospects and how he would feel about himself when he was fifty. Only by combining these two kinds of expertise could an appropriate decision become clear.

After Alice and I became lawyers and practiced employment law for the Youngstown office of the federal Legal Services administration, the same logic recommended itself in our relations with workers. We might know how to file a charge with the National Labor Relations Board, what redress was possible if the employer terminated a pension plan, or whether complaining to the Equal Employment Opportunity Commission was likely to be fruitful. But the client was the expert about the shopfloor practices at a particular place of employment, how particular language in a contract had been interpreted over the years, and what had been the experience of rank-and-file candidates at that particular local union.

As an example of accompaniment consider the trajectory of an organization of steel industry retirees that named itself Solidarity USA. In July 1986 LTV Steel, one of the largest remaining companies in our Valley, declared bankruptcy and simultaneously canceled health insurance for LTV Steel retirees. At least one man died, afraid to return to a hospital for his heart condition without insurance. Delores Hrycyk was the wife of an LTV Steel retiree. She worked as a receptionist in the office of an eye doctor three floors below our Legal Services office. Ms. Hrycyk telephoned local radio talk shows and asked them to announce a rally in downtown Youngstown the next Saturday. She informed me that I would be her lawyer and directed me to come. About a thousand persons attended.

Solidarity USA developed a modus operandi. We learned from experience that asking for an appointment was futile. So we would write a letter to LTV Steel, a health care provider like Blue Cross, or the Steelworkers union. We would not ask for an appointment. We would inform the recipient that Solidarity USA intended to appear at their front door on a particular day. We hoped that they would meet with us. In any event they could expect a very large picket line. Whoever it was always met with us, but usually asked to meet with the lawyers (ourselves) or with a designated number of persons. We would always reply politely, No, we have a committee and we want you to hear from all of us. The committee including Alice would go upstairs while I continued to walk on the picket line outside with most of the retirees. By the time LTV Steel emerged from bankruptcy, retirees had regained most of the pension and health care benefits they had initially lost.

One last point about "accompaniment" is that it can only come about if you—that is, the lawyer, doctor, teacher, clergyman or other professional person—stay in the community over a period of years. People get to know you and trust you. When the first Iraq War began the Workers Solidarity Club to which Alice and I belonged decided to picket against the war every day in downtown Youngstown. I could hardly absent myself because the picketing site was only a few yards from the office building in which we worked, but inwardly I told myself that this might be the end of our stay in the Mahoning Valley. In fact nothing changed. One retiree told me at a meeting in our office, "Lynd, you know I disagree with you about the war." Another approached me as we walked along a sidewalk to a meeting in Cleveland and said quietly, "Staughton, you know I agree with you about the war." But our activity on behalf of Solidarity USA went on as before. It was as if both men said to themselves, What else would you expect from Staughton?

I feel strongly that if more professionals on the Left would take up residence in communities other than Cambridge, New York City, and Berkeley, and stay there for a while, social change in this country might come a lot more quickly.

### B. Solidarity Unionism

In Youngstown, more than twenty-five years ago, several of us began to meet once a month at the local union hall of Utility Workers Local 118. The local had just been through a strike during which the central labor body provided very little help. I was asked to teach a class and told attenders that I wished to devote it to the question, What has gone wrong with the trade unions? Why are we all broken-hearted lovers?

The only evening I remember clearly was a discussion of a new encyclical by the Pope entitled, "On Human Labor." The Pope said that there were two kinds of work: for money, and for the glory of God. All one long evening the late Bob Schindler, an electric lineman for Ohio Edison, maintained that when he went up on the pole he did so for the glory of God. It turned out that when Bob and his crew were called out in an ice storm the company expected them to repair the line but to report the need to turn the power back on to headquarters. Rather than leave an elderly woman to suffer through another freezing night Bob's crew would fully restore electric service, much as unemployed workers did in the 1930s.

At the end of the class we did not want to stop meeting. We adopted the name Workers Solidarity Club of Youngstown. For the next twenty years there was a place where workers in need of help could go on the second Wednesday of every month. During at least two long and bitter strikes the support of the Club ensured the survival of the local unions involved. At the end of every meeting we formed a circle and sang the first and last verses of "Solidarity Forever."

Over the years several members of the Workers Solidarity Club used their annual vacations to visit revolutionary Nicaragua. Ned Mann, one of Ed Mann's sons, helped to construct a vent over a particularly smoky furnace at Nicaragua's only steel mill. Bob Schindler (who didn't know a word of Spanish) worked as part of an electric maintenance crew in Managua. A young man named Benjamin Linder had been killed in northern Nicaragua working on electrification for villages there. Bob Schindler went back the next year to help to finish the electrification project.

Others from the Club attended a workers' school south of Mexico City supported by the Frente Auténtico del Trabajo, the network of Mexican independent unions. African American participants experienced another world that, while not free of racial prejudice, was far more hospitable than the United States.

So what is solidarity? Most obviously, we find it in the conduct of certain radical martyrs. When the so-called Haymarket anarchists were being rounded up after the Chicago bombing of May 1886, Albert Parsons made it out of town and took up residence, in disguise, near Milwaukee. His comrades were put on trial for their lives. Parsons returned to Chicago, walked into the courtroom, and was tried, convicted, and hanged with the others.

In Mexico, the painter Frida Kahlo spent her adult life in great physical pain after a near-fatal streetcar accident crushed her spine and pelvis, leaving her unable to bear children. She finally had her first Mexican solo show in 1953 and went to the opening on a stretcher. She would lose a leg to gangrene. In June 1954 she had herself pushed in a wheelchair to join a protest against the action of the United States in overthrowing the democratically-elected Arbenz government in Guatemala. A few days later she died.

So this is one kind of solidarity. The Left did not invent it. As is stated in the Gospel according to St. John, ch. 15, v. 13: "Greater love hath no man than this, that a man lay down his life for his friends."

There is another kind of solidarity: the day-to-day practice of poor and oppressed persons who turn to each other in the belief that "an injury to one is an injury to all." In his book *Weapons of the Weak* (New Haven: Yale University Press, 1985), the anthropologist James C. Scott describes that kind of solidarity well. Scott rejects the concept of "hegemony" if that is understood to mean that what the peasant or worker ordinarily dares to express is all that the subordinate thinks or feels. At those rare historical moments when the weak openly confront their masters, it is not so much that "a new consciousness, a new anger, a new ideology" has come into being, but rather that what was there all along is fully displayed.

Scott also insists that the cries of "bread" and "land" so often at the core of peasant resistance arise from "the basic material needs of the peasant household." More generally,

> [t]o require of lower-class resistance that it somehow be "principled" or "selfless" is not only utopian and a slander on the moral status of fundamental material needs; it is, more fundamentally, a misconstruction of the basis of class struggle. . . . "Bread-and-butter" issues are the essence of lower-class politics and resistance.

Crucially, for Scott

> forms of resistance that are individual and unobtrusive are not only what a Marxist might expect from petty commodity producers and rural laborers, but have certain advantages. Unlike hierarchical formal organizations, there is no center, no leadership, no identifiable structure that can be co-opted or neutralized. What is lacking in terms of centralization may be compensated for by flexibility and persistence. These forms of resistance will win no set-piece battles, but they are admirably adapted to long-run campaigns of attrition.

Moreover, while the forms of resistance Scott studies may be individual, "this is not to say that they are uncoordinated. . . . [A] concept of coordination derived from formal and bureaucratic settings is of little assistance in understanding actions in small communities with dense informal networks and rich, historically deep, cultures of resistance to outside claims."

Scott studies peasants. Where do we find in the activity of industrial workers a comparable practice of the idea that an injury to one is an injury to all?

The most striking form of solidarity I have encountered during more than thirty years in Youngstown as a lawyer for rank-and-file workers, and as a labor historian, is the conduct of some workers during layoffs.

Labor historians are in general agreement that the signature achievement of CIO industrial unionism is the seniority system. The need for institutionalized seniority must have seemed obvious in the 1930s. In Youngstown, it was still the practice then for workers to assemble at the mill gate in the morning and to be individually called to work by the foreman much as in a longshore "shape-up." *Quid pro quos* for steady work included giving the foreman free meals at the worker's home, or worse.

But during layoffs, the mechanical application of seniority puts the most recently-hired workers on the street with nothing while older workers not only keep their full-time jobs but may continue to work overtime. Precisely in shops where the spirit of solidarity is strongest workers may refuse to follow collectively bargained seniority language and will instead divide work equally among all members of the "family at work," regardless of date of hire.

It happened among Illinois coal miners during the 1920s, among countless industrial workers in the early 1930s, and continues sporadically today. In the Youngstown Legal Services office where I worked in the 1980s, when President Reagan cut our budget by 20 percent the lawyers all reduced their work week by one day (while leaving untouched the weekly salary of non-lawyers who were underpaid to begin with). Alice and I experienced the same thing with an independent union of visiting nurses that we helped to organize. Perhaps the clearest description of the process that I know is the following account by Mia Giunta, an organizer for the United Electrical Workers, about a plant called F-Dyne Electric in Bridgeport, Connecticut; see *The New Rank and File*, ed. Staughton Lynd and Alice Lynd (Ithaca, NY: Cornell University Press, 2000).

> There were layoffs in 1978, 1979, right after the contract was signed.
> Under the contract, the layoffs went according to seniority. We felt terrible, thinking of some of the workers who would be put out on the street. There was a Portuguese woman named Albertina who had little children. She was crying but she said, "It's OK. It's all right." The other women said, "That's unfair."
> The workers took up a collection for her. I felt very guilty, and tried to talk to Albertina to make sure that she and the kids would be all right. We just didn't want to see her go.
> When the next bunch of layoffs came along, somebody suggested, "We'll all work a few hours less each week. That

way everybody can stay. Everybody will have health insurance."
And . . . that became the tradition in that factory.

The contract was never amended. Every time there was
a layoff, we would sign a side agreement that everyone would
agree to cut back.

An easy way to remember the basic idea of solidarity unionism is
to think: Horizontal not vertical. Mainstream trade unionism beyond the
arena of the local union is relentlessly vertical. Too often, rank-and-file
candidates for local union office imagine that the obvious next step for
them is to seek higher office, as international union staff man, regional
director, even international union president. The Left, for the past seventy-five years, has lent itself to the fantasy that salvation will come from
above by the election of a John L. Lewis, Philip Murray, Walter Reuther,
Arnold Miller, Ed Sadlowski, Ron Carey, John Sweeney, Andrew Stern,
or Richard Trumka.

Instead we should encourage successful rank-and-file candidates for
local union office to look horizontally to their counterparts in other local
unions in the same industry or community. This was labor's formula for
success during its most creative and successful years in memory, the early
1930s. During those years there were successful local general strikes in
Minneapolis, Toledo, San Francisco, and other, smaller industrial towns.
During those years local labor parties sprang up like mushrooms across the
United States. Today some organizers in the IWW, for example at Starbucks
stores in New York City, once again espouse solidarity unionism.

### C. "Mandar Obediciendo"

Finally, and more briefly, I offer one more kind of orientation: the
Mayan idea that central governments should "mandar obediciendo," that
is, lead by obeying.

You will recognize the close kinship between this idea and the concept of solidarity unionism. It calls for separate emphasis because of the
preoccupation of socialists for the past century and a half with "taking
state power."

I glimpsed the problem with the strategy of taking state power as
a teenager, riding back and forth between home and high school on the
7th Avenue subway in New York City. A book by an ex-Trotskyist named
James Burnham made the essential point. The transition from feudalism to capitalism was prepared by a long process in which the emerging
middle class created new institutions within the interstices of feudal society: free cities, guilds, Protestant congregations, banks and corporations,
a new court system, and finally, parliaments. National political power

passed to a new class only after that class had created a new society within the shell of the old.

Burnham argued that nothing like this was possible within capitalism. Trade unions were the obvious candidates for prefigurative institutions comparable to medieval cities. But trade unions, at least mainstream trade unions like the AF of L and CIO, were inextricably part of the existing scheme of things. They might ameliorate the hardships of capitalism but they did not offer an alternative.

From age fifteen to age sixty-five, I could find no persuasive answer to Burnham's reasoning. Then came the Zapatista insurgency in Chiapas. As I read the communiques from the Lacondón jungle I realized that at least from a time shortly after their initial public appearance, the Zapatistas were saying: "We don't want to take state power. If we can create a space that will help others to make the national government more democratic, well and good. But our task, as we see it, is to bring into being self-governing local entities linked together horizontally so as to present whoever occupies the seats of government in Mexico City with a force so powerful that it becomes necessary to govern in obedience to what Subcomandante Marcos calls 'the below.'"

Needless to say this ideology articulated the practice of hundreds of years of common life in Mayan communities. Anthropologist June Nash describes what happens at a Chiapas *asamblea*. Villagers gather to confront those of their number whom they have asked to perform particular "*cargos*," or tasks. At town meetings in the United States political representatives expect to answer questions and do most of the talking. In Chiapas elected village functionaries are expected to listen.

To be sure, as in any political jurisdiction of significant size, the *asambleas* must send delegates to a representative body. But they are instructed delegates. Thus, when Zapatista delegates met in San Cristóbal with spokespersons from the national government to seek negotiated agreements, questions arose that had not been discussed in the *asambleas* and as to which the delegates had not been instructed. As I imagine the dialogue it went something like this:

> ZAPATISTA DELEGATES: This is a new subject. We have to go back to the villages to get instructions.
> GOVERNMENT SPOKESPERSONS: How long will that take?
> ZAPATISTA DELEGATES: We can't be sure, but probably only a couple of weeks.
> GOVERNMENT SPOKESPERSONS: What!!!

Please note that I am not denying the need for national governments, national trade union federations, and the like. The issue is who directs whom. Thus in Bolivia, when Evo Morales was elected president, in his inaugural address he said that he expected *"mandar obediciendo,"* to govern in obedience to those who had elected him.

As I said at the end of a book called *Wobblies and Zapatistas*, a joint product of myself and Andrej Grubacic: "[F]inding my way beyond what I have called 'Burnham's dilemma,' imagining a transition that will not culminate in a single apocalyptic moment but rather express itself in unending creation of self-acting entities that are horizontally linked, is a source of quiet joy."

### *III*

Now you know everything I do, and I shall stop.

Actually, I am glad that there does not exist a map, a formula or equation within which we must act to get from Here to There. It's more fun this way, to move forward experimentally, sometimes to stumble but at other times to glimpse things genuinely new, always to be open to the unexpected and the unimagined and the not-yet-fully-in-being.

There is a poem by D. H. Lawrence which says it. The poem ends:

> What is the knocking?
> What is the knocking at the door in the night?
> It is somebody come to do us harm.
> No, no, it is the three strange angels.
> Admit them, admit them.

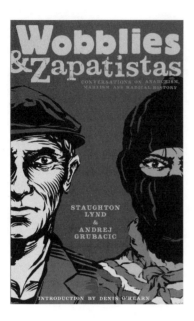

ALSO AVAILABLE FROM PM PRESS

*Wobblies & Zapatistas:*
*Conversations on Anarchism,*
*Marxism, and Radical History*
by Staughton Lynd &
Andrej Grubacic
ISBN: 978-1-60486-041-2
$20.00

*Wobblies & Zapatistas* offers the reader an encounter between two generations and two traditions. Andrej Grubacic is an anarchist from the Balkans. Staughton Lynd is a lifelong pacifist, influenced by Marxism. They meet in dialogue in an effort to bring together the anarchist and Marxist traditions, to discuss the writing of history by those who make it, and to remind us of the idea that "my country is the world." Encompassing a Left libertarian perspective and an emphatically activist standpoint, these conversations are meant to be read in the clubs and affinity groups of the new Movement.

The authors accompany us on a journey through modern revolutions, direct actions, anti-globalist counter summits, Freedom Schools, Zapatista cooperatives, Haymarket and Petrograd, Hanoi and Belgrade, 'intentional' communities, wildcat strikes, early Protestant communities, Native American democratic practices, the Workers' Solidarity Club of Youngstown, occupied factories, self-organized councils and soviets, the lives of forgotten revolutionaries, Quaker meetings, antiwar movements, and prison rebellions. The book invites the attention of readers who believe that a better world, on the other side of capitalism and state bureaucracy, may indeed be possible.

*"Here we have the best of a non-dogmatic Marxism listening to a most creative and humane anarchism. But this book is never weighted down by unforgiving theory. Just the opposite: it is a series of conversations where the reader feels fully present."*
–Margaret Randall, author of *Sandino's Daughters, When I Look Into the Mirror and See You*, and *Narrative of Power*

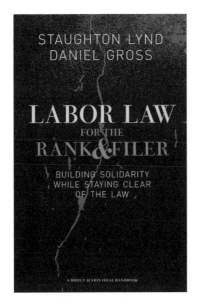

Have you ever felt your blood boil at work but lacked the tools to fight back and win? Or have you acted together with your co-workers, made progress, but wondered what to do next? If you are in a union, do you find that the union operates top-down just like the boss and ignores the will of its members?

*Labor Law for the Rank and Filer: Building Solidarity While Staying Clear of the Law* is a guerrilla legal handbook for workers in a precarious global economy. Blending cutting-edge legal strategies for winning justice at work with a theory of dramatic social change from below, Staughton Lynd and Daniel Gross deliver a practical guide for making work better while re-invigorating the labor movement.

*Labor Law for the Rank and Filer* demonstrates how a powerful model of organizing called "Solidarity Unionism" can help workers avoid the pitfalls of the legal system and utilize direct action to win. This new revised and expanded edition includes new cases governing fundamental labor rights as well as an added section on Practicing Solidarity Unionism. This new section includes chapters discussing the hard-hitting tactic of working to rule; organizing under the principle that no one is illegal, and building grassroots solidarity across borders to challenge neoliberalism, among several other new topics. Illustrative stories of workers' struggles make the legal principles come alive.

*"Some things are too important to leave to so called "experts": our livelihoods, our dignity and our rights. In this book, Staughton Lynd and Daniel Gross have provided us with a very necessary, empowering, and accessible tool for protecting our own rights as workers."*
—Nicole Schulman, co-editor *Wobblies! A Graphic History* and *World War 3 Illustrated*

ALSO AVAILABLE FROM PM PRESS

*Don't Mourn, Balkanize!:*
*Essays After Yugoslavia*
by Andrej Grubacic

ISBN: 978-1-60486-302-4
$20.00

*Don't Mourn, Balkanize!* is the first book written from the radical left perspective on the topic of Yugoslav space after the dismantling of the country. In this collection of essays, commentaries and interviews, written between 2002 and 2010, Andrej Grubacic speaks about the politics of balkanization—about the trial of Slobodan Milosevic, the assassination of Prime Minister Zoran Djindjic, neoliberal structural adjustment, humanitarian intervention, supervised independence of Kosovo, occupation of Bosnia, and other episodes of Power which he situates in the long historical context of colonialism, conquest and intervention.

But he also tells the story of the balkanization of politics, of the Balkans seen from below. A space of bogumils—those medieval heretics who fought against Crusades and churches—and a place of anti-Ottoman resistance; a home to hajduks and klefti, pirates and rebels; a refuge of feminists and socialists, of anti-fascists and partisans; of new social movements of occupied and recovered factories; a place of dreamers of all sorts struggling both against provincial "peninsularity" as well as against occupations, foreign interventions and that process which is now, in a strange inversion of history, often described by that fashionable term, "balkanization."

For Grubacic, political activist and radical sociologist, Yugoslavia was never just a country—it was an idea. Like the Balkans itself, it was a project of inter-ethnic co-existence, a trans-ethnic and pluricultural space of many diverse worlds. Political ideas of inter-ethnic cooperation and mutual aid as we had known them in Yugoslavia were destroyed by the beginning of the 1990s—disappeared in the combined madness of ethno-nationalist hysteria and humanitarian imperialism. This remarkable collection chronicles political experiences of the author who is himself a Yugoslav, a man without a country; but also, as an anarchist, a man without a state. This book is an important reading for those on the Left who are struggling to understand the intertwined legacy of inter-ethnic conflict and inter-ethnic solidarity in contemporary, post-Yugoslav history.

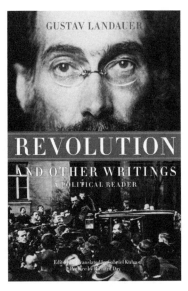

*"Landauer is the most important agitator of the radical and revolutionary movement in the entire country."* This is how Gustav Landauer is described in a German police file from 1893. Twenty-six years later, Landauer would die at the hands of reactionary soldiers who overthrew the Bavarian Council Republic, a three-week attempt to realize libertarian socialism amidst the turmoil of post-World War I Germany. It was the last chapter in the life of an activist, writer, and mystic who Paul Avrich calls "the most influential German anarchist intellectual of the twentieth century."

This is the first comprehensive collection of Landauer writings in English. It includes one of his major works, *Revolution*, thirty additional essays and articles, and a selection of correspondence. The texts cover Landauer's entire political biography, from his early anarchism of the 1890s to his philosophical reflections at the turn of the century, the subsequent establishment of the Socialist Bund, his tireless agitation against the war, and the final days among the revolutionaries in Munich. Additional chapters collect Landauer's articles on radical politics in the US and Mexico, and illustrate the scope of his writing with texts on corporate capital, language, education, and Judaism. The book includes an extensive introduction, commentary, and bibliographical information, compiled by the editor and translator Gabriel Kuhn as well as a preface by Richard Day.

*"At once an individualist and a socialist, a Romantic and a mystic, a militant and an advocate of passive resistance… He was also the most influential German anarchist intellectual of the twentieth century."*
—Paul Avrich, author of *Anarchist Voices*

ALSO AVAILABLE FROM PM PRESS

*Demanding the Impossible:*
*A History of Anarchism*
by Peter Marshall

ISBN: 978-1-60486-064-1
$28.95

Navigating the broad 'river of anarchy', from Taoism to Situationism, from Ranters to Punk rockers, from individualists to communists, from anarcho-syndicalists to anarcha-feminists, *Demanding the Impossible* is an authoritative and lively study of a widely misunderstood subject. It explores the key anarchist concepts of society and the state, freedom and equality, authority and power and investigates the successes and failure of the anarchist movements throughout the world. While remaining sympathetic to anarchism, it presents a balanced and critical account. It covers not only the classic anarchist thinkers, such as Godwin, Proudhon, Bakunin, Kropotkin, Reclus and Emma Goldman, but also other libertarian figures, such as Nietzsche, Camus, Gandhi, Foucault and Chomsky. No other book on anarchism covers so much so incisively.

In this updated edition, a new epilogue examines the most recent developments, including 'post-anarchism' and 'anarcho-primitivism' as well as the anarchist contribution to the peace, green and 'Global Justice' movements.

*Demanding the Impossible* is essential reading for anyone wishing to understand what anarchists stand for and what they have achieved. It will also appeal to those who want to discover how anarchism offers an inspiring and original body of ideas and practices which is more relevant than ever in the twenty-first century.

"Demanding the Impossible *is the book I always recommend when asked—as I often am—for something on the history and ideas of anarchism."*
    —Noam Chomsky

*"Attractively written and fully referenced…bound to be the standard history."*
    —Colin Ward, *Times Educational Supplement*

# FRIENDS OF

In the year since its founding —and on a mere shoestring —PM Press has risen to the formidable challenge of publishing and distributing knowledge and entertainment for the struggles ahead. With over 40 releases in 2009, we have published an impressive and stimulating array of literature, art, music, politics, and culture. Using every available medium, we've succeeded in connecting those hungry for ideas and information to those putting them into practice.

Friends of PM allows you to directly help impact, amplify, and revitalize the discourse and actions of radical writers, filmmakers, and artists. It provides us with a stable foundation from which we can build upon our early successes and provides a much-needed subsidy for the materials that can't necessarily pay their own way. You can help make that happen—and receive every new title automatically delivered to your door once a month—by joining as a Friend of PM Press. Here are your options:

- $25 a month: Get all books and pamphlets plus 50% discount on all webstore purchases.
- $25 a month: Get all CDs and DVDs plus 50% discount on all webstore purchases.
- $40 a month: Get all PM Press releases plus 50% discount on all webstore purchases
- $100 a month: Sustainer. - Everything plus PM merchandise, free downloads, and 50% discount on all webstore purchases.

Just go to WWW.PMPRESS.ORG to sign up. Your card will be billed once a month, until you tell us to stop. Or until our efforts succeed in bringing the revolution around. Or the financial meltdown of Capital makes plastic redundant. Whichever comes first.

 PM Press was founded at the end of 2007 by a small collection of folks with decades of publishing, media, and organizing experience. PM co-founder Ramsey Kanaan started AK Press as a young teenager in Scotland almost 30 years ago and, together with his fellow PM Press coconspirators, has published and distributed hundreds of books, pamphlets, CDs, and DVDs. Members of PM have founded enduring book fairs, spearheaded victorious tenant organizing campaigns, and worked closely with bookstores, academic conferences, and even rock bands to deliver political and challenging ideas to all walks of life. We're old enough to know what we're doing and young enough to know what's at stake.

We seek to create radical and stimulating fiction and nonfiction books, pamphlets, t-shirts, visual and audio materials to entertain, educate and inspire you. We aim to distribute these through every available channel with every available technology - whether that means you are seeing anarchist classics at our bookfair stalls; reading our latest vegan cookbook at the café; downloading geeky fiction e-books; or digging new music and timely videos from our website.

PM Press is always on the lookout for talented and skilled volunteers, artists, activists and writers to work with. If you have a great idea for a project or can contribute in some way, please get in touch.

PM Press
PO Box 23912
Oakland CA 94623
510-658-3906
www.pmpress.org